GORDON R. LOWE

The Growth of Personality

from Infancy to Old Age

PENGUIN BOOKS

Penguin Books Ltd, Harmondsworth, Middlesex, England
Penguin Books Inc., 7110 Ambassador Road, Baltimore, Maryland 21207, U.S.A.
Penguin Books Australia Ltd, Ringwood, Victoria, Australia
Penguin Books Canada Ltd, 41 Steelcase Road West, Markham, Ontario, Canada

—

First published 1972
Reprinted 1974

—

Copyright © Gordon R. Lowe, 1972

—

Made and printed in Great Britain by
Cox & Wyman Ltd,
London, Reading and Fakenham
Set in Intertype Plantin

TO ANDY

Contents

Acknowledgements

IN writing this book the ideas of Dr Douglas C. Levin, with whom I worked in Montreal from 1958 to 1964, have perhaps influenced me most. It was he who first drew my attention to Erikson's developmental theory. More important, however, he encouraged me to make clinical connections between ordinary behaviour on the one hand, and metapsychological concepts on the other. I am grateful for his teaching, and for his friendship, during those formative and exciting years at the Montreal General Hospital.

Other colleagues and friends of that period also helped and influenced me, perhaps more than they themselves realized; for example, Dr Peter G. Edgell, Dr Kingsley Ferguson, Professor Ernest Poser, and J. Alec Sproule. To each of these people, for different reasons, I owe special thanks.

Miss Carol Rice, who typed two complete drafts of the book, deserves special mention. Her secretarial skills and her personal enthusiasm contributed greatly to the work. The help of Miss Lynne Setter with the final stages of typing and amending is gratefully acknowledged.

Without the initial insight of Mr Charles Clark, the subsequent suggestions of Mr Dieter Pevsner, and the overall editorial help of Miss Julia Vellacott, all of Penguin Books, the book in its present form would not have been possible.

The understanding and support of my wife Wilma, and my daughter Laura, have contributed more than I can say to both the work and the fun involved in writing the book.

Preface

THIS book is about people. It is about you, and me, and every-body we know. Its purpose is to show how we can increase our understanding of others, and ourselves, and thus make better sense of our everyday living.

To do this it is not enough merely to describe what people do; we must also find out *why* they do it. Why, for example, are some people argumentative and domineering, while others are shy and hesitant? Why do some people become desperate for attention, and go to any lengths to obtain it? Why are some people greedy, selfish, and cynical, while others are kindly and easy to get along with? In general, what prompts people to behave as they do? We know what people are – but how did they get that way?

One obvious answer is that 'things happened to them'. This is perfectly true. Things do happen to people, and change them. It is, however, equally true that people happen to things, and change *them*. Everyday living is a continuous two-way trans-action between ourselves and our environment. We must con-sider therefore not only the external events 'out there' in the environment, but also the events within ourselves, our 'inner life' of personal experiences, feelings and emotions, attitudes, impulses, strivings and aspirations.

But are we not all different? Well, of course we are; but we are not utterly different. There are similarities as well as differences. Although individual personality and life experi-ences vary from person to person the variety is not infinite. Each of us is in one sense unique, and in another typical. What-ever our personality, and whatever sort of a life we have had, we all have in common certain characteristics and certain experiences. These features, which make us all alike, constitute our starting point.

OUR PSYCHIC 'APPARATUS'

Taking inner life first, all human beings possess consciousness. When psychologists talk of the 'conscious' mind, the 'subconscious', and the 'unconscious', they are simply recognizing that human beings function simultaneously at several different levels of awareness. Taking you, the reader, as an example, your conscious mind consists of everything you are fully aware of at this moment; for example, this printed page. Your subconscious mind consists of those experiences which you are not aware of at this moment, but could become so if you wanted to; for example, your recollection of what you had for breakfast this morning. Notice also that other people may, by drawing your attention to some *current* experience of which you are not fully aware, pull that experience into your conscious mind and make you fully aware of it. At this moment, for example, you are not fully aware of the taste in your mouth – but you are now. You do not consciously experience the pressure of your clothes – but you do now. At any given moment you are being bombarded by countless stimuli, but only some of these stimuli will register clearly in your conscious mind.

Your *unconscious* mind contains all those experiences, impulses, drives and feelings of which you cannot become aware under ordinary circumstances. At first sight this seems paradoxical. If we cannot become aware of our unconscious how do we know we have one? The answer is simply that we can become aware of our unconscious feelings in certain extraordinary circumstances, such as psychoanalytic or hypnotic treatment, in times of very extreme stress, in dreams, in certain types of mental illness, and so on. Sometimes even in everyday living our unconscious feelings may almost reach our conscious minds, and indeed may distress or bewilder us when they do. Freud, in his *Psychopathology of Everyday Life*, pointed out that many social howlers, such as embarrassing slips of the tongue, are produced by a temporary lapse of censorship within ourselves, so that our polite social self conflicts with our not-so-polite unconscious attitudes. Thus, when expecting unwelcome guests we might greet their arrival with 'What, so soon?' instead of our intended 'Ah, at last!'; and on their departure blurt out 'Ah, at last!' instead of 'What, so soon?' Similarly, we might find ourselves taking an instant, powerful and apparently quite unjustified dislike to someone we have just met for the first time, and about whom we know literally nothing. This 'Dr Fell' situation is usually due also to an unconscious reaction. It may be, for example, that the individual reminds us strongly of someone we disliked in the past and have long 'forgotten'. Thus, unconscious feelings, even when derived from experiences in the remote past, may continue to influence our behaviour.

This division of consciousness into conscious, subconscious, and unconscious levels of awareness is now accepted by most psychologists. One group of psychologists, the psychoanalysts, have mapped out the human psyche in a more detailed way which is roughly parallel to the above distinctions. Psychoanalytic theory divides our psyche into three parts: the 'ego', the 'superego' and the 'id'. The Latin names are almost self-explanatory. The ego is, roughly speaking, the self: it is what we refer to whenever we use the word 'I'. The ego often acts as a kind of buffer between our superego and our id, and we are on the whole conscious of it. The superego can be called our conscience. As we know, its imperatives are mainly negative; it is much more likely to veto, forbid, discourage, and say generally 'thou shalt not' than it is to encourage and say 'thou shalt'. The superego is partly conscious and partly unconscious, depending on whether its pronouncements are derived from recent and remembered experiences, or from forgotten experiences in the past, e.g. early family influences. The id, which is unconscious, contains our crude, primitive, instinctive urges, mainly sexual or aggressive, which if uncontrolled would demand immediate gratification at any cost, regardless of consequences.

We are not born with an ego and a superego (or a sense of self and a conscience) but acquire them in rudimentary form in childhood. During the rest of our lives they are continually modified by our everyday experiences. We are, however, born with an id. A baby is, psychologically speaking, almost pure id. The moment he feels an instinctive urge he clamours for its instant gratification; and it is only his relative helplessness and physical ineffectiveness that stops him from acting on that impulse. An adult who acted solely on id-impulses would be a monster. For example, if he accidentally jostled a casual passer-by he would not step aside or apologize; he would smash and destroy the passer-by as an insufferable obstacle, tearing him apart with bare hands and, to obtain more crude pleasure, might then dance on his remains singing comic songs. If he were then to see an attractive member of the opposite sex – but here we should perhaps follow the example of the Victorian novelists, who marked this point with a long line of asterisks.

Comparison between the two parallel psychic systems we have outlined may be clarified by looking at the diagrams on the page opposite.

The arrows indicate that the systems are never static, but are normally held in a dynamic equilibrium of powerful forces. It should be emphasized also that these pieces of psychic apparatus are not 'real', in the sense that the various parts of our physical brain are real. They are no more than convenient psychological ideas or concepts; indeed, they are merely hypotheses. We use them in psychology because otherwise a great deal of our human behaviour would remain mysterious and inexplicable.

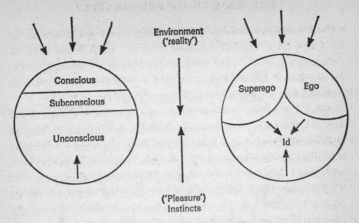

EGO DEFENCE MECHANISMS

It is clear that our individual egos are under considerable and continuous pressure from several sources. Our id-impulses, surging within us, search unceasingly for immediate expression; our superegos continually veto, prohibit, and restrict the expression of id-impulses; and the environment, although it varies in its influence (sometimes tempting, sometimes frustrating) always interests, stimulates and arouses us. Our ego has to be sufficiently integrated to withstand these onslaughts, yet flexible enough to accommodate their variations. In this conflicted situation, our egos survive and deal with these pressures largely by using a set of complicated and interrelated psychological techniques; they are usually referred to collectively as 'ego defence mechanisms'. These defensive techniques can be seen to some degree in all of us. Normal people call on them only in conditions of special stress, and when they *are* required they do not predominate for long. (We shall see later that in different psychological disorders different ego defence mechanisms are so predominant that they involve most of the individual patient's energy and interest.) Some of the more common defence mechanisms are as follows:

Repression is a largely unconscious device which we may use whenever we are confronted with a fact so distressing or repugnant to us that we try to deny it. We say, in effect, 'it ain't so'. It involves a flat refusal to accept a demonstrable fact; not consciously (this would be merely *suppression*) but without our being aware that we have done so. We might for example 'forget' that we have an oppointment with the dentist – we repress the knowledge, pushing it down into our unconscious. The repression may be complete, so that we have no conscious awareness whatever of the unpleasant fact, but quite often it is only partial. Thus, as the time of our dental appointment draws near we might feel vaguely uneasy, and wonder whether we haven't forgotten something; but this minor anxiety is much more tolerable than the traumatic actuality involved in keeping the appointment.

Projection occurs when we deny an unacceptable characteristic in ourselves, then ascribe it to someone or something else. We say, again unconsciously, 'It's not me, it's them.' This very common defence mechanism may become exceedingly destructive, depending on the malignance of the original characteristic projected. Mild forms may be observed in everyday life, e.g. any husband-and-wife argument in which each partner blames the other for tendencies that in fact both show. A more serious form was exemplified in Somerset Maugham's short story 'Rain', in which the clergyman denied, or repressed, his own libidinous impulses, ascribed them (i.e. projected them on) to the prostitute, and attempted to punish (or 'save') her for having them. The climax of the story came when his projective defence mechanism broke down and the minister suddenly became aware of his own 'intolerable' impulses. He acted out his libidinal impulses towards the prostitute and then, unable to deny any longer this evidence of his feelings, committed suicide. It is important to notice that projection, like other mechanisms, allows us a good deal of concealed gratification, in that once we have successfully accomplished it we can then belabour to our hearts' content the person who now 'demonstrates' what we can't stand in ourselves. Often when we hear vehement tirades and denunciations we may suspect a projective element in the denouncer. It is the vehemence, and the concealed malicious satisfaction, that give the game away.

Introjection is in a sense the converse of projection: when we introject we are not expelling undesirable features of ourselves, but incorporating the (to us) desirable features of others. Instead of saying 'It's not me, it's them,' we say 'It's not them, it's me.' (The unconscious is notoriously ungrammatical.) This does not imply that these characteristics (for example, the moral values of others) are really desirable, but only that we think so at the time, at least unconsciously. As we shall see later, children introject many of their parents' standards as a normal part of growing up, and adults introject many standards of their immediate society, or even of the institutions or professions within which they earn their living. The problem with introjection is that the standards or characteristics may be adopted in a wholesale, undiscriminating, exaggerated, or distorted form. Introjection is a more extreme form of *identification* which is more conscious, partial, and temporary, e.g. 'I'm *like* them.' And identification is in turn a more extreme form of mere *imitation*, e.g. 'I'm acting like them.'

Displacement involves saying, in effect, 'It's *this* I love or hate, not that.' The original feeling is consciously retained but it is unconsciously redirected on to some more acceptable substitute object. A man who has been criticized by his boss may not express his anger against the boss but against his wife when he gets home; the wife, also displacing her anger, proceeds to take it out on her children, who may in turn take it out on the dog, who takes it out on the cat, who takes it out on the canary – and so on, down the line. Any hierarchical system of human relationships facilitates displacement as a defence mechanism. Good-will as well as ill-will may be displaced in the same way.

In *rationalization* we present ourselves as acting rationally when in fact we are acting emotionally. A classic example of rationalization is the 'sour grapes' situation, where we decry the value of something unobtainable and thus conceal the humiliating fact that we have failed to get what we want.

Reaction formation involves establishing whole patterns of behaviour and feelings, developed as a massive defence against some intolerable and otherwise uncontrollable urge. This is defensiveness extended almost into a way of life. It is perhaps seen most clearly in the obsessive-compulsive personality (see Chapter 2), but some theorists, assuming that we are all basically nasty, would say that any civilized way of life is really a reaction formation against our naturally barbaric impulses. We can often see a grain of truth in this point of view. A ruthless business tycoon who has clawed his way to the top, stamping on the faces of all who got in his way, may become terrified at his own ruthlessness and dedicate his life suddenly and completely to 'good works'. Similarly, the mother who cannot bear her own 'unnatural' lack of maternal feeling (or who herself feels maternally neglected), may over-compensate by smothering her children with attention all through their lives. Her whole life may become a systematic attempt to refute publicly an unacceptable truth about herself. In making such interpretations, we should keep in mind that reaction formations *are* so only when they can be shown conclusively to be so. It is only when the underlying impulse shows through the defence mechanism that we may suspect that there is something wrong underneath.

Sublimation is similar to reaction formation in that it involves a fairly wholesale disgui.e and re-expression of unacceptable unconscious impulses in terms of acceptable conscious ones. Sublimation is, however, more positive and less defensive than reaction formation, in that the original impulse is considered to be 'transformed'; for instance, an ugly woman, unconsciously resentful of the good looks of other women, might open a beauty salon and make a career of enhancing their beauty, thus sublimating her own resentment. Here again we should guard against any tendency to consider all positive human activities as nothing but sublimations of something less attractive. Unless there is some discernible element of falseness or caricature in the behaviour (i.e. so that the initial impulse, however well disguised, may still be seen), the activity cannot be regarded as a sublimation.

Fantasy is one of the commonest defence mechanisms which we all tend to use when bored or disgruntled. If reality displeases us too much we may simply transform it by daydreaming; we elaborate our internal world according to our needs at the time, and at the expense of the outer world. Most of us are aware of this tendency, if not during the fantasy, then afterwards when we are brought back to reality. We know we have been 'making believe'.

These defence mechanisms, plus *regression*, which is central to our developmental outline and is discussed in more detail later in this preface (p. xxii), represent some of the ways in which the ego retains its integrity; or, in plain language, the ways in which we try to make life more bearable for ourselves.

DEVELOPMENTAL MILESTONES

Having outlined these common features of our inner lives, we now turn to the environmental or external events which we all share. In his ordinary living, every human being experiences many critical and intense life-situations; for example, being an infant, being looked after by parents, being at school, being married, being a parent, earning a living, and dying. These are psychological milestones in human development, and represent personal crises which each of us must resolve as best he can. We are inevitably confronted by the crises simply in growing older. They involve us in vital personal relationships with all the important people in our lives: our mother, our father, our brothers and sisters, our friends and neighbours, the opposite sex, our teachers and employers, our husbands and wives, and, in turn, our children. It is on these basic human crises that we shall concentrate.

Our format or framework is, naturally, developmental. That is, we shall be considering, in their developmental order, infancy, early childhood, the play age, the school age, adolescence, young adulthood, adulthood and old age. We shall be asking: what is the central psychological issue, and what concerns us most, at each stage of development? In each crisis, what are the satisfactory and the unsatisfactory resolutions? And how influential are the earlier resolutions (good, bad, or indifferent) in our later lives? As we discuss each growth stage we shall take the point of view of the individual who is in that phase of development.

NORMAL AND ABNORMAL

Psychologists are sometimes criticized for ignoring mental health. Some of them seem to imply that mental illness is universal, and that everybody (with the possible exception of the psychologist) is so sick as to require urgent and extensive psychoanalytic treatment. On the whole, this is merely an occupational bias which need not be taken too seriously. At its worst, however, it takes the form of insisting that unpleasant or ignoble motives are always more real and valid than our pleasant or kindly ones. Now there is no doubt whatever that we often have nasty motives, and that we conceal them or disguise them as noble altruism. We shall in fact be examining such deceptions in considerable detail. But our search for concealed motives does not commit us to the view that all the pleasant ones are nothing but unpleasant ones in disguise. Being 'nice' is not always, or solely, a defence against being nasty. Those who insist, despite all evidence to the contrary, that friendly, constructive, helpful behaviour is always 'really' (at some mystic level of psychological insight) a rampant but craftily concealed selfishness, are showing a compulsion to believe the worst of people – which itself invites psychological interpretation. This kind of bias will probably be minimized by the developmental framework of this book, which allows us to consider constructive as well as destructive behaviour, health as well as illness, and normality as well as abnormality.

Psychologists usually distinguish at least three meanings of 'normal': the statistical, where we are normal if we are in the majority; the (hypothetical) ideal, where we are normal if we are perfect; and the adaptive, where we are normal if our reaction is appropriate to a given situation. These meanings, which overlap to a considerable degree, may be subsumed under *developmental normality*, in terms of which we are normal if we function predominantly according to our age. This is, if you like, 'maturity', so long as we realize that we may be mature in this sense at any given stage of development, and not merely when we are given the key of the door. There are as many forms of developmental normality as there are developmental phases. We should recognize also that the same psychological functionings may be healthy or normal at one stage of development, and unhealthy and abnormal at another. For example, it is natural for a child of six to be predominantly concerned with his intense feelings for both of his parents; it is not at all natural for an adult of thirty to be similarly preoccupied.

We shall describe illness or abnormality in two ways: (a) as a failure to resolve satisfactorily the psychological crisis appropriate to a given age group, and (b) as 'regression' to ways of functioning appropriate to earlier age levels. Thus, the thirty-year-old adult mentioned above is abnormal both because he is *not* living like a thirty-year-old adult and also because he *is* living like a six-year-old child. This double criterion for illness allows us to interrelate those psychological breakdowns due to current stresses and those due to unresolved earlier conflicts. Probably all mental illnesses are due to a combination of both factors, but in any given illness one or other factor may predominate.

REGRESSION

Since the idea of regression is central to our developmental outline we should clarify the use we intend to make of it. Regression occurs when a person under stress reverts to a less complex and less differentiated mode of living than is appropriate to his particular age; that is, he reacts to stress with immature behaviour. Regression is quite common in everyday living. The newly-married housewife, who, having burned her first cake, bursts into tears, or the husband who, frustrated by his inability to follow the instructions on a do-it-yourself kit, hurls his hammer through the window, are both people regressing under stress. However understandable their reactions, they are, clinically speaking, behaving like very young children. For some people, however, regression is not brief and temporary, but may become a way of life. They may relive, over and over again, episodes or stages in their earlier lives. In this broader, more inclusive meaning of regression, the individual's reversion or slipping back to earlier, more primitive ways of functioning may take biological, psychological, and social forms.

Since we are giving regression such a broad meaning, we should remember that the concept is limited by certain clinical facts. The actual behaviour of regressed adults is never identical with the behaviour of individuals at an earlier developmental level, only comparable. Adult patients are not children, only *like* children. Also, regression is always partial, so that the regressed individual will continue to behave in some ways that are quite appropriate for his age. Even when regression is severe, behaviour is never utterly consistent: symptoms vary considerably from day to day and even from hour to hour.

A further qualification is that regression is not always sick. Psychoanalysts usually assume that no basic psychological crisis is ever fully resolved, and that traces of early partly resolved conflicts and partly satisfied needs will always persist into later life. If the frustration of early needs is a necessary part of ordinary living, then our tendency to regress to early developmental levels must be regarded as normal to precisely the same extent as the original frustration was inevitable. Such regressions cannot indicate abnormality. At most they represent a certain psychological vulnerability common to us all. It has even been suggested that some forms of regression may actually be advantageous to us, in that they are regressions in the service of the ego, e.g. unconscious creative processes. To regress in this sense may be regarded as *reculer pour mieux sauter*.

These considerations alone should make us very careful about trying to match specific developmental stages with specific types of illness in a one-to-one or once-for-all fashion. This is why, throughout the book, we shall be considering only the *predominant* features of any given situation. When I consider illness or regression in each basic situation, I shall describe psychologically sick people in terms of their *similarity* to younger people. Regressive illness is considered to occur when we cannot *easily* be distracted from earlier crises; when we neglect for them the *urgent* demands of current reality. Regression becomes pathological when one (or more than one) earlier mode of functioning *predominates* in our lives.

We shall assume that an individual of any age may regress to any stage, or stages, through which he has already developed; that the stage to which he regresses is the one in which his earlier conflicts were least adequately resolved; that the form of his illness is determined by the normal psychological crisis of the 'regression stage'; and that the earlier the stage to which he regresses, the more severe the illness.

I hope that this developmental framework, on which the book as a whole is based, will systematize and to some extent integrate the various psychological theories about human beings. In particular I wish to avoid sterile controversy, such as the (now old-fashioned) contest between psychoanalysis and behaviourism. Psychoanalysis deals with symptoms as determined by their antecedents; it focuses on the past, and on the genesis or origin of the symptom. Behaviourism deals with the symptom as determined by its consequences; it focuses on the present, and how symptoms are maintained here and now. Psychoanalysis asks, 'What caused the symptom?', and answers mainly in terms of individual unconscious processes. Behaviourism asks, 'What maintains the symptom?' and usually answers in terms of observable social reinforcements, i.e. rewards and encouragement as opposed to punishment and discouragement. Psychoanalysis, assuming that the symptom reflects, or is a 'sign' of, something else, tries to give the patient 'insight'. Behaviourism, assuming that the symptom *is* the illness, regards it as merely a bad habit that the patient must be encouraged to unlearn.

The difference between these theories is not one of truth and falsity, but merely one of basic assumption. Controversy is possible only when the assumptions are regarded as facts, instead of convenient hypotheses which are confirmed sufficiently for some, but not all, practical purposes. The developmental approach is the one most appropriate to our present purpose, and is adopted here solely because of its convenience.

THE TABLES

In the Tables (see Appendices pp. 259, 260) some of the main psychological approaches to personality have been not merely juxtaposed but integrated, in the hope that this will emphasize similarities as well as differences, and in order that each may act as a corrective on the others. Although Erikson contributes more to Table I than either Freud or Piaget, this is merely because his developmental outline is the most comprehensive. Erikson not only gives due weight to biological, psychological and social modes of functioning, and to health as well as illness; his outline also covers the whole life span, and does not come to an abrupt end in adolescence or early adulthood. Table I is intended to provide a highly condensed summary of human development in terms of age, major physical changes, major psychological preoccupations and intellectual features, and significant social changes.

Table II, which has to do only with illness, may require a word of explanation. Levin's table, based on Erikson's eight stages, was originally described as 'A concise table of the predominant content of the direct or precursive form of the psychiatric primitives as these appear serially through the eight stages.' Levin's 'psychiatric primitives' are simply those basic clinical concepts which are usually called anxiety, depression and identity pathology.[1] Simply put, his table represents a systematic analysis of emotion as it predominates in mental

1. Although most of us know roughly what we mean by 'identity', it is not easy to describe precisely. D. C. Levin (1963) describes it generally as 'the sense of the continuity of human life from the cradle

illnesses when these are considered as developmental regressions. Levin himself is fully aware that his table represents a gross oversimplification of human emotion. He emphasizes that his table 'is to be taken as relating to psychiatric theory . . . in the same way that a multiplication table is related to the whole of mathematics.'

The second part of Table II is taken largely from Foulds (1965), who classifies illnesses in terms of the degree of psychological disintegration involved. He regards illness as failure in personal relations, a failure increasing in severity along the following continuum: personality disorder, personal illness, integrated psychosis, disintegrated psychosis. In Table II Fould's integration–disintegration continuum has been modified developmentally so that illnesses may be considered not only as disintegrative but also as regressive.[2]

If you object that this elaborate frame of reference is not neat and tidy, I may reply with truth that neither are people.

It is in fact the tables which, in summarizing the book as a

-----

to the grave', and of course he spells out its various negative forms as shown in Table II. You, the reader, may grasp the meaning of identity in a more personal way by thinking deliberately about your own sense of 'self'. For example, you have a certain sense of your self at the present moment; this present self is considerably different from the self you were, say, five years ago; and will presumably be very different from the self you will be, say, five years from now. Yet despite the fact that your sense of self changes with time and experience, there is something within you that does not change but continues as a constant. This may be regarded as your identity. In this sense, we may even see identity in others. For example, an older man may give a boyish grin which suddenly lets us see what he must have been like in his youth; or a young girl may frown seriously, and we suddenly get a glimpse of what she will be like later in life. What we are seeing on such occasions is the continuity of self over time; we are catching a glimpse of identity.

2. Although the work of several authors has been incorporated into Tables I and II, this does not mean that these authors are in any way responsible for the use made of their work in this book.

whole, indicate how close I intend to stand to human beings in order to see them clearly. They indicate our focus on humanity. We can illustrate this by an analogy with television viewing. If we stand too close to our television screen we do not see people clearly: we only see parts of them. Many textbooks of psychology adopt this viewpoint, and deal with preselected and partial aspects of people, such as their learning processes, their perception, or their attention. Similarly, if we stand right up against our television screen we do not even see parts of people, but only wavy lines and whirling points of light. The psychological textbook taking this viewpoint might deal with neurone impulses and synapses, or glandular secretions, or biochemical units, or stimuli and responses; it would not really be about *people* at all. If, on the other hand, we stand too far away from our television screen we see only broad, blurred patterns. Textbooks as distant as this from people tend to lose sight of them altogether, and deal with groups, trends, national and cultural patterns, or even with statistical formulae. I have attempted in the tables to indicate a viewpoint somewhere in the middle distance, where we require neither a microscope nor a telescope, but where we may use our own eyes and recognize clearly individuals as whole persons, interacting with other whole persons in the ordinary situations of everyday life.

Two major omissions in the book should be pointed out. Although the biological determinants of personality will always be given due weight, we shall not be considering, as such, the personality of individuals whose disturbance is clearly physical; nor shall we deal with the personalities of mentally defective people. In all our discussions of basic interpersonal situations we shall regard both physique and intelligence as 'constants'.

One final word of caution to the reader. When some people first realize how many things can go terribly wrong even in quite ordinary psychological development, and how many apparently adequate adjustments conceal hidden conflicts, they begin to see all kinds of psychological disasters and catastrophes in the lives and personalities of those around them. Some of these people are in fact transformed by their new-found insight into psychological zealots. Self-appointed spokesmen for Sigmund Freud, they rush towards their friends and acquaintances determined to stamp out mental illness wherever they think they see it. And they see it everywhere. One can hardly offer the most harmless comment, like 'It's a fine day,' without these individuals nudging themselves gleefully and muttering 'Aha! I know what that means; that's *very* significant.'

This book provides no justification whatever for such enthusiastic extravagances. It is a guide to understanding personality, not a do-it-yourself psychotherapy. It is intended to help the reader see why people's lives sometimes go wrong; it will not explain how they should be put right. The light-hearted prescription of psychological remedies, without adequate training and experience, is exceedingly dangerous and may do irreversible psychological damage.

If any reader, having read this book and mastered its contents to his own satisfaction, finds that he cannot resist the temptation to psychodynamite the people he knows, he is earnestly urged (for his own sake) to begin with the individual who confronts him when he stands before a mirror.

CHAPTER ONE

Infancy (0–2 years)

... shadow-peopled infancy
SHELLEY, *Prometheus Unbound*

INTRODUCTION[1]

IT is in some ways unfortunate that human growth begins with infancy for there is no area in psychology more bedevilled with controversy and dispute than the psychology of infants. The disputation is perhaps inevitable. Infants, especially when we try to consider them from their own point of view, are not easy to understand. They cannot tell us what is going on in their inner life; and even if they could we would almost certainly find we did not understand them. We can of course see that the behaviour of babies is exceedingly unstructured and almost random; and we can surmise that their subjective experiences are correspondingly blurred, fleeting and diffuse. But we do not know that it *must* be so. Indeed, as adults who have long forgotten our own infancy, we *cannot* ever know directly (or even by first-hand report) what it is like to be a baby. What knowledge we do have depends very heavily on inferences, analogies, hypotheses, and more or less educated guesses. This means also that when we come to consider the regressions to infancy shown by some adults, our descriptions of these people will be no more valid than our best inferences about the infants they resemble.

1. Readers who are not especially interested in the background theoretical problems of infant psychology may skip this Introduction and start reading on page 11.

Since our knowledge of the infant's psychology (and of adults who show infantile regression) is so heavily inferential, we will first consider the kinds of evidence from which our inferences must be drawn. We have in fact three main sources of information: (*a*) the biological facts of growth and maturation; (*b*) the observable behaviour of babies, both animal and human; and (*c*) our knowledge of the more basic instinctive and emotional needs of living creatures.

(*a*) Biological

The psychology of the infant may be clarified to some extent if we begin even before the beginning, as it were, by glancing briefly at his life before he is born. During the pre-natal period his functioning, especially in relationship to his mother, is of course much more biological than it is psychological or social. In these first nine months, during which the infant lives as a foetus in the moist, even warmth of his mother's inside, he resembles in many ways the protozoic sea-animal whose needs for oxygen and nourishing minerals are supplied by the sea-water, and whose existence may be described as 'drifting, receptive, passive, and without direction or motility'.

It is probably safe to assume therefore that in the pre-natal period the psychological life of the infant is rudimentary. For instance, there can be no awareness of space in the womb. The foetus does not have to move from here to there for food and shelter. Nor can there be any sense of time: the foetus cannot experience even the rhythmic and cyclical changes in his own physical needs.

Nevertheless, although the pre-natal infant may not be 'conscious', he is very much alive and active, even before his mother becomes aware of his first stirrings in the womb. Indeed, in the months from conception to birth he is recapitulating the whole of mankind's evolution. He starts as a small blob of protoplasm, changes into a kind of fish (his gills are observable), then into a

2

near-reptile, and finally into the monkey-like creature which foreshadows his ultimately human form. Of course the infant's condensation of centuries of ancestral evolution into nine months of pre-natal development does not imply intention on his part. Recapitulation is not something he initiates; it is merely something that happens to him because he is a member of the human species.

The physical influences which play upon the infant during the pre-natal period may determine, in crucial ways, what he will be like after he is born. For example, if the mother is over-exposed to X-ray radiation, or if she catches German measles, he may be born malformed. If the mother is addicted to drugs, he may be born similarly addicted. The timing of such influences, that is, the precise point during the pre-natal period when the infant suffers the infection (whatever it happens to be), is of prime importance. At any given time, the most vulnerable organs are the ones which are differentiating and developing most rapidly at that time. If the infant is infected before the end of the fourth week of pregnancy, he is likely to suffer spina bifida or anencephaly; by the end of the seventh week, cardiac malformations; before the end of the ninth week, cleft lip; and so on (Millen, 1963). The risk of damage is greatest during the first month of pregnancy and diminishes gradually until about the fourth month. Among mothers who have German measles during the first twelve weeks, sixteen per cent of the children who are born alive may have cataract, deafness, heart lesions, or subsequent retardations; but if the mother's illness occurs in the fourth month, the only risk is deafness.

In these scales (which are still only rough guides) we see that if we know the time of the noxious stimulus we can predict the probable effect; and if we know the effect we can calculate the probable time of the noxious stimulus. These scales are based essentially on our knowledge of the basic sequences and critical periods of the differentiation of organs in embryonic growth.

The general sequence of development in the embryo (embryo-genesis) is of course the same for all human beings. The first organs formed are the mouth and the intestines; a little later, the anus. Muscles appear, the jaw muscles first, and later the sexual glands.

Now there is a marked similarity between the growth of the embryo and subsequent psychological development, that is, between the stages of physical development before birth and the stages of bio-psychological development after birth. The post-natal development of human beings, without exception, centres successively on certain zones of the body: first the mouth, then the anal system, then the genitals – the order is invariable. Psychological development 'lags a long way behind the somatic development, like a late version or repetition of the same process' (Abraham, 1924). As the growth of the embryo recapitulates evolution, so psychological development recapitulates that of the embryo.

These parallels between physical and psychological development apply to both health and illness. If the foetus is malformed, from the type of physical malformation and from knowledge of the ages at which the different organs develop we can tell at what age the foetus was infected. If we consider which aspects of *mental* development are most affected, from knowledge of the age at which various *mental* functions are normally developed, we can draw similar inferences about the ages at which adverse *psychological* factors made their impact.

We suggested earlier that the pre-natal infant was not conscious. We should recognize, however, that psychologists disagree as to when precisely the infant may be said to become conscious, or to become a person capable of social relationships with others. Even though pre-natal infants can respond to stimulation, whether from the mother or her outside environment, and even though this capacity is certainly a part of what we usually mean by 'consciousness', most psychologists tend

4

not to regard the pre-natal infant as conscious. It is in fact doubtful whether any genuine psychological interaction (as distinct from merely biological interaction) takes place between the mother and the foetus. The popular belief that young mothers may increase the physical attractiveness of their unborn child by looking at nothing but beautiful paintings and statues in art galleries during their pregnancy cannot really be supported by psychological evidence. There is of course little doubt that mother–foetus relationships do occur; for example, a mother undergoing extreme emotional stress may cause hyperactivity in her foetus, and after birth such infants may cry a lot, be generally irritable, and have great difficulty in sleeping, feeding, and excreting. But if these effects are caused by psychological factors, the precise factors are not known.

The infant's earliest psychological needs are inferred largely from our knowledge of his biological needs, from which indeed they are scarcely distinguishable. It is usually assumed that he does have needs, e.g. for food, warmth, support, protection. It is, however, also assumed that he cannot be aware of these needs, simply because there is, in the very nature of his pre-natal life, no delay between the arousal of such a need and its gratification, e.g. he can never feel hungry because his hunger is satisfied the very instant it occurs. In general it is assumed that the unborn baby enjoys in the womb a unique freedom from basic frustration.[2]

When the baby is born he obviously becomes much easier to observe directly. It would seem logical therefore to precede any description of his inner life with a brief description of his typical behaviour. That is, before attempting to infer what he is feeling, we should first observe what he is doing.

2. Some psychoanalysts have assumed also that throughout our life we unconsciously wish to return to this state of pre-natal bliss. Such speculations are interesting, but probably unverifiable. The evidence usually offered, e.g. the fact that many adults adopt the foetal position during sleep, is itself highly inferential.

(b) Behaviour

Psychologists have studied infant behaviour in two ways: by observing it directly, and by comparing it with the behaviour of lower animals. While the information provided by these behavioural studies does help us to understand the psychology of infants, we should remember that our inferences, from (i) what the infant does to (ii) what he must be experiencing, should always be drawn with the greatest caution.

Many studies have been concerned with the effect of stimulation on infants. These investigations have clearly shown that even young infants are able to distinguish between different sensory stimuli. The process may not be started by the new-born infant himself, but as soon as he feels stimuli impinging upon him he seems to be able to discriminate selectively. It has been demonstrated that new-born infants can give specific motor responses to thermal, tactile, taste, auditory, and visual stimulation even on the first day of life. As well as activity involving the infant's whole body, he makes many specific movements of turning towards, trying to maintain contact with, and turning away from, different external stimuli. The fact that some of these specific movements are positive and others negative suggests that even the new-born infant is capable of selecting between different kinds of stimuli and that his sensual adventuring, whether out into his environment or merely over his own body, is not entirely random.

New-born infants also seem to derive pleasure from stimulation as such. They are, within the first twenty-four hours, *attracted* to stimuli: not only those closely related to their desire to nurse (e.g. finger-touch on the lip, stroking of the cheek, warmth of the cheek, taste of lactose solution); but also to other stimuli such as warmth on the sole of the foot, the smell of anise, and a moderate light. This 'enjoyment' of stimulation is more than the mere appetite for stimulation. It would appear that even new-born infants are not simply surviving the 'cata-strophe of birth' but may have a positive, although rudimen-tary, zest for living.

The infant also seems to derive pleasure from stimulation only when the stimulation is optimal. He will be restless and search actively when he is under-stimulated; but he will be restless also when he is over-stimulated, whether from within (e.g. by hunger) or from without (e.g. by a bright light). Also, the same stimuli that will attract the infant when he is re-freshed will repel him when he is tired.

In this context maternal influence may be understood in terms of the degree to which the mother can protect her infant from over- or under-stimulation. Stimulation is optimal when the mother recognizes her child's needs and adjusts his environ-ment accordingly. This means full-time and whole-hearted ten-derness and watchfulness on her part. If she is distracted, perhaps by her own problems or anxieties, the infant is liable to suffer over- or under-stimulation. There are of course wide in-dividual differences in babies. Babies who are initially active will develop normally even when stimulation, whether mater-nal or otherwise, is kept to the bare minimum consistent with good physical care; while inactive babies will develop normally only if frequently stimulated. Similarly, 'dummies' or 'pacifiers' will calm highly aroused infants, but will arouse calm ones.

We should also remember that although babies actively search for and enjoy stimulation they are not always seeking. Piaget (1952) observed that infants in the first and second days of life showed only an eager concentration, with their torso and limbs quite still, when they were sucking. Nor of course are infants always restless and active; when newly born they spend eighty per cent of their time sleeping.

Much of the infant's stimulation comes not from objects in his environment, but from people. Three stages of development in the infant's social behaviour have been distinguished. From birth until three months he seeks sensory stimulation as such. What he requires, however, is not stimulation specifically from people but merely stimulation that is sufficiently varied. If he is deprived of this general stimulation he may be seriously harmed. Between three and seven months his interest is genuinely social, but still indiscriminate. He distinguishes people from the rest of his environment but not from each other; so that at this time he will be comforted by literally anyone who supplies his needs. After seven months he is able to discriminate between people, and actively seeks general sensory contact with his mother and other familiar and preferred figures.

Animal studies have sometimes thrown light on human infant behaviour. The need in infants for stimulation was almost unwittingly confirmed by an experiment with young white rats. One group of rats was given extensive handling, another group was given mild electric shocks, while a third group was simply left in the nest. The rats most adversely affected were the unhandled ones, not (as expected) the shocked ones. Stimulation as such was found to be beneficial, in the sense that both the handled and the shocked rats developed faster, and in later life coped better with stress.

The complexities of early mother–child relationships were well demonstrated by a series of experiments with monkeys. By substituting wire-and-terrycloth mothers Harlow (1962a and b) showed that, when feeding, baby monkeys respond to the tactile stimulation in nursing as much as to the nursing itself. However, follow-up studies showed that infant monkeys brought up with these mother-surrogates did not breed well in later life. Although it was found later that the effects were less damaging if baby monkeys were allowed to interact more with their peers, the essentially adverse effect of deprivation has been confirmed in many other studies.

These studies warn us that important factors may operate in

a given experimental situation, yet remain undetected until powerful side-effects emerge later in follow-up studies. In any experimental situation hidden variables are a constant possibility, and they are perhaps most likely to be present in studies of early influences in the rearing of infants, whether human or animal. Even the finding that the damage caused by maternal deprivation may be offset to an indefinite extent by increased interactions with peers requires careful interpretation; for the two situations may not really be equivalent. It may be that losing a mother is not so bad if you can gain a few friends, but did Harlow's monkeys regain exactly what they had lost?

There is also the general difficulty about animal studies – inferences drawn from them tend to become invalid if pushed too far. Some animal experimenters have made inferences from, say, rats to children, with a facility that they would not dream of allowing themselves in making inferences between other species, say, from rats to cats. The biological and developmental differences between species (e.g. the initial superiority and later inferiority of monkeys in relation to children) makes comparison between them a very delicate matter indeed. A single inference, from child behaviour to child psychology, is complicated enough; a double inference, from animal behaviour to child behaviour to child psychology, has an enormous potential for error at each step.

On the other hand, many of the variables isolated in animal studies confirm those discovered in investigations into human development; for instance, the infant's need for general stimulation; the impairment he suffers when the mother is absent, or when nursing is drastically interfered with; the occurrence of critical ages for the development of the specific functions; and the importance of social interaction with other people besides the mother.

(c) Instincts, Needs and Emotions

When we turn from the study of infant behaviour, human or animal, to the study of infant *experience*, we find that experiential studies – those concerned with the infant's motivation, personality, consciousness, cognition, emotions and inner life generally – have to cope not only with all the problems of behavioural studies but with others as well. The overriding qualification to any theory of infant psychology is that the infant's own awareness of what is happening around him and within him, his 'consciousness', is bound to be extremely diffuse. It would in fact be astonishing if his inner subjective experiences were any better differentiated than his biological and cognitive–perceptual apparatus. We may assume with some confidence that infantile consciousness is not well articulated in itself, and is not therefore likely to make firm contact with external reality.

In trying to understand the inner life of infants one great danger is that we become 'adultomorphic', and reinterpret infant behaviour in terms of similar adult behaviour. For example, in one attempt to distinguish stages in the emotional development of babies during the first year, it was found that they could show diffuse excitement at birth, distress and delight at three months, anger and disgust by the fifth month, fear by the seventh month, elation and affection between ten and twelve months. Despite the rough parallel between this finding and other scales, the fact remains that our observation is necessarily limited to emotion that can be identified and described. If infants do not show identifiable and describable emotions we often conclude that they have no emotions whatever. This is one form of adultomorphy.

Again, it has sometimes been assumed by investigators that babies who bite, suck, and touch are being 'sadistic', 'aggressive', and 'libidinous'. If we, as adults, were to behave like such infants our behaviour might reasonably be described as sadistic, and so on. However, it is not us, but the infant, with whom we are concerned, and we are not entitled to assume that he has the same reasons as we might have for behaving in a particular way. To project adult motivation into infant behaviour is another form of adultomorphy.

Some investigators are so adultomorphic that they will not allow the infant any consciousness at all. From the study which showed that infants first seek stimulation in general, some would conclude that the infant 'must be' totally unaware of his mother until he is seven months old. However, no one is suggesting that the infant has a highly developed consciousness, like our own. Like the foetus, he may be profoundly influenced by his mother without being *fully* aware of it. In this sense, his early interaction with his mother may be regarded as his first personal relationship so long as we do not insist that the influence of each upon the other is psychologically equivalent in terms of intention and consciousness. The relationship, if not reciprocal, is at least mutual.

CRISES IN INFANCY

When a child is born, the psychological changes he goes through – however vaguely he perceives them – are almost certainly as profound as the biological changes. Birth is a disencapsulation, and the regions of the infant's 'life space' are utterly transformed – his mother, once the whole of his environment, is now, suddenly, merely a small part of it. His new, expanded environment bombards him with stimuli. If at birth he is slapped he may feel pain for the first time. He may feel cold, exposed and unsupported. And so on. These changes must have a considerable influence on his subjective (inner) life. At the most primitive level, he must suddenly become aware of all those needs (hunger, for instance) which before birth had been satisfied in the very moment of their occurrence. There is now a delay between his feeling of need and its gratification. If his mother is attentive and loving the periods of delay may be very short; but the point is that delays do occur, where before they did not.

The infant's awareness of his own needs does not, however, necessarily entail any clear sense of himself as a self. If all his perceptions of his environment are (so far as we can observe and deduce) incoherent and transitory, then so is his perception of his own identity and inner life. Even the physical boundaries of his own 'body image' have to be learned. For example, he may watch his own hand move in and out of his field of vision many times before he begins to suspect that he himself has anything to do with the phenomenon, or even that the hand is his, and is connected to his arm and his body.

It is also unlikely that the infant can distinguish clearly between his inner and outer world. We have no reason to suppose that the young infant has any clear idea of where he stops and his environment begins. It is more likely that he experiences himself and his surroundings not as interacting but as interpenetrating. For him, the boundaries between the two are probably permeable, and only later do they become mutually exclusive enough to allow him to differentiate effectively between 'me' and 'not-me'.

The differentiation between 'me' and 'not-me' is probably never achieved once and for all by human beings, but is continually being tested and modified in the light of experience. Even in adults the differentiation may blur in certain circumstances, such as drug or alcohol intoxication, moments of extreme introspection, states of fatigue, prolonged concentration or isolation, or perhaps even in the condition known as falling in love. In certain illnesses, as we shall see later, the central symptom is the inability to distinguish between feelings that are ours and those that may be attributed to others. There may also be a cultural difference: some countries, and especially the Oriental ones, do not make such clear distinctions or have such water-tight categories in their normal conceptualizations of reality as in the West.

The infant's sense of time and causality is probably as unclear as his awareness of himself and objects in space. If he finds that whenever he roars for food nourishment comes, he may have a vague feeling that he is controlling reality. However, he is almost certainly not capable, as some authorities have suggested, of purposefully directed action of such a complex nature. He does not really have the intellectual apparatus to be described accurately as suffering from 'delusions of omnipotence'; any delusion involves complex and well-integrated thought processes. At most, he is confusing *post hoc* with *propter hoc*, and failing to realize that the mere sequence of events – nourishment following the need for it – does not necessarily imply that his need directly causes his nourishment to materialize.

It is generally agreed that the infant does enter into 'a state of permanent exchange with the environment'. It is also generally agreed that although the infant himself is so undifferentiated, his main mode of function is 'incorporative' (see Appendix, Table 1). That is, he takes in his outside world. Although he incorporates reality with all his senses, his predominant mode of incorporation is oral. The mouth is the most highly developed part of the body at birth, and very young infants do not merely test their world for satisfactoriness; they actually taste it. Babies will refer all objects to their mouth for evaluation. Freud referred to this as the first oral stage of sucking. Later, when the infant feels his new teeth thrusting painfully through his gums he reaches a second oral stage of biting. At this stage he is still predominantly incorporative but perhaps less so than before. Certainly his perceptual and muscular apparatus has developed considerably. 'The eyes, first part of a passive system of accepting impressions as they come along, have now learned to focus, to isolate, to "grasp" objects from the vaguer background and to follow them. The organs of hearing sensitivity have learned to discern significant sounds, to localize them and to guide an appropriate change in position ... the arms have learned to reach out determinedly and the hands to grasp firmly' (Erikson, 1959).

The visual system in fact matures very rapidly in babies. Within two months they show visual 'shape constancy'; that is, they recognize a square object as square even when they see it subjectively as oblong, for example, when it is not viewed directly at right angles to the surface. Also, normal adult visual accommodation, or the capacity of the lens of the eyes to change its curvature when viewing objects close at hand, is present by the fourth month. Babies tend to focus during the early weeks on objects eight to nine inches away; in most cases this will be the mother's face during feeding, but in any case, babies of four to six weeks do show a preference for the human face. Disturbed (e.g. autistic) children will avert their gaze and show more interest in objects, and the faces of animals.

It is on the basis of these biologically inevitable changes in feeding, teething, and eventual weaning that an infant's subjective inner life develops. His personality is in fact determined largely by his capacity to cope with these successive critical events. Erikson's analysis of infantile psychology, for example, starts with the relationship between the infant's inner and outer world. As inner feelings of comfort and discomfort recur in fairly regular cycles they eventually become familiar to the infant. As they integrate he begins to develop a rudimentary memory, a vague sense of his own continuity – in short, a primitive identity. These inner events gradually become associated with outer events and people, especially his mother. The sequence may be thought of as: inner discomfort (e.g. hunger) – outer event (mother's feeding) – comfort ... discomfort – outer event – comfort ... and so on, so that there is eventually a satisfactory correspondence between inner and outer events. If his mother continues to provide from outside the comfort and welfare that is consistent and hence predictable, she becomes for the infant a psychological certainty; a source of constant reassurance to him that his needs will be met by his new environment. It is from this reassurance that babies develop what Erikson calls *basic trust*. From what the infant incorporates, from its taste, its regularity, and its synchronous occurrence in relation to his needs, he derives his first rough estimate of how good or how bad the world is going to be for him.

At this early stage, trust shows behaviourally in the ease with which the baby feeds, in the depth of his sleep, and in the relaxation of his bowels. A little later it is shown when the infant will let his mother out of his sight without undue anxiety or rage. The baby who smiles also demonstrates trust in Erikson's sense. We should note however that in the earliest days the smile may indicate mere physical well-being in the infant, a sense of being 'all right' or of 'feeling good in his own skin'; a little later his smile seems to be less self-centred, but still largely imitative; only after some months is it a genuinely social response. Thus the infant who has achieved basic trust should be able to do all these things well.

It is interesting to notice that these criteria for health in infancy, namely, eating, sleeping, and excretion, continue to be basic for the rest of our lives. When we fall ill as adults, the first things we are asked by the doctor are, 'Is your appetite good?' 'Do you sleep well?' 'Did you "go" today?'

The infant who has achieved satisfactory adjustment to his world at the sucking stage cannot rest on his laurels for long. As his growth continues and his teeth begin to thrust painfully through his gums, he finds himself involved in a short-lived but genuine psychological conflict. To obtain the relief he requires from his new teeth he will be impelled to bite; but on the other hand, if he attempts to bite the nearest object, namely his mother, she will either withdraw or retaliate, thus leaving him worse off than before. Most infants are of course helped through this crisis by their mother providing a substitute such as a hard biscuit, and eventually the child learns how to continue sucking without biting. In psychological terms he will have achieved a compromise, without impairing his sense of personal identity or having his basic trust undermined.

Weaning, which is equally inevitable for all infants, is usually considered to involve some loss to the child. It is important that it should be as gentle and as gradual as possible for 'even under favourable circumstances this stage seems to introduce into the psychic life a sense of division' (Erikson, 1959).

Thus, as birth, feeding, teething and weaning successively make their psychological impact on the infant, they determine his first psychological crisis. What he has to cope with in his earliest experiences is his rudimentary but perhaps intense impression of 'having been deprived, of having been divided, and of having been abandoned' (Erikson, 1959).

Many investigators regard these earliest experiences in infancy as having a profound, indeed a disproportionate, effect on later life. It has even been suggested that the effect varies inversely with age. At first sight it is not easy to see why this should be so. It may be that when in later life we combine present and past experiences, we attend selectively to those aspects which confirm our own expectations, that is, we tend to see as adults what we were brought up to expect to find in life. If we experience contradictions we regard them as anomalous. In addition, our expectations may not only misrepresent the environment but may actually change it. If, for example, our early experiences have been consistently discouraging and have given us a low opinion of ourselves, we will as adults tend to behave in a rather abject fashion. Such an attitude eventually encourages others to accept our self-evaluation and make them treat us with a certain disdain, which otherwise they might not have done. The whole process confirms the initial self-derogation, thus completing the circle. The scarcity of landmarks in early experience may tend to make each one relatively more impressive; so that later experiences, if they are to be comparably impressive, must be very intense and important. A person of limited experience (as all young children are) tends to see quite minor events in life as major ones simply because he knows nothing else with which to compare them; a person of considerable experience, on the other hand, can accommodate even major events without undue excitement. We might add also that the novelty of an event increases its impact; and in infancy most events are novel.

Psychoanalysts take it for granted that the infantile (or any subsequent) crisis is never fully resolved. Thus basic trust is established against, despite, and throughout the infant's combined impressions of deprivation, division and abandonment. Nor is trust ever established once and for all. 'What the child acquires at a given stage is a certain ratio between the positive and the negative which, if the balance is towards the positive, will help him to meet later crises with a better chance for unimpaired total development' (Erikson, 1959).

ILLNESS IN INFANCY

The main criteria for illness in infants, as we might expect, are not so much psychological as biological and behavioural, for example, difficulty in sleeping, feeding and excreting, over-activity or under-activity, backwardness in perceptual or muscular development, and so on. The infant's biological development depends largely upon his inherited constitution and the stimulation he receives from his environment, while his psychological development depends largely on the stimulation and care he receives from other people.

The close connection and indeed the overlap between biological, psychological, and social influences in infancy has been
repeatedly demonstrated by many studies of the relationship
between mother and child. For example, it has been found that
both boys and girls whose mothers were described as 'warm'
(i.e. friendly and expressive) showed fewer difficulties such as
finickiness in feeding, temper tantrums, and lack of independence. It seems clear that the quality as well as the quantity of mothering is important. At this early stage, when the
infant is parasitic and totally demanding, without scruple or
regard for the needs of his mother, it would probably be hard
for him to have 'too much of a good thing'. Only in later years,
when incessant satisfaction of basic needs becomes less necessary and hence less appropriate, can his development be stifled
by a 'smother-mother'. As for the quality of the mothering he
receives, the infant may not be able to fully conceptualize the
difference in 'feel' between a loving, solicitous mother and, say,
an impatient, overworked, anxious, impersonal nurse who dis-
likes children; but to say he cannot ever be affected by such
differences goes far beyond, and in fact against, the evidence
which we have about the sensitivity of babies.

On the negative side it is generally thought that infants deprived of ordinary maternal care suffer an irreversible impairment of their capacity to respond warmly to people around
them. However, despite this general agreement about the adverse effects of maternal deprivation and lack of stimulation,
the precise effects of these influences are not yet fully known.
Maternal deprivation varies both in quantity and quality; in
other words, we must always ask not only whether or not deprivation occurred, but also how much and what kind of deprivation. The effects of deprivation depend on many factors: the
developmental stage of the child, the period of separation, the
quality of the relationship with his mother, the availability of
satisfactory substitutes, and other experiences at the time or

later which may help or further damage the child. We should also remember that deprivation need not be objectively real to produce a bad psychological effect on the infant; it is enough for him to feel deprived. We tend to forget that children's reactions to the outside world are not only diffuse but also exaggerated and intense. For instance, if a mother suddenly stops feeding her infant to answer the phone, he may not understand her absence. He will probably think she has left him to starve.

The purely experiential aspects of impaired relationships in infancy cannot of course be observed directly. They are inferred from the critical events of infancy. If birth, sucking, teething or weaning are too traumatic, the infant is believed to suffer an exaggerated sense of deprivation, division or abandonment – in Erikson's terms *a basic mistrust*. The infant may experience a sense of chaos when inner and outer events in his experience do not correspond. He may feel isolated, withdrawn, out of contact with his environment, or he may experience vague fears that there is insufficient nourishment for him. The basic mistrust of such infants involves an almost somatic bewilderment, apprehension, and discouragement.

When basic mistrust is extreme, infants may relapse into 'symbiotic' relationships in which there is a psychological fusion of mother and child. The infant is extremely clinging and 'melts into' the mother's body; he can neither differentiate himself from her nor function independently of her. Another severe form of basic mistrust shows in the autistic infant, who is unable to respond at all to any kind of outside stimulation.

It is doubtful whether these infantile impairments should be understood in psychological or merely in biological and genetic terms. Some investigators have extended the idea of regression to include both psychological and biological characteristics and therefore regard such infants as regressing in both senses. On the other hand, since the psychological past of infants is by definition extremely short, other investigators have preferred to regard the regression of infants as entirely biological. Psychological symptoms in infancy may be due to a 'lag in maturation'. In the words of one investigator, 'the neurological hierarchy and control remain primitive, resembling in many respects the organization of behaviour found in the foetal stages of development.' That is, just as regressed adults may show infantile characteristics, regressed infants may show foetal characteristics.

The general criteria for psychological failure in infants may therefore be regarded as the converse of the criteria for success already outlined in the preceding section. Psychological symptoms in infants may show when any of the following behavioural features becomes predominant: difficulty in sleeping, feeding, excreting; hyperactivity, restlessness and irritability; apathy, lack of energy, diminished responsiveness, perceptual and muscular retardation. The subjective or experiential aspects of such failures in infancy may be inferred as follows (see Appendix, Table II): A sense of *chaos*, when the infant fails to match inner and outer events; *anxiety*, showing in the form of a vague but extreme fear that there may not be enough to eat; *depression*, e.g. a profound, almost somatic feeling of loss. These negative feelings are subsumed under 'basic mistrust', and stem from the basic infantile experiences of deprivation, division and abandonment.

REGRESSIONS TO INFANCY

I emphasized in my preface that regression is not always pathological, and, when temporary, can even be beneficial. Some regressions, such as making a bawdy joke, having a dingdong row to get it out of our system, submerging our identity in a football crowd, or getting mildly drunk, are merely reactions in which we take a break from civilized 'coping behaviour' so that we can return to everyday problems refreshed and more effective.

Regressions even to infancy are sometimes normal. That is, if we are adopting the view that early needs, including those of infancy, are inevitably frustrated (if only because we are pushed by our biological growth into the next developmental stage), we must accept also that we shall remain psychologically vulnerable regarding those needs for the rest of our life. Our individual vulnerability depends of course on the extent to which the needs were frustrated, but we are *all* vulnerable to some extent; we all lived through roughly the same infantile experiences. So before considering people whose regression to infancy is pathological, we should first consider what allowance we must make for the normal regressions which represent merely our common vulnerability.

One measure of our vulnerability may show in our responsiveness to modern advertising. Advertising depends on creating a demand, or, in psychological terms, deliberately arousing needs. Advertisements become much more effective if they can arouse those basic and universal needs which in our normal development are inevitably left unsatisfied. The principle itself is simple. The advertiser first reactivates our earlier needs, then attempts to demonstrate that his product will satisfy them. Our response to such advertising is not so much rational as emotional; in fact, because the 'persuaders' are so well 'hidden' we are often not aware that we have been manipulated.

The earliest needs of infancy, for example, may be aroused by advertisements for beds and electric blankets, which re-create pictorially the warmth, support and comfort that we enjoyed in our earliest months. One current advertisement shows a blonde young lady snuggling down into her voluptuously soft bed, obviously enjoying that exquisite comfort which most of us suddenly become aware of when the alarm clock summons us in the morning. This type of advertisement is selling not the bed or the blanket, nor even the blonde, but the snuggle. Similarly, in selling insurance our latent anxieties about primitive security (for instance, the vague fear of unforeseen accidents) are first aroused, and then allayed by emphasis on the safety and security of the given firm's insurance policy. Often the advertised security is offered visually, in the form of a thick and apparently everlasting wall around the potential customer.

Oral needs of the sucking variety are reactivated in advertisements for smoking or drinking. Their effectiveness is tested empirically, according to sound psychological principles. Television commercials for smoking, for example, used to feature some sunlit, woodland scene by a waterfall, where a good-looking couple were observed blowing cigarette smoke into each other's faces, murmuring mellifluously how much they enjoyed the experience. It was soon found that the effectiveness of this commercial could be greatly increased if the couple were brought forward from the middle distance to the immediate foreground, emphasizing close-ups of their inhalations with the camera focused directly on the mouth. Similar techniques are used in beer advertisements, most of which appeal directly to the infantile logic that if it looks good and tastes good it *must* do you good. Oral aspects are particularly stressed. In one, a beer-drinker uses a tankard with a glass bottom. First the beer is drawn, and the viewer clearly sees and hears it foaming and splashing; the drinker's mouth begins to work in anticipation; there is a close-up of his lips actually closing over the rim of the tankard; and as he slowly drains it the camera is trained on the bottom of the glass so that the beer can be seen swirling down the drinker's throat. By the time the commercial is over the excited viewer is probably half-way across the room for his beer, or on his way to the telephone to order a dozen crates.

The biting phase of orality is recreated in advertisements for chewing gum, and for all the 'crunchy, munchy' products.

These sell us the reassurance that 'it's all right' to bite. Some stress the message that basic tensions will be relieved, or some disaster averted, by chewing the product. Others actually portray the disaster, but caricature its relationship to biting; a young man takes a bite of a crunchy bar of chocolate and the whole environment collapses in consequence. The 'world dissolution' is exaggerated just enough to produce a comic rather than an anxiety-provoking effect, but otherwise the situation is remarkably similar to that of the teething infant who bites inappropriately, and for whom the result (within his own frame of reference) would be equally cataclysmic. After all, when an infant realizes that his mother has withdrawn from him he has no way of knowing that this is a temporary and involuntary reaction; his experience is exceedingly limited and his powers of deduction negligible.

The infantile apprehension that the world will not provide enough to eat, or that there might not be enough food to go around, is of course aroused by many advertisements offering ways of storing security. We are urged to 'save for a rainy (i.e. foodless) day', or are offered elaborate storage containers, such as refrigerators and freezers, in which we may preserve any excess perishable foods that we cannot eat at the time. (The alleged tendency of even Eskimos to buy refrigerators is thus psychologically explicable.) Most housewives do keep a store of tinned food as a precaution against sudden social demands or their own temporary oversights; and if the store becomes depleted, by say the advent of unexpected guests, she feels anxious and uneasy until her 'tins cupboard' is as full again as she 'requires'.

Our vulnerability to all these appeals represents a normal temporary and partial regression to the infantile level. In fact we may regard such vulnerability as evidence of the extent to which our earliest needs were unsatisfied. It is the persistence of these needs into adult life that allows the advertiser to make predictions about us with an accuracy that is very much better than chance. The advertiser in fact measures his accuracy mathematically, in sales figures.

Also within the normal range are those people whom we tend to describe in language which, although non-technical, has oral connotations. For example, we call some individuals 'parasites' – a term of opprobrium whose literal meaning refers to a typically oral-dependent tendency. Such people are considered to be dedicated to their own oral satisfaction and will demand, explicitly or implicitly, continuous welfare from those around them. They are greedy people, addicted to 'taking', and will go to considerable lengths to avoid giving anything to anybody. This consistent refusal to recognize that others have an equal right to receive is in many ways comparable to the attitude of the infant to its mother. Infants are, technically speaking, parasitic on their maternal hostess, and behave with no consideration whatever for her needs.

An oral-incorporative tendency may of course be expressed not only in terms of food and support but also in terms of love. Some adults, for example, show a babyish dependency on others and will cling to any strong figure in their environment. Others are exceedingly ingratiating, cannot bear not to be loved, and will do almost anything to ensure continuous supplies of affection. This is not quite the natural wish to be thought well of, or to have affectionate friends, but a rather compulsive and chronic need for supplies which tends to dominate the whole of a person's life, and in fact to prevent the forming of spontaneous and mutual friendships. The tendency is probably related more closely to the weaning than the sucking phase of infancy.

Within the normal range there are of course many differences in degree regarding oral-incorporative and oral-dependent tendencies, and some forms are more obvious than others. The chronic glutton, for example, who is compelled to satisfy his oral needs by direct and excessive gormandizing, is merely a more extreme example of, say, the socialite who never gives a party but always manages to get himself invited to parties given by other people. In all such cases the behaviour may be chronic without being pathological in the strict sense. The orality is perhaps unpleasant or irritating, but it is not socially intolerable. In addition, when we criticize such individuals we are implying that their oral tendencies are not really beyond their own control – they can be 'blamed' for it.

Similarly, some forms of aggression are usually described in oral terms. Individuals who are unnecessarily brusque in their relationships with other people are often thought of as snappish or even biting. Examples may be found in many rural villages, but of course elsewhere also. These typically crusty old curmudgeons were once popularized in song by Bing Crosby, 'The Pessimistic Character with the Crab-Apple Face'. Their angry, cynical disillusionment is a common result of chronic personal disappointment, and often centres around matters of basic welfare. But although they are not happy people, they cannot be called pathological either. Many of them are in fact well tolerated by their communities as eccentrics.

The above examples by no means exhaust the variety of 'oral characters' who can be observed in everyday life, but they are enough to show the kind of allowance we must make for any oral tendency before we begin to regard it as pathological. Although a tendency of this kind may be consistent and last a long time, it does not really become pathological until it also predominates over positive tendencies in the individual's personality. All the characters described may well possess many positive characteristics also, such as the ability to hold a job or raise a family. In fact, in many people the negative characteristics of their personality do not merely co-exist with the positive characteristics, but are transformed or sublimated into positive tendencies. A person may choose a job, for example, not to avoid, or compensate for an unsatisfied oral need, but because it actually exemplifies that need and allows its continued expression in a socially acceptable form. (Analysis of sublimations would involve us in highly sophisticated psychodynamic theorizing far beyond the limits of our present purpose. We need only recognize that such extensions are logically possible.)

PATHOLOGICAL REGRESSIONS

We turn now to those infantile regressions which are regarded as pathological. Some people revert to infantile behaviour as a way of life. Just as in infancy the psychological and social aspects of experience are often difficult to distinguish from biological aspects, so those patients tend to be diagnosed both in psychosocial terms and also in constitutional-organic terms. Many psychologists who have investigated the relative contribution of psychological and physical factors in different illnesses have attempted to interpret the one set of factors in terms of the other, that is, to regard apparently biological aspects as really psychological, or vice versa. It seems more appropriate, however, to accept the dispute, now many years old, as evidence that both sets of factors do interact in infantile regressions, as indeed they do in infancy itself.

It is worth dwelling on this point for a moment, for we have in the past been too inclined to consider illness as *either* physical *or* mental, as if these two aspects of human functioning were always mutually exclusive. Most clinicians nowadays are beginning to suspect that the actual form an illness takes is less important than the fact that illness has occurred at all. It has been found that, in the life of an individual illnesses occur not at random but in 'clusters' lasting about seven years, and in correspondence with periods of environmental stress. During these periods patients become more susceptible to *all* kinds of illness, so that there is a parallel between the occurrence of mental and physical illnesses. Thus, not only are we more vulnerable at some times than others, but our vulnerability is general. The eventual form of the illness may be determined merely by our 'line of least resistance' (or greatest satisfaction) at the time. The classification of an illness as mental or physical is in fact largely a matter of therapeutic convenience. Clearly it is more useful to regard a broken leg as a physical illness, and a broken heart as a psychological illness, but sometimes the diagnosis is not so simple. If the patient with the broken leg has already broken it half a dozen times in the preceding few months we should become interested in more than the mere physical result currently presenting itself. We should begin to think in terms of accident-proneness, which of course implies a very considerable psychological component. Similarly, the patient with a broken heart may develop severe physical effects, such as an inability to stomach food. Diagnostic classification depends very largely upon where we decide to stop looking for related causes, and this in the last analysis is a matter of practical convenience.

If we consider illnesses as being due to stress we can distinguish psychological and physical aspects in all of them. Indeed, one way of conceptualizing the relationship between psychological and physical aspects is to regard them as lying at opposite ends of a symptom-continuum. Thus, the most direct, superficial, flexible, and relatively short-term form of reaction to stress would be psychological; here the individual feels bad, considers that he has an emotional problem and is treated mainly by psychological means. If the problem remains unresolved and stress persists over a long enough period, the continuing psychological stress (e.g. anxiety) may produce physiological changes (e.g. peptic ulcer) and the individual may then be said to suffer from a psychosomatic illness in which physical and psychological components are equally predominant. Such physical symptoms may produce irreversible physical deterioration, and thus come to represent the long-term and indirect effects of the initial, unresolved psychological problem. That is, the physical symptoms may represent a psychological problem that has, as it were, petrified into a physical problem, either because the stress itself has been extreme and unrelieved, or because the individual himself has lacked the basic resources to deal with it at the level of a psychological problem.

Such petrified problems are usually presented as chronic physical symptoms to G.P.s, or in extreme cases, to surgeons. At this stage, such patients do not regard the illness as alien but as an integral part of themselves; it has become part of their identity. It is sometimes impossible, and often inadvisable, to convince such patients that their illness is all in the mind. If they had been able to accept that, they would not have had to develop the physical symptom in the first place. In a sense, the physical symptom (which identifies them as a patient in need of help) is their necessary defence against the realization that their original and continuing problem is essentially psychological. This is why such patients will resist furiously, even to the extent of manufacturing new and virulent symptoms, any suggestion that their problem is essentially psychological. They prefer to be regarded as physical patients requiring medication rather than psychological patients from whom distressing insight and personal effort might be required in treatment. To attempt to translate the petrified problem back into psychological terms may actually make the patient worse, and might in some cases lead to a breakdown ending in death. Of all patients who are endangered by such rule-of-thumb interpretations, the psychosomatic patient is the clearest example, quite apart from the ever-present risk of overlooking a genuinely independent physical ailment. In this respect there is, for diagnosticians and therapists alike, really a double danger; the preoccupation with psychological symptoms to the exclusion of related physical factors, and the over-emphasis on physical symptoms to the exclusion of related psychological factors.

We can see that a symptom is in itself a very complicated event. It is a signal, or a sign, that the individual is not able to cope with a continuing stress. It is also a plea that attention be paid to his plight. It is also an expression of resentment at not getting enough attention. It may also, and especially when genuinely painful or unpleasant, represent the patient's attempt to punish himself for demanding such extra attention. Patients often dislike themselves for the demands they cannot help making.

Does this mean that some symptoms are not genuine, or that symptoms may be adopted voluntarily? Surely nobody would voluntarily adopt a symptom which beyond all doubt causes them severe pain and continuous distress? The first point to note here is that some symptoms develop in an attempt to avoid something worse – worse in the eyes of the patient. For him, his symptom is the lesser of two evils. We have to keep in mind also the fact that symptoms often bring the patient a secondary gain. That is, they often prevent his doing something that unconsciously he doesn't want to do. Most of us have experienced minor symptoms of this sort. On Monday mornings we may have a vague malaise or faint headache, which we feel might be cured if we did not go to work that morning. Students confronted by exams for which they are ill-prepared may develop a stomach upset. The tired businessman, too prostrate with fatigue to mow his lawn, leaps out of his armchair with alacrity when his bachelor friend invites him for a game of golf. And so on.

Turning back now to apply these principles to infantile-regressive illnesses, the most obvious example would be *addiction* to drugs, alcohol, etc. Psychologically, addictions represent a chronic and compulsive need for 'intake'; to gratify oral-incorporative needs. They involve also a physical craving, or body-need which may have a constitutional, organic, genetic, or biochemical origin. In extreme form such regressions also involve progressive physical damage; the individual simply cannot do without his particular nourishment, even although he eventually begins to deteriorate physically through taking it.

To take alcohol, for example – we are not talking here of the mild 'social drinker', nor even of the majority of members in Alcoholics Anonymous, who can, with some support, abstain for relatively long periods without undue distress; but of the genuinely addicted hard drinker who will sacrifice his family, career, friends, and ultimately himself to his need for the bottle; and who will, if unable to obtain alcohol in the ordinary drinkable form, resort to methylated spirits, hair oil, boot polish, or any noxious substance which contains a modicum of alcohol. Some alcoholics in Glasgow have obtained a cheap alcoholic kick from a bottle of ordinary milk through which they have bubbled household gas. A more extreme example was shown by one patient who in desperation boiled the shellac off old gramophone records and then drank the water. At this stage drinking becomes a direct attack on the body, and in this sense may be regarded as a self-destructive form of depressive behaviour. Alcoholism of this kind is usually irreversible and often fatal.

Similarly, *suicide* involves physical components in that its end result is death. Psychologically, it is predominantly depressive in content, involving a profound and exaggerated sense of loss, comparable to the effects of a traumatic weaning experience. Taking one's own life reflects a conviction that the world is never going to be good enough, that there is no hope anywhere, and that the only way to end intolerable despair is to kill it, even though one kills oneself in the process. This implies that in the suicide there is not only depression but anger. (Some authorities have suggested that the two are in fact one; that depression *is* anger, turned against oneself because it has nowhere else to go.) Suicide often involves an element of hurting or punishing others (as implied in the typical suicide note) and to that extent implies anger in the ordinary sense. Certainly it is true that the person most likely to commit suicide is not the profound melancholic submerged in total despondency, but the same individual when he becomes angry as well as depressed. Many such patients commit suicide just when, clinically speaking, they appear to be getting better, i.e. expressing more positive feelings. The genuinely suicidal patient is almost invariably successful. His suicide is prompted not by adverse external circumstances but by his own inner urges. Such individuals, however, do not really intend to commit suicide or make a conscious decision to do so; nor are they making a suicidal gesture merely to get attention; they are driven to suicide by powerful forces over which they have very little control. At this level of death-wish the individual is scarcely a reasonable person; he is in fact functioning negatively at a near-biological level. In other words, granted that suicide is predominantly depressive, its end result – death – suggests that infantile depression may take a physiological form.

There are of course many illnesses which show a *partial* regression to the psycho-physical functioning of infancy. For example, the conversion hysteric (see Chapter 3) shows features of both infancy and later childhood, the former being expressed mainly in physical symptoms and the latter in psychosocial symptoms. While each main symptom may refer to one specific stage of development, the total complex of symptoms in some illnesses requires simultaneous reference to more than one stage. Such illnesses are therefore multi-level regressions.

A good example of a multi-level regression illness is the *psychopath*. The psychopathic individual is usually impulsive and anti-social, but lacks any feelings of guilt or shame. He seems to be unable to love, to feel sympathy, or even to form lasting personal relationships, although he can often behave as if he did have those capacities.

His main symptom, his lack of empathy, has been explained in various ways; for example, as a basic constitutional defect with which he was born, or as a result of early rearing which was so unstable and transient that empathy never had time or opportunity to develop. In either case the impairment is so basic that it involves regression to (or fixation at) an infantile level of emotional experience. The aggressive aspects of psychopathy expressed impulsively and with no thought of consequences, are similar to some forms of 'aggression' seen in young infants. In the biting phase, a teething infant bites not when he chooses but when he must. The violence of the psychopath is equally blind and senseless. His criminal and anti-social actions are unthinking and irresponsible; they are not conscious systematic attempts to pay back society for early frustrations and deprivation. They are no more malevolent than the enraged reactions of a baby who suddenly feels a powerful impulse and cannot have it immediately gratified. In infancy the capacity to anticipate consequences and to have consideration for the feelings of others has not yet developed. In psychopaths these capacities never develop.

In contrast to the genetic and oral-aggressive features of psychopathy, the amorality, lack of conscience, and the inability to feel shame and guilt represent a developmental impairment that is not infantile but Oedipal. Since conscience does not usually develop in human beings until around the age of five to seven years (see Chapter 3), the lack of conscience in psychopathy is more usefully regarded as a failure at that age rather than at an earlier one. To conceptualize psychopathy as a multi-level regression rather than a simple or direct regression to only one stage is in keeping with the observable clinical complexities of the illness.

As a final example of multi-level regression we may consider *homosexuality*. Clinical explanations of homosexuality usually involve simultaneous reference to at least three developmental levels. There may be a genetic component in that the individual is constitutionally over-similar to the opposite sex in his physical characteristics. (Extreme oral deprivation in infancy may leave him also with an exaggerated need for physical contact, regardless of sex.) These basic tendencies may be enhanced later by Oedipal conflicts with both parents (see Chapter 3), and in any later stage specific social opportunities may result in the active expression of his latent homosexual characteristics. Thus, genetic-infantile, Oedipal, and later developmental features may all require mention in the full clinical description of the homosexual.

We have considered all these illnesses in terms of their infantile-regressive characteristics. Clearly, some patients will be more regressed than others – those whose biological impairments are more pronounced, or who show more infantile than other forms of regression. Such patients have never been ordered or graded in terms of the developmental regression, and we have followed the tradition here. They could be ordered in this way quite easily, but it seems preferable to use them as specific examples of the complexity involved in evaluating regressions generally, and particularly regressions to infancy.

Let us now look at those illnesses which have been ordered, at least in terms of the degree of psychological 'disintegration' involved (See Table II). These are the psychoses:[3] paranoid

3. A general distinction is usually drawn between psychosis and neurosis. On the whole, psychosis involves the individual's whole personality, entails a loss or impairment in his capacity to maintain adequate contact with reality (e.g. the environment, including other people) and precludes insight on the part of the patient: he doesn't consider himself to be ill. In neurosis, on the other hand, only a part or aspect of the personality is affected, contact with reality is not so much lost as distorted, the patient usually knows he is ill, and is often

psychosis, manic-depressive psychosis, and schizophrenia (paranoid, simple, catatonic and hebephrenic).[4] They are listed in order, from least to most malignant, disintegrated, or regressive.

Paranoid psychosis is perhaps the clearest example of a psychotic illness where the patient has regressed to infancy, yet not all the way back to its earliest phases. The typical features of paranoid psychosis are predominantly psychological and non-organic; they seldom represent total impairment or disintegration, and do not always completely disrupt the patient's ordinary living.

The central defence mechanism of paranoid psychosis is projection (see Preface, p. xvi), in which the patient ascribes to others his own unacceptable impulses and feelings. He lives his life on the principle 'it's not me, it's them', and is proof against any demonstration to the contrary. This complicated manoeuvre not only makes him suspect the motives of others, but also allows him to punish them, often in a grandiose, exalted, or bizarre fashion, for having such motives. Paranoid projection involves a fairly high level of integrated infantile behaviour over which the paranoid himself and the changing events of the real world have considerable influence. This does not mean that the individual can voluntarily control his tendency to project (if he can, he is normal) but only that he still has some influence over the form and content of his projection. Such control is actually more typical of the anal regressions discussed in Chapter 2 than of infantile regressions as such.

---

sufficiently disturbed by his symptoms to seek treatment. It is possible to regard the two types of illness as continuous with one another, the psychosis representing a more serious and total breakdown than the neurosis; and for convenience we shall regard them so here, recognizing however that they also have many important clinical differences.

4. The *organic* psychoses fall outside the scope of our developmental outline.

Obsessive-compulsive patients whose condition has worsened often become paranoid, suggesting that paranoia is on the borderline between anal and infantile levels of regression.

Mild forms of paranoia are observable, and are sometimes actually preferred, in certain social circumstances. For example, Holt (1960) described one of his patients as a 'beady-eyed, handle-bar-mustachioed young detective' in Kansas, whose test results and clinical history showed a clear paranoid break with reality, yet whose extreme sharpness of perception and chronically suspicious turn of mind had not prevented him from becoming an excellent detective; on the contrary, they enhanced his efficiency. Psychological symptoms never occur in a vacuum, but always in a certain social context; they can be evaluated only in relation to the environment of the person who manifests them. Paranoid suspiciousness would be quite out of place, say, in the League of Nations, but might be highly adaptive to the requirements of M.I.5. In clinical diagnosis we must always keep in mind that a person may be psychologically sick in the sense of falling short of some hypothetical ideal yet socially healthy in the sense of being well adapted to a given community.

At the other end of the scale the extreme paranoid may have dangerous delusions (false beliefs) and florid hallucinations (false perceptions), and thus be incapable of fitting into any society except that of a mental hospital. Even so, he may be distinguished from the paranoid *schizophrenic* (with whom he shares some symptoms, as the diagnostic label suggests), by his greater degree of general psychological integration. He is less helpless than the schizophrenic because he is more able to manufacture an inner or false world and arrange it to suit his own needs. In technical terms, he has better psychological defences. He often excludes or ignores the external world, but on the whole he is more likely merely to misinterpret it; he can at least recognize that there is such a world. The paranoid patient's overweening fears and suspicions of the motives of others are much less cosmic than those of other psychotics; in fact they usually refer to specific events or people, most of whom are real. Even his suspicions that others are talking about him may contain a grain of truth, or become true as his own behaviour begins to exclude him from community life.

Manic-depressive (or affective) psychosis shows clinically in gross fluctuations of mood, ranging from wild elation or euphoria on the one hand to despondency and profound hopelessness on the other. Both extremes are usually controlled nowadays by drugs. Without medication manic patients are constantly restless, excited, and uninhibited to the point of exhausting other people and eventually themselves. They are so easily distracted that they can hardly concentrate on any one thing long enough to carry on an ordinary brief conversation. It is as if they cannot make sense, either of incoming stimuli or of their own reactions. While 'high' they are capable of maintaining their excited behaviour without sleep or nourishment. They give a first impression of being the life and soul of the party, but for them the party goes on for ever. Their behaviour is often playful and flirtatious but may also become rather malicious.

The depressive phase is typified by just the opposite tendencies. The patient becomes sad and melancholic, filled with guilt and remorse for all the world's troubles, to the exclusion of any interest in ordinary everyday affairs. Behaviour is usually sluggish and inactive, but some depressives will try to harm themselves by tearing at their hair or body, by mutilating themselves, or by suicide, (which, as suggested above, may sometimes be regarded as the ultimate form of regressive depression); while others, (the so-called 'agitated' depressive) will show the diffuse excitement of an anxiety state even while their predominant mood is one of despondency.

The illness is cyclical, so that patients alternate unpredictably between elation and depression, sometimes with an intermediate and relatively brief period of normal mood. This cyclical nature of manic-depressive psychosis, and the complete absence of relationship between the cycles and the current real events in the patient's life, allow us to draw a parallel between the illness as seen in adults and the experiences of infancy. We suggested earlier that an infant, while nursing, might develop a rudimentary sense of time, a sense of his own identity, and a rough indication of 'how good' the world was, i.e. according to whether his inner needs were in fact being met appropriately by outer events. All infants experience a primitive cycle (pain or discomfort), followed by satiation when fed (pleasure or comfort), followed in time by hunger again, and so on. An infant who is severely frustrated in infancy, and cannot obtain a satisfactory correlation between his needs and his satisfactions may well become fixated at that emotional level, and may in later life find himself caught helplessly in a similar emotional cycle of alternating despair and elation which recur according to his own laws and out of all relation to the environment.

This theory becomes more plausible if we consider our own fairly normal changes in mood. We all, have our ups and downs, and if life is treating us well or badly, as the case may be, there is no problem in accounting for those variations. But sometimes the changes do not correspond to external events. For example, we may begin to feel vaguely anxious if we feel we have been enjoying *too much* good fortune. We find ourselves saying, 'It's too good to last, you know', as if we were anticipating some *inevitable* adversity. Similarly, if we have had an unusually prolonged run of bad luck, we begin to feel that things must take a turn for the better, even when all evidence may indicate otherwise. Even in normal people the cycle of variations in mood does not always correspond exactly to the cycle of external variations in events. If the alternations of these cycles derive from our infantile experiences of welfare, we would expect that in normal people the cycles will be more or less 'in phase', while in severely disturbed individuals, such as manic-depressives, the disparity between them may become gross and exaggerated.

Again, if we find ourselves down in the dumps we often force ourselves to do something; we push ourselves into some activity which will distract us from our mild depression. The more profound the gloom, the more vigorous and varied the activity required to offset it.

There is a frantic quality in manic behaviour which resembles the behaviour of infants when deprived in basic ways; while psychotic depression in manic-depressive patients often resembles the stuporous inactivity of autistic children, i.e. children who have been grossly frustrated and discouraged by what is to them a bewildering and senseless world. Clinically, manic behaviour is in fact usually interpreted as a psychological defence against depression. That is, the behaviour of the manic-depressive is taken to represent the frenetic activity of someone who is literally going mad in his attempts to avoid or deny a growing despair. This is of course a 'tiger by the tail' situation, and may be resolved only when the patient becomes so exhausted that he collapses and cannot then prevent his despondency from sweeping over him.

Schizophrenia, besides representing the most extreme form of psychological regression among the psychoses, is in many ways also the most complicated. It has been sub-classified into a group of illnesses referred to collectively as 'the schizophrenias': paranoid, simple, catatonic, and hebephrenic. Many of the extreme forms of schizophrenic symptoms are nowadays fairly well controlled by various drugs, so that in the following descriptions we shall often be describing not what we actually see in schizophrenic patients but what we would see if the patient were not under medication.

Just as schizophrenia as a whole represents the most regressed class of psychoses, the sub-classes within schizophrenia may be ordered roughly according to their respective degrees of regression. Generally, the more severe the schizophrenia, the earlier the level of infantile impairment, the greater the mental and emotional defects, and the more apparent the influence of physical factors. The less severely disturbed schizophrenics, while still predominantly infantile, may be understood mainly in terms of extreme psychological or social difficulties. Many such schizophrenics retain some elements of mental functioning; it has been shown that the perception of some adult schizophrenics was similar to that of five-year-old children. Before taking each specific form of schizophrenia in turn, therefore, we should look briefly at some psychosocial features of less disturbed schizophrenics.

Bateson and his colleagues related some forms of schizophrenia directly to childhood experience of severe conflict in the more basic personal relationships. These authors described how some schizophrenics regress into infantile confusion from a chronic interpersonal deadlock, or 'double-bind' situation, within their family. The most damaging form of double-bind is that initiated by a mother who persistently places her child in a situation which is essentially contradictory, but in which she nevertheless forces the child to respond as if the situation were not contradictory. For example, if the child spontaneously throws its arms around its mother's neck and cuddles her, the mother, unable to respond naturally to the child's need, will withdraw. When the child withdraws also because of this rebuff the mother may say, 'You should love your mother'. By simultaneously offering the child mutually antagonistic signals of her expectations, she eventually produces a disintegration in the child's developing personality, which shows as a schizophrenic bewilderment, even when the child is confronted by ordinary situations. Such 'schizo-phreno-genic' or 'schizo-genic' mothers are unable to let their children grow into independence, yet are themselves too disturbed to provide any useful psychological model for them.

The family relationships of schizophrenics are seldom genuinely harmonious, although they may sometimes involve a false harmony or 'pseudo-mutuality'. Mild tendencies in this direction may be seen in any family which denies spontaneous feelings, or sacrifices them to some false or exaggerated ideal, such as respectability, family tradition, etc. Schizophrenia tends to occur in families where such abnormal interactions are unrelieved, inescapable, intense, and prolonged. Two typical patterns have been described as 'marital schism', in which one parent steadily undermines the other's influence over the children; and 'marital skew', where the pathological rearing of the child by one parent is passively accepted by the other. In families showing either schism or skew the basic impairment usually has its source in the original relationship between the parents. When the parents completely fail to achieve genuine intimacy (see Chapter 6) with each other the resulting mutual isolation or lopsidedness in their relationship is bound to have serious adverse effects on the emotional development of their children.

It seems likely that less severely disturbed schizophrenics often live in families in which the dominant parent is the father rather than the mother. Even if the father is tyrannical, harsh, and oppressive, the child will not be so severely disturbed if his mother is sufficiently easy-going, warm and loving. If she is dominating and restrictive, however, the disturbance is greater in the schizophrenic child, even when the father is easy-going – a pathological mother seems to produce deeper abnormalities in the child than a pathological father, other influences on the child being equal.

Thus the schizophrenic may attempt to retreat from the anxiety and tension produced by realistic interpersonal situations into a self-constructed 'pseudo-community' consisting of delusions and hallucinations. Just as ordinary people indulge in a daydream when reality is too harsh, too boring, or too discouraging, so schizophrenics resort to daydreaming, with the important difference that they cannot voluntarily regain contact with reality. Their confused dream world *is* their reality. Attempts to reach schizophrenics by social means, such as encouragement or censure, usually increase the disturbance, especially if these attempts involve too much emotion for them to deal with. On the other hand, schizophrenics do respond better to an even, constant, open friendliness than to a formal and rigid personal approach.

The treatment of schizophrenics nowadays is often not confined to the patient alone, for it is recognized that his disturbance may be merely a reflection of his sick family background. In such families the abnormalities sometimes balance out in a way which produces apparent homeostasis. Indeed, in a family where the apparent harmony is so false, precarious, and largely accidental, it is often the relatively healthy member who, unable to stand the universal illness within which he is forced to live, eventually breaks down and is referred for treatment. In this sense, treatment may sometimes be carried out on the wrong person. Very often in such cases, as the patient improves, the other members of the family, unable in their turn to accommodate the healthier influence of the patient reintroduced to the fold, may break down themselves.

We have probably said enough already about schizophrenia to emphasize its complexity. Schizophrenia certainly is complex – at least as complex as infancy – and there is always a temptation to over-simplify the illness. In a bold attempt to clarify the confusion, one writer stated bluntly: 'schizophrenia is a disease which has its origin somewhere between conception and prior to termination of the prenatal period and it is caused by the mother's inability to love her child.' Such over-simplifications do not really do justice to the complexities of the illness and it is more appropriate to recognize these complexities, and try to order and interrelate the known biological, psychological, and social elements within a stable framework of different levels of developmental regression. There are as many important differences in the various forms of schizophrenia as there are between children of ages ranging from conception to about two years old. Let us now turn to these differences.

It is usually implied that in the less severe forms of schizophrenia, such as *paranoid schizophrenia*, symptoms may be not only regressive but also restitutive. That is, some symptoms represent a breaking down or disintegration of personality, while others suggest an attempt to restore integration in the personality. The regressive symptoms include feelings of depersonalization and loss, extreme passivity or withdrawal, magical thinking, in which objects and their symbols are not distinguished, and fantasies of world dissolution. Restitutive symptoms on the other hand represent the schizophrenic's attempt to regain contact with reality; for example, bizarre language, hallucinations and delusions, grandiosity, unrealistic feelings of omnipotence and fantasies of world reconstruction – all indicating that a certain degree of personality integration has been retained. These restitutive features are fairly typical of the paranoid schizophrenic. The more regressive psychotic symptoms he shows, the more likely that the qualifying word 'paranoid' will be dropped from his diagnosis.

Simple schizophrenia usually starts slowly – the patient gradually becomes apathetic, less intelligent in his behaviour, and more and more withdrawn from his environment. This usually entails also a deterioration in personal habits, but the degree of psychological disintegration is on the whole less marked than in catatonic and hebephrenic schizophrenia. Regression seldom reaches the vegetative level, where organic features may be as predominant as psychological symptoms. On the other hand, the illness is usually progressive, involving an increasing over-expansion of inner reality at the expense of outer reality.

The most severely regressed forms of schizophrenia are the *catatonic* and *hebephrenic* varieties, both of which involve a deterioration and disintegration of function which is as much organic as psychological. The *catatonic schizophrenic,* for example, typically shows phases of complete stupor in which he is unresponsive to any kind of stimulation from the environment, even to the point of basic reflex failure. If someone made as if to throw a knife at him, he would make no move to dodge or defend himself, but would simply allow the knife to pierce him. On occasion, he may emerge suddenly and without warning from his stupor, showing an extremely violent, senseless, wild type of behaviour which is equally impervious to the influence of other people around him. There is a gross deterioration in personal habits (e.g. infantile incontinence) and this may degenerate eventually into a form of living that is more vegetative than human. Although many of these characteristics resemble to some extent the normal behaviour of very young babies, it is probably more appropriate to regard catatonia as comparable to gross exaggerations or extreme caricatures of infantile behaviour. Very young babies, although helpless, can nevertheless act on their basic reflexes, and although some of them may be either unusually withdrawn and unresponsive ('autistic'), or unusually active and restless, their behaviour is still a very pale reflection of the catatonic stupor or furor.

The functioning of the *hebephrenic schizophrenic* is similarly disintegrated. In all his reactions he shows gross bizarreness, illogicality, and a silly absurdity. His speech, for example, often consisists of a 'word salad', in which words occur not in organized sentences, but all mixed up at random. Insofar as speech reflects inner cognitive functioning, the subjective world of such patients must be senseless and diffuse. (Compare the inner world of the young infant, once hypothesized by William James as 'a booming, buzzing confusion'.) The inability of such schizophrenics to make sense of incoming stimuli by distinguishing the important from the trivial, and their high degree of distractability, have been well demonstrated by experimental psychologists. Indeed, this nuclear type of schizophrenic may have more in common with brain-damaged patients than with the other types of schizophrenics.

According to the reports of schizophrenics themselves, they often experience feelings of strangeness and unreality about their own identity and their external environment, for example, a sense of flatness or remoteness. Schizophrenics whose condition is severe also experience gross disturbances of 'body image', their awareness of their body. The adualism of the infant, who is not clear about the boundaries between himself and objects in the environment, is similar to this disturbance of the schizophrenic, who may feel that environmental objects are inside his body, or that parts of his body are 'out there' in the environment. The difference of course is that the adualistic perceptions of the infant normally become clarified in time, while those of the schizophrenic do not.

At the most extreme end of the schizophrenic scale all mental function is lost. As Freeman (1958) put it: 'Mental function may then consist solely of bodily activity.'

A final example of infantile regression is a chronic illness well known to every experienced welfare worker, but for which there is no psychiatric label. This illness is found in people whose biological resources are poor, whose subsequent family and social history is consistently catastrophic, and whose psychological assets from any point of view are grossly insufficient. They are sometimes referred to as inadequate

or 'multi-problem' individuals, and are often solitary and no-
madic, e.g. tramps, hobos, destitutes.

The lives of these people may be regarded as a re-enactment
of the crisis of early infancy. Indeed there is a sense in which
they have not so much regressed to infancy, but have always
been fixated there. Like infants, their psychological and
social functioning is diffuse. They have no integrated skills,
capacities, aptitudes, or abilities – only needs. Their interpersonal relationships are infantile and essentially oral-
incorporative, in that others are perceived not as people but
merely as potential sources of supply. So insatiable is their need
for welfare that their life becomes one long despairing search for
perpetual hosts. Inevitably they run out of these very quickly,
for no ordinary person, no matter how kindly disposed, can
supply such a hunger. Sooner or later, therefore, the inadequate
individual will gravitate towards some artificial but more permanent source of supply, such as a charitable or welfare
institution, which of course is specifically designed for giving.
He may attach himself permanently to the institution, manufacturing whatever qualifications are required, in an attempt to
make the giving perpetual. Eventually he becomes one of the
hard core cases, with files several inches thick. Thus the continuing existence of the inadequate individual, like that of
infants generally, depends strictly on the world's goodwill.

The individual with this pattern of living cannot respond to
the usual forms of therapy; still less can he respond to the
exhortations sometimes offered by would-be do-gooders to
'buck up', or 'get a grip on yourself'. Psychologically there is
nothing there to get a grip of. Because his oral needs are so
gross he can never feel, even for a brief moment, that he has
been 'born with a silver spoon in his mouth'.

SUMMARY

We introduced this chapter by listing the sources from which we derive our knowledge of infant psychology, emphasizing the problems involved in making inferences from infant to adult forms of functioning. We outlined the normal crises of infancy, with their satisfactory (trusting) and unsatisfactory (mistrustful) resolutions, as these are expressed in biological, psychological, and social modes.

In discussing regressions to infancy we attempted to indicate the 'allowance' we should make for 'normal' regressions, then considered pathological regressions. Illnesses are ranked as more severe when they involved total or near-total regression, when the regression was to earlier phases of infancy; and when regression involved physical factors. These criteria were applied to several clinical illnesses (addiction, suicide, psychopathy, homosexuality) but without ranking these formally in order of severity. Then, following more traditional diagnostic classification, we ranked the main psychotic illnesses in order of severity: paranoid psychosis, manic-depressive psychosis, schizophrenia (paranoid, simple, catatonic and hebephrenic). We finally described the 'inadequate' personality, which exemplified in a general way most of our criteria for infantile regression.

Referring back to the first rows in Tables I and II we may differentiate these illnesses in terms of which basic feeling predominates – anxiety, depression, an impaired sense of identity. When psychotic or Stage I *anxiety* predominates, we see in the patient a fear of 'starvation'. This fear, even when extreme, is rarely expressed directly, except by infants; in regressed adults it is usually shown symbolically – a fear that the world, or the self, is coming to an end. Every so often we hear of people who proclaim that the end of the world is at hand, and are even prepared to specify the date on which the event is to take place.

When it does not take place, these individuals are reassured only temporarily, and prophesy world disintegration once more when their psychotic anxiety level becomes sufficiently high. The same anxiety appears in a more scientific and less 'religious' form in people who take active and elaborate precautions against the effects of the H-bomb. One such person emigrated with his family from Canada to New Zealand (then thought to be the safest place for 'fall-out drift'), where he proceeded to build a personal dugout; he then filled his shelter with foodstuffs – and weapons, to fight off all would-be invaders who had not had his foresight. Such people show only partial regression to Stage I anxiety, so long as their lives are otherwise reasonable. (Those who cannot bear to experience Stage I anxiety may, for example, become megalomanic, i.e. the extreme denial of infantile vulnerability and helplessness. Milder reactions may show as extreme acquisitiveness. And so on.)

When psychotic *depression* predominates we see in the patient 'a lonely and withdrawn mood, a feeling of being out of reach and out of touch' (D. C. Levin, 1963). This is more extreme than the relatively common feeling of loneliness; it is a feeling of being totally abandoned in a world that is utterly empty.

Finally, when psychotic or Stage I *identity pathology* predominates we see in the patient a complete inability to test reality (to reorganize and deal with it appropriately); his inability to make any sense of everyday events reflects an infantile incoherence and a disintegration of his total personality.

CHAPTER TWO

Early Childhood (2–4 years)

Great contest follows and much learned
dust involves the combatants . . .
COWPER, *The Task*

INTRODUCTION

WE saw in Chapter 1 that the infant is uniquely difficult to understand because his behaviour is so unstructured and his subjective experiences so blurred and fleeting that adult concepts are not adequate to describe them properly. These particular problems are much less troublesome to the investigators of early childhood, the period roughly between two and five years. A child at this age is certainly well enough integrated in all his psychological functions to be regarded as a person, capable of genuine reciprocity in his social interactions.

In describing the psychological crises of early childhood we shall assume first that our hypothetical young child is normal. That is, that he has done well enough in his infancy to have achieved a sufficient preponderance of trust over mistrust to enable him to face the early crises of childhood with at least a reasonable chance of finding satisfactory solutions. To a considerable extent his being in this situation is a matter of luck and good fortune. The infant, although by no means passive, is helplessly dependent on his own ancestry, his biological heredity, and the particular environment in which he finds himself. If these are not good there is not much he can do about it. Infancy is a period in which 'things happen to us', more than 'we happen to things'. The young child, however, has much more direct influence on what happens to him and can intentionally bring that influence to bear on his own life. He is much more personally responsible for what happens to him in early childhood than in his infancy, and this responsibility increases as he continues to develop. This means that his own contribution to the eventual outcome of all subsequent crises, whether good, bad or indifferent, increases progressively as he grows up.

The central problem of the young child is that his bio-psycho-social situation is uniquely and inherently antithetical in its own nature, even before any complications have arisen. Early childhood consists of a series of interrelated dilemmas in which the young child, whatever effort he makes, is both 'damned if he does, and damned if he doesn't'. The antithetical, almost contradictory, quality of this whole stage of development also determines the young child's personal relationships. To understand this we should first consider certain biological, psychological, and social changes which mark the end of infancy, and are precursors of early childhood proper.

The biological changes come as a result of simple maturation which at the beginning of this period is still very rapid. The child's bone structure has developed and his muscles have matured to the point where his movements are not merely reflex, but voluntary as well. For the first time, he himself may choose to flex or extend his muscles; he may hold them rigid or let them relax; in short, he can use his own muscles as and when he wishes. In the process of exercising this new ability he stands on his own two feet, and soon afterwards walks alone without help. Similarly, he learns that he can control the evacuation of his own bowels and bladder. We shall see that each of these new achievements relates directly to the new personal relationships in which the young child inevitably becomes involved during this period. (It is in fact because of the importance of such physical changes, and specifically those of the anal system, that

this period is usually referred to as 'the anal stage' of development.) Meantime, we may assume at the common-sense level of
ordinary introspection that the young child obtains some
pleasure from the exercise of his new-found biological autonomy. It is, after all, a new skill. The evacuation and retention of
bowel and bladder contents, for example, involve basic physical
tensions, and their self-regulation must surely provide some
gratification to the child. We need not be committed to all the
more extreme psychoanalytic theories concerning the young
child's attitude to his own faeces; the point is simply that he
probably derives pleasure at the biological level, not only from
elimination and retention as such, but also from his own ability
to regulate these functions.

The psychological precursors stem naturally from the earlier
achievements of the infant. As early as seven or eight months
after birth, it will be remembered, the infant can clearly identify and show specific preference for his mother. This perceptual achievement has not only an objective aspect (the
infant's recognition of his mother) but, we may infer, a subjective aspect as well, namely the infant's recognition of himself as *separate from* his mother. If, even in infancy, such
differential perception is possible, then by early childhood both
social and self-perception must have much greater clarity and
scope. We need not debate whether or not the young child's
perception of himself is as clear or even as fully conscious as his
perception of another. The point is simply that by the age of two
he has a much firmer and stronger sense of his own identity.

This development of the ego in the young child goes hand in
hand with the development of his intellectual powers. According to Piaget, the child of two has passed through the phase of
'sensori-motor intelligence' and is beginning to demonstrate
'conceptual intelligence'. Stimuli are no longer mere sensory
events but also have meaning; the young child's sensations
have developed into percepts and may even be elaborated into

elementary concepts. His cognitive capacity now includes rudimentary symbolism.

The bridge between cognitive development and ego-development in the young child is, almost certainly, language. In language development the child's increasing ability to make sounds, and their increasing approximation to adult sounds, result both from his enjoyment of his own sounds and also from the reinforcement he derives from speaking like his parent. When a child begins to speak, he often develops a kind of wilfulness. He begins to assert his own opinions and to make some of his own decisions. The development of volition and the use of language are closely related and it is not coincidental that a young child is often heard exercising his new-found linguistic ability to express his wish for autonomy against his environment; the most frequent words he uses are 'no!' and 'mine!'

Psychologists have found wide individual differences among children in the time they begin to speak. Although children usually speak their first word around the end of the first year, variations range from eight to twenty months of age. Gifted children average around eleven months. The rate of subsequent speech development, however, seems to be determined largely by psychological and social factors. For example, children with retarded speech development are often over-dependent; while children whose retardation is general are often detached in social relationships. Again, only children, although they do not have significantly different personalities from sibling children, are usually above average in speech development, presumably because they are more exposed to adult influences.

Language allows the child to formulate and conceptualize. He can make his 'declaration of independence' in words as well as deeds. He can grasp that people and objects continue to exist even when he is not actually perceiving them. He can conceive the idea of 'absence'.

We saw in Chapter 1 how the infant who achieves trust (in

Erikson's sense) has succeeded in tolerating, without undue rage or fear, the absence of his mother. The young child must do better. He must learn and accept that when his mother is absent it is often because she is interested in other things and other people. He must face the fact that sometimes others will be given priority over himself. He no longer has exclusive rights over his mother's love.

Perhaps no infant ever has such rights in the first place. Some psychoanalytic writers have suggested that at least the infant *thinks* he has absolute rights in mother-love during his infancy, and talk of the infantile 'delusion of omnipotence' which, they suggest, is dispelled traumatically in early childhood. This point of view depends so heavily on knowing the nature and content of the infant's inner life that it can probably never be either proved or disproved. We need not argue the point, for there is no reason to suppose that mother-love itself is ever absolute. Babies make such inordinate demands on mothers that it would be astonishing if her feelings were never ambivalent. The mother's ambivalence towards her child probably also increases as he develops: by the time the infant reaches early childhood his mother has had to cope with his peremptory feeding demands, has lost many hours of necessary sleep during his teething, and has washed many acres of soiled nappies; and all this in addition to her everyday household chores, the endless needs of other members of her family, and perhaps a full-time job as well. Such stresses are bound to have negative effects, for although motherhood is a profound and important experience for a young woman it does not of itself transform her into a saint.

The natural ambivalence of mothers may be reflected in many ways, perhaps even in the nursery rhymes they have crooned to fractious infants for many generations. The sleepless baby may be soothed and comforted by the opening lines of 'Rock-a-bye-Baby'; but if he continues to be sleepless, a certain natural irritation, not to say ominousness, begins to creep into the lullaby as it continues: 'the cradle will fall, and *down* will come baby, cradle and all'.

Most mothers lavish unconditional care and attention on newly-born babies, because they seem so vulnerable. But as the months pass, and the infant shows every sign of continued survival, their love gradually becomes more conditional. At first it may depend on the baby's crying, and on the way he suckles. By early childhood it is conditional also upon the child's toilet training, and his social behaviour generally. Not that the mother does not love her child; but merely that she will tend to love him more if he 'behaves himself', i.e. gives her no unnecessary trouble.

These changes in the mother have a profound influence on the young child. The way his mother treats him gives him an idea of the way she feels about him. This idea, of course, may be considerably distorted and exaggerated, because the child's mental and perceptual processes are by no means fully developed even towards the end of this phase. Nevertheless, what the child gradually acquires from his awareness of how others feel about him is a sense of his own worth as a person; 'I am loved' becomes 'I am lovable'. The child's sense of personal worth is confirmed, modified and refined ever afterwards by elaborate systems of rewards and punishments from parents and other people around him.

In summary, then, the psychological crises of early childhood are determined to a large extent by their bio-psycho-social forerunners. From the biological maturation of his body the child derives a new capacity for mobility and self-regulation; from the psychological and cognitive changes he derives a new sense of identity and separateness, and can project (through language and symbolic thought processes) beyond the immediate here and now; from the social changes, and especially from his mother, he derives a sense of his own worth as a person. These precursors, interacting with one another, are central to his personal relationships at this stage of development.

All these precursors have one essential feature in common, namely a certain antithetical quality. Biological self-regulation, for example, involves the control of physical alternatives that are mutually exclusive; one cannot both flex and extend muscles at the same time; nor can they be held rigid and relaxed simultaneously. In the self-control of bowel movements one cannot at once expel and retain. The oppositeness of these alternatives does not matter a great deal, except that the child obtains *pleasure* from both kinds of activity. What he enjoys, at least to begin with, is the exercise of self-regulation *as such* – the form it takes is of secondary importance. His mother, too, represents an inherent contradiction; she administers both reward and punishment, approval and disapproval. Thus, in the interaction between child and mother, the child becomes more independent and self-assertive while the mother is more ambivalent and more inclined to regulate her child's behaviour for her own convenience.

THE CRISIS OF EARLY CHILDHOOD

Although life for the young child of two to four years is full of stress and strain we must not assume that it is necessarily traumatic. There are, it is true, new problems for the child to solve and difficult relationships for him to master; but there are also new satisfactions to be gained. He will discover, for example, that love and attention are obtainable not merely at the whim of his environment but through his own efforts; and also that these will come from other people as well as his mother.[1] Again,

1. A study by Harlow (1962) not only demonstrates this latter possibility but suggests that there is a critical period for the acceptability of 'substitute' love objects. If substitutes are offered before the child is ready it is doubtful whether he can regard them as genuinely equivalent.

when the mother *is* distracted by her own interests the child may find he can share these interests with her. Chess (1959) makes the point satirically: 'so much has been written about parent–child hostility, the child's resentment of dependency and similar aspects . . . that the psychologically well-read mother may hope for no more than that she will not show up too badly in her child's analysis when he becomes a maladjusted adult'.

We suggested above that the young child of two to five years is predominantly striving for *autonomy* and for *self-esteem*. These central features of his personal relationships cannot always be clearly separated. For example, when he manages for the first time to stand up he will be gratified by his achievement, especially since it is lavishly rewarded by adults around him; but, being now better able to make comparisons regarding stature generally, he will also become more aware of his own smallness in relation to other people.

One can approximate this childhood situation by observing how the size, proportion, and spatial relationships of objects and persons change when viewed from the floor on all fours. Even a table has a different significance when seen from a position lower than its surface. A young child who stands for the first time is like the climber who has scaled the foothills and enjoys his achievement – until he realizes that although this gives him elevation over the plains, it draws his attention to the mountain range towering above him.

Similarly, when the young child manages to walk without support, his autonomy and sense of personal achievement is enhanced; but, since a walking and climbing child is more troublesome than a crawling child, the ever-present adults may show mixed feelings about his new mobility, and his self-esteem may suffer. So autonomy and self-esteem, although they often vary concomitantly, may sometimes have an inverse relationship – the more of one, the less of the other.

In toilet training, for instance, young children are strongly encouraged to believe that a good boy is a clean boy, while a bad boy is a dirty boy. Solicitous adults may also be heard assuring their children that cleanliness is next to godliness.

What the child has to learn is how to exercise his autonomy sufficiently to establish his self-esteem, but not so extremely as to invoke overwhelming social retaliation that would undermine his self-esteem. He has to learn to compromise. For this he requires surroundings that allow him to make genuine choices, yet at the same time make him aware of realistic limits. A delicate balance must be maintained between the encouragement of autonomy ('stand on your own feet') and discouragement of its excesses ('don't stand on mine'). As the child slowly learns that others besides himself have needs and expect some consideration, his capacity for manipulating and being manipulated become clarified. Only if this is successful will he develop a flexible, good-humoured acceptance of others and of himself. Erikson (1959) suggests that we should 'be firm and tolerant with the child at this stage, and he will be firm and tolerant with himself. He will feel pride at being an autonomous person; he will grant autonomy to others'. In other words, 'easy does it'.

Although the child of two to four is involved in genuine social relationships, his involvement is still fairly limited. Piaget, in his well-known study of Swiss children, found that the two- to three-year-old child was markedly individualistic, but that this behaviour consisted largely of physical movements; he regarded marbles, for example, merely as objects to be pushed about, dropped, poured into folds in the upholstery, and so on. He followed no specific rules in his game, nor did he show any general sense of obligation. Later, however, between the ages of four and six, the child, now 'egocentric' (see Table I), is aware of codified rules, and makes some show of imitating them, e.g. if he is alone he plays a game with himself. The use he makes of these rules is limited if he is with others; he does not try to win or even to integrate his activities with those of the others – so far as he is concerned, everybody can win at once. He considers all rules to have their source in adults, but although he gives their rules an almost divine, sacred status, his behaviour shows a good deal of egocentric rebellion against them. Again we see the inherently contradictory element in the situation.

Other childhood studies agree generally with Piaget's findings. Before two, children tend to play on their own, paying little or no attention to any prospective partners who might be available. This represents in a sense the one-person social situation. Children do not really play cooperatively until well into their second year, and even then cooperation is minimal. Between the ages of two and four to five years social interaction does occur, but only between two children at a time, even when three children are present. The social situation here is essentially a two-person one. Not until the age of five and later do three or more children interact simultaneously and show cooperation, rivalry, sympathy and friendship. This 3-plus person situation will be discussed more fully in Chapter 3.

Autonomy in early childhood is extremely complex. The basic situation is one in which the child, confronted at every turn by his more or less ambivalent or conditionally-loving mother, actively searches for autonomy and for more opportunities to exercise his own choice. In such a situation the fundamental question is, 'Who decides?', the child, or someone else? Since the central issue is one of control, the encounter between the child and his mother is always a contest, and often a head-on collision. The contest has, however, many battlefronts; it is not confined to the bathroom, any more than the earlier mother–child relationships were confined to the dining-room.[2] Although toilet-training is one of the more obvious areas of child-mother contention the question of control, or 'Who decides?', extends beyond excretory impulses to impulses of all kinds, and hence to all of the child's personal relationships.

The pervasiveness of the contest can be better understood if we think of it in terms of 'holding on' or 'letting go' (Erikson, 1950). At the physiological level what is held or released is of course the body's waste matter; the question here is simply 'Who decides when I go to the bathroom?' All the schedules and schemes for training the child answer the question one way or another, ranging from 'Go only when you are told', to 'Go whenever you feel like it'. Many mothers institute such training schedules as early as possible, and then tell their friends with modest pride that their child was completely trained in his first year. Such training is, however, premature, and runs counter to the child's natural development. Until the age of about eighteen months most children simply do not have the necessary physical equipment to control themselves. It may be, therefore, that those mothers who have trained their child before this point are merely more sensitive to the child's warning signals, or faster on their feet when it comes to acting on those signals. Such training habits are essentially artificial, and may interfere with the later genuine training in which the child often cooperates spontaneously, simply because he is then ready and willing to

2. The specific question, 'Who decides when I go to the bathroom?', generalized to 'Who decides?' has no genuine counterpart prior to the anal stage. It is true that the outcome of the oral question, 'Who decides when I eat?', (the establishment of feeding schedules based on the child's or the mother's convenience) is analogous in form to the outcome of the anal question, (the establishment of toilet schedules); but the infant has no control over his hunger, or himself, or those who provide his basic gratifications: while the young child of two to four years does have some capacity for control, whether or not he is allowed to exercise it.

exercise his new ability to choose for himself in this area. Most children achieve control by the age of three.

At the emotional level, what is held in or let out is the child's feelings. Anger, for example, may be bottled up, or may be loosed destructively in a furious attempt to disfigure or obliterate the world that frustrates him. The question here is, 'Who decides how I express my feelings?' At the level of more ordinary behaviour, 'holding on' or 'letting go' show simply in the child's attitude and habits regarding objects. He may collect trivial objects, not with any thought of saving for a rainy day (see Chapter 1), but merely for the pleasure of holding or controlling that small part of his world. (A few months earlier he was obtaining pleasure from alternately relinquishing and retrieving objects, especially in the game where a toy is handed back and forth between himself and some friendly adult.) At the level of social interaction with others, he may 'hold' people, either by grabbing them possessively, or by making them wait; alternatively he may 'let them go' by excluding them from his private world, or by waiting for nobody.

The essential contradictions in all these areas of functioning, whether biological, psychological or social, show in the contrariness, or mutinous negativism, which typifies the young child's behaviour at this stage of development. A stubborn contradictoriness, often accompanied by fairly extreme changes in mood can be seen in most normal children of this age. The legendary little girl who 'when she was good was very, very good', but 'when she was bad she was horrid', was probably within this age group, and in its earlier phases. Such negativistic behaviour becomes a matter for clinical concern only when it persists into and beyond the later phases of this period.

Most children of this age show a form of behaviour which appears to be negativistic but is not really so, namely the tendency to perform and take pleasure in actions that are repetitive. This is the age, for example, at which the child, finding a wooden spoon and an empty tin can, is liable to hammer the latter with the former monotonously for hours at a time, merely to hear the rhythmic noise continue. The irritated parent, having reached the age when peace and quiet seem more desirable, usually interprets such behaviour in adult terms as a deliberate attempt to provoke. The child himself, however, is often (although not always) merely trying to master a tiny part of his environment; indeed, much of his play at this age reflects such an attempt. Other children are not irritated when they encounter such repetitive ritualistic forms of learning in their contemporaries.

Health, or satisfactory solutions to the crises central to this phase of development, shows in the child who manipulates neither himself nor those around him to an extreme degree, who is capable of genuine mutual regulation with others, and who can, within his own natural and social limits, compromise. When he grows up he can 'hold on' when this is appropriate, but without feeling the need for cruel clutching or taking a death grip; similarly he will be able to let go when *this* is appropriate, being able to 'let well alone', to 'live and let live', but without feeling the need for a destructive loosening of natural bonds, or for obliterating all forms of opposition.

DISTURBANCES IN EARLY CHILDHOOD

When the personal relationships of a child break down, the impairment may show in several different ways. At the physiological level he may refuse, or seem unable to achieve, toilet training and control. Psychologically he may become over-assertive, aggressive and hostile, defiantly pretending a false independence he has not really achieved. He may go in the other direction and become over-dependent, regressing to earlier forms of control, such as thumb-sucking or whining. In more severe cases where the breakdown is made worse by sudden or prolonged separation from his mother, a sensitive child may regress to infancy because his earlier fears of division or abandonment have also been reawakened – he will show 'separation anxiety'. As well as the alternatives of 'fight' and 'flight', the young child who is baffled by inconsistent training may freeze into a chronic state of ambivalence, in which self-assertion alternates with dependence, aggression with submissiveness, cruelty with gentleness, orderliness with disorderliness, cleanliness with dirtiness; he may make a futile attempt to express the alternatives in these antitheses simultaneously.

Any of these breakdowns in interpersonal relationships in childhood may result from faulty parental control. The question 'Who decides?' has many wrong answers, and many of these are given not by children but by adults. Some parents, for example, over-control their child, saying, in effect, 'always me, never you'. Others under-control, saying, in effect, 'always you, never me', and become so permissive in their training that from the child's point of view they are psychologically 'not there'. Others again are quite inconsistent, saying, in effect, 'maybe you, maybe me, but neither of us will know in advance'. Any of these parental faults may produce any of the above reactions in children.

To understand the child at this age we must not only observe his behaviour, but also consider how he feels when he fails to resolve his psychological crises adequately. Here there are very few experimental studies; and we have to depend much more on clinical findings, and on the integration of these findings into coherent psychodynamic theories.

As we have seen, this stage of development is inevitably (although not entirely) a continual battle between the child and his environment, including other people. It seems unquestionable that when the child is thwarted or frustrated in his struggle for autonomy he will feel anger. Since nearly every-thing that frustrates him is bigger and more powerful than he is, we may safely infer that he also feels fear, although he may control this fear. Erikson (1950, 1959) has suggested that just as the achievement of genuine autonomy gives the child self-esteem and a firm sense of his own personal worth, so his failure to achieve autonomy will produce feelings of shame and doubts about his personal value.[3]

If the child's dilemma becomes insoluble and persists too long, his need to control or manipulate others may be turn-ed against himself. Erikson (1959) tells us that when this happens,

he will overmanipulate himself, he will develop a precocious con-

3. In ordinary conversation we do not always distinguish shame from guilt. Erikson (1959) suggests that 'shame supposes that one is completely exposed and conscious of being looked at – in a word, self-conscious. One is visible and not yet ready to be visible. That is why we dream of shame as a situation in which we are stared at in a condi-tion of incomplete dress, in night attire, "with one's pants down". Shame is early expressed in an impulse to bury one's face or to sink there and then into the ground ... too much shaming does not result in a sense of propriety but in a secret determination to try to get away with things when unseen, if indeed it does not result in deliberate shamelessness'. Shame, then, is a vague diffuse sense of falling short of some ideal. We feel that our 'fault' (in Biblical terms) is a sin of om-ission; we have left undone that which we ought to have done. Guilt, on the other hand, refers to some specific wrong thing we have actu-ally done. We feel here that our fault is a sin of commission; we have done that which we ought not to have done. Erikson suggests that the emotion which predominates in disorders of early childhood is shame rather than guilt (guilt predominates in the disorders occurring in the next stage of development). D. C. Levin (1963) has suggested also that fear and doubt about impending disgrace, and a sense of personal worthlessness, are also dominant emotions in the disorders of early childhood. These formulations and suggestions are not of course precise descriptions; but they do indicate generally the kind of emo-tional reactions that are hypothesized by psychoanalytic investigators.

science. Instead of taking possession of things in order to test them by repetitive play he becomes obsessed by his own repetitiveness. He will want to have everything 'just so' and only in a given sequence and tempo. By such infantile obsessiveness, by dawdling for example, or becoming a stickler for certain rituals, the child then learns to gain power over his parents and nurses in areas where he could not find large-scale mutual regulation with them. Such hollow victory then is the infantile model for 'compulsion neurosis'.

This is a pathological extreme. Most normal young children show mild forms of the same tendency; they may, for example, demand a bedtime story, and insist that it be told in precisely the same words every night before they will go to sleep ('Who decides when my waking hours have come to an end?').

Experimental studies of early childhood, although numerous, have tended to be limited in scope. On the other hand, since autonomy is complex it is not surprising that most experimenters have restricted themselves to studying one or other of its principal aspects, and have then concentrated on its more extreme or negative forms. The main forms of autonomy investigated have been those which show in toilet training, childhood aggression, and childhood dependency.

Failure to achieve toilet control is seldom due to some physical disability. Psychologists have found that it is usually due to faults in toilet training, or to a breakdown of control in 'dry' children when they were involved in family crises, separation, or major changes in their life situation. In other words, it seems likely that autonomy even at the physiological level has important psychosocial components. This suggestion is confirmed by many studies. Among mothers, for example, there are wide individual differences regarding the timing and duration of toilet training – which might start any time between five and thirty-four months, and might last (from start to completion) from one month to seventeen months. When training started later, it was usually shorter.

Although the mother's influence may show most clearly in toilet training, it will certainly be felt by the child in many other situations. For example, the more 'cold' the mother, the more likely the child is to have severe emotional upset because of toilet training; and the more anxiety she has about sex the greater the likelihood that she will start toilet training early. The same kind of mother is also less likely to breast-feed her child in infancy. Warm, tolerant mothers, who administer less corporal punishment, are much gentler in their toilet training, and as individuals show higher esteem for themselves and for their husbands. These examples demonstrate the complexity of personal relationships in early childhood, and the consequent difficulty of investigating even the more obvious biological aspects of autonomy.

Some of the earlier psychological studies were far too naïve and one-sided. The classic example is J. B. Watson's (1928) peremptory instructions to parents regarding toilet training. He wrote:

the infant from eight months onward should have a special toilet seat into which he can be safely strapped. *The child should be left in the bathroom without toys and with the door closed.* Under no circumstances should the door be left open or the mother or nurse stay with the child. This is a rule which seems to be almost universally broken. When broken it leads to dawdling, loud conversation and in general to unsocial and dependent behaviour.

In contrast with this attitude ('always me, never you'), one mother, an extremely jolly, easy-going woman, insisted that it was really no bother to keep wiping up her daughter's little indiscretions ('always you, never me') . . .

If it is true, as we suggested earlier in this chapter, that the young child himself actively contributes to the crises in which he is involved, it is equally true that much of his behaviour is not self-initiated, but is a direct reaction to the attitudes of those around him. Parental attitudes tend not to be confined to specific situations such as toilet training, or to vary from one situation to another, but to spread to all situations in which the parent has any influence. A parent with strict coercive regulations about toilet training tends to be equally strict about everything else. Not that the one is necessarily the cause of the other, but merely that all expressions of strictness tend to reflect the parent's basic personality, of which he may be relatively unaware. 'Rigid' parents tend to produce 'rigid' children, simply because the child spends much of his time trying to please his parents, and therefore imitates them to the best of his ability. Many of his reactions occur only in relation to specific parental attitudes, and would be different if he had different parents. Indeed, parental attitudes, whether pathological or benign, may be seen reverberating in their influence through several generations in a given family. Both the sins and the virtues of the parents may be visited on the heads of the children 'even unto the third and fourth generation'.

Autonomy conflicts may be expressed in either aggressive or dependent forms of behaviour, and psychologists have studied these intensively. Unfortunately neither aggression nor dependency is easy to define, and many of the attempted definitions are determined not by facts but by value judgements.

Such studies are nevertheless relevant to this stage of development. Take aggression, for example; it is obviously important to investigate it in its earliest clearly defined forms. Aggression pervades adult life and, indeed, has pervaded the history of mankind. It is hardly surprising that society's strictures against aggression are comparable to its strictures against sexuality. Freud himself, although he was more concerned with sexuality, regarded aggression as an equally basic and biologically-rooted drive. Perhaps infants cannot be said to show anger so much as rage, which, however intense it may be, is diffuse, formless, and global. But certainly by early childhood the young child is well enough integrated in his emotional and psychological development to show anger; and his anger may be expressed not only in aggressive behaviour but also in hostile attitudes. In addition, the young child of two to four years cannot escape some frustration and conflict. He may conceivably be so lucky as to find himself in ideal surroundings, where most of his desires could be gratified; but no environment, however ideal, can gratify desires that are in themselves self-contradictory. This connection between frustration and anger is not only a common-sense assumption but a scientific hypothesis now well supported.

REGRESSIONS TO EARLY CHILDHOOD

Before outlining the various forms of pathological regression to the anal stage, we should first consider what allowance to make for 'normal' regression. The distinction between normal and pathological is harder to draw for anality than for orality. Oral tendencies, except for very mild forms, or highly symbolic forms such as acquisitiveness, are in the main essentially pathological. In contrast, many forms of anal regression – even when extreme or directly expressed – are tolerated by society; indeed, some forms have become, in our society, even preferred. In the following discussion, therefore, some readers may wish to make their own 'cut-off', that is, to establish for themselves the point at which anal-regressive tendencies become pathological.

In Chapter 1 normal regression to the oral stage was illustrated by our responsiveness to advertisements based on the typical needs of infants. Here, normal regression to the anal stage can be seen in our response to advertisements based on the typical needs of young children of two to four years old. As we might expect, the appropriate types of advertisement first undermine, then reinforce, our sense of autonomy; they stimulate, then promise to abolish, our sense of shame; they arouse, then diminish, our fears of impending disgrace; they reactivate, then dispel, our doubts regarding the validity of our own self-esteem. In general, there are two main types of advertisement; those which have to do with 'control', and those which have to do with our sense of personal worth.

Advertisers usually promise autonomy in the form of increased power and control over others ('There's a tiger in my tank'); over one's self ('Give up smoking in seven days, or your money back'); or over one's environment, in the form of aids to orderliness and tidiness which cater to our need to have 'a place for everything and everything in its place'. In such advertisements one can usually detect a latent competitive element as well as the more obvious appeal to our desire for more autonomy and control. Those that promise to enhance our sense of personal worth focus on the possession of objects, which we buy not because we need them, but because they have prestige value. This appeal is so important and widespread that the sale of unnecessary objects has become an essential, and perhaps irreversible, feature of our national economy, for example in the 'planned obsolescence', not of objects, but merely of fashions and styles. Enhancement of personal worth is also, and not at all surprisingly, promised by advertisements focused on personal cleanliness and hygiene. One of the most effective sales campaigns was based on the two whispered initials 'B.O.' We are now conditioned to the conviction that people should not smell like people, but only like the latest brand of toothpaste or toilet soap. We are good (boys and girls) if we are clean, better if we are cleaner, and best if we are cleanest. The detergent advertisements in particular ('whiter than white, whiter than bright') not only imply a contest between the consumer and her neighbours, but demonstrate how she can win the contest and be shinier than all of them.

Advertisers have even recognized, and of course exploited, the contradictory features of childhood competitiveness. They often use a trivial and 'easy' competition ('write your slogan on the entry form') as an additional inducement to buy; though they ensure that the vast majority of competitors will win nothing (compare football pools, bingo, and the like). Similarly, the contradictory features of childhood autonomy have been exploited. Advertisers learned quickly that too much autonomy or power could be disturbing to the ordinary man in the street; automobiles are now advertised as faster *and* safer.

Many anal traits are not merely tolerated, but are actively encouraged, by society. Salesmen, for example, are often specifically trained to be competitive or 'aggressive', and to regard their professional relationship with the customer as a contest. Our schools and educational system, and of course our militaristic training schemes, encourage the same characteristics in all of us (see Chapter 4). But in general, given the extent to which society promotes such contention, we cannot be considered pathological when we respond appropriately. We are normal in both the adaptive and statistical senses (see Preface, p. xxi). Whether contentious behaviour is normal in the 'ideal' sense is another matter, and one which probably involves value judgements beyond the scope of psychology.

Merely from our analysis of early childhood, and quite apart from any subsequent social training or conditioning, we might expect to find both contentiousness and the wish to be considered superior in normal adults. Their occurrence however makes it difficult to classify, for example, the argumentative person who lives with a chip on his shoulder. Such individuals do not carry on ordinary conversations with others; they merely take issue. They are forever 'throwing down the gauntlet', challenging, disputing, contradicting, forcing their opinions on others, and persisting until they have irritated everyone into battling with them. There is no placating them. They are compelled not only to create contests, but also to ensure that the contests never have any constructive outcome. Such chronic battling, in so far as it is a neurotic perpetuation of the contest situation of early childhood, will of course never establish a more secure sense of autonomy; on the contrary, its stridency guarantees an equally contentious attitude in others.

Similarly, it is difficult to classify the 'exclusiveness' of many people who wish to be considered superior. This may become so extreme as to lead to social isolation, but many ordinary people do restrict their social world artificially until their own power and prestige becomes undisputed. These are the people who (perhaps because earlier they have failed to obtain autonomy or self-esteem from the world at large) form an elite, or an 'in' group of 'select' members. The group, once formed, looks down contemptuously on everyone who is not a member, and indeed treats outsiders 'like dirt'. These tiny caste systems may be based on a variety of different principles; on common interests, as in a club; on blood-lines, as in the aristocracy; on money, as in a group of 'sound' businessmen; on similarity of ideas, as in a group of 'sound' scholars; on nationality, on geographical location, on a sense of family – in fact, on any principle, real or imaginary, which allows the members to regard themselves as superior to everyone else. The qualifications for entry into such groups usually become diffused into a group mystique, and eventually may become undefinable. The members may then safely exercise their superiority; they make sure others envy them, but at the same time preclude them from joining. When entrance qualifications are simultaneously essential and non-specific, only the 'in' group has control.

The essential vagueness of such entrance qualifications may often be disguised by the group's apparent preoccupation with rules and regulations. Many individuals, once they have joined the self-defined elect, spend most of their time devising legalistic controls to the point where even the group itself is ruled and regulated. Protocol becomes important not as a means of establishing reasonable order, but merely for its own sake. Most of us have at some time been baffled and thwarted by these attitudes in our dealings with public officials, large institutions, or, indeed, with most professions.

The wish to control, when extreme, usually implies a fear of that which is to be controlled, namely, spontaneity in all its many forms. Similarly, the wish to be superior or exclusive, when extreme, usually implies a fear of anything that is 'inferior' or 'outside', and ultimately a fear of being 'contaminated'.

Many everyday social situations are dominated and spoiled by individuals with anal tendencies. When we meet them, say at a party, they are instantly recognizable. Within five minutes of their arrival they have managed to deflate all enthusiasm, stifle all hilarity; that is, they take over, making it 'their' party and ensuring that enjoyment is possible only under their constrictive regulation and control. They assert their own inhibitions until everybody becomes equally inhibited. They are dragons of decorum, of social rules and regulations. If a would-be reveller makes a joke, they don't laugh, and somehow manage to imply that the joke should never have been made, or that those who laughed at it have lost prestige or approbation by doing so. Although they systematically belittle or repel everyone around them, they will not 'let go' of them afterwards. When the others, naturally enough, make as if to withdraw or move away, they will insist, with temporary charm, that they stay. These people invariably cause resentment because, although they are so adept at snubbing and creating uncomfortable situations, their impenetrable sense of superiority makes it look like everybody else's fault. Recently, a mild form of this characteristic has been humorously and aptly described by

Stephen Potter as 'one-upmanship' or 'gamesmanship'. Potter's general philosophy lacks malice, but the basic principle (domination of a situation) is the same. Essentially it is a means of controlling a situation by putting others off balance, exploiting their politeness, and stifling their spontaneity. A more severe form of the same attitude is perhaps represented by the 'Britisher abroad' stereotype – someone who condescends to 'foreigners' or 'natives', disparaging them because they do not speak English and show no gratitude for the condescension.

A much more severe form of anal contentiousness is seen in the 'pseudo-idealist'. Such individuals proclaim moral standards which are not only unbelievably exalted, but savagely strict. For them, life consists of rigid, mutually exclusive, antithetical categories; right *or* wrong, good *or* bad, black *or* white, all *or* nothing, now *or* never, and, ultimately, me *or* you. They are self-appointed judges of everything, constantly proclaiming 'no compromise', insisting on justice though the heavens fall – even though everybody concerned is devastated in the process.

In everyday living this tendency is usually confined to a mere querulous petulance: 'I know my rights' (and will insist on them even though I gain no practical advantage whatever but merely the dreary satisfaction of making others toe my line); or, 'it's the principle of the thing' (never the money, or the fact that one is irritated, etc.). In America such individuals are usually described as 'people who would rather be right than be President'. The savage ruthlessness of anal pseudo-idealists is often carefully disguised as noble benevolence – 'this hurts me more than it hurts you', or 'I'll do you good' (i.e. impose some stupid principle on you) 'though it slay you'.

Other forms of anality may result in 'vendetta' situations. These are by no means confined to gangsterdom, the criminal underworld, or the Sicilian Mafia. In many areas of everyday life we hear people proclaiming, and acting blindly upon, the old rule of an eye for an eye, even harming themselves as well as their victim. Many parents, teachers, lawyers, or demagogues show these anal tendencies. In international affairs, for example, we see many politicians who, instead of evaluating their foreign policies in terms of 'What good will it do?' assert blindly that 'This *must* be done'. Such assertions inevitably arouse antagonism in the chosen 'beneficiary', and the ensuing contest may degenerate into the unedifying spectacle of two national leaders scowling belligerently at one another across their respective boundary fences (and behaving in a way which we should never tolerate in our own children), each refusing to yield an inch to the other, and both justifying their anal behaviour in terms of 'the honour of the country', 'the need for defence' (never 'attack'), 'national expediency', 'justifiable retribution', and the like. Sometimes the situation becomes farcical when the two protagonists use silly pretexts for their determination never to negotiate sensibly – the shape of the conference table is wrong, the meeting-place is not mathematically half-way between the two countries, the agenda conceals some imaginary advantage to one side, and so on; but on other occasions the contest may develop into total war. In such disputes the public issue, however nobly formulated, is really irrelevant to the underlying private issue of 'Who decides?'

The social damage caused by people with such anal characteristics is incalculable. Moreover, their constrictiveness, vengefulness, ruthlessness, and hunger for power is not always easy to detect. They seem at first sight exceptionally fine people, noble, altruistic, hard-working, eminently respectable; only later do we find that they are as mean as the devil. We are of course aware of any exaggerated and direct attempt at domination. It is, however, more difficult to detect the latent domination in someone who merely shows an implacable and paralysing resistance to any sort of spontaneous activity, to growth, to change and particularly to anything creative. We may sense that the avowed motives are hypocritical; that moral superiority conceals its opposite; and that eternal cross-bearing and martyrdom ('nobody knows how much I suffer') is false. Nevertheless we often find ourselves trapped in contest. These people, as we say, 'bring out the worst in us'; that is, they stimulate our own latent anal needs.

We should perhaps pause here for a moment to elaborate the psychodynamics involved. It seems clear that an attempt to dominate, and an overweening assumption of moral superiority, are both challenging. The statement, 'I am a fine fellow, while you are beneath contempt' will provoke us just as much as the statement 'I am always right and you are always wrong'. Both statements are provocative. Rebellion incited by the anal instigator is then interpreted as a vicious and unprovoked attack, which clearly justifies the most sadistic counter-attack. This is usually the beginning of an interminable series of vengeful encounters, which become progressively more ruthless and ever more nobly motivated, until finally the anal individual can persuade himself that he has a duty to unleash the full fury of his hatred. Until this point is reached, however, the individual usually conceals, both from others and himself, the basic purpose of his contentiousness and striving for superiority; that is, to offset his chronic sense of shame and doubt about his own autonomy and self-esteem. When his attempts fail (and he himself ensures their failure) we are likely to see appalling outbursts of sadistic behaviour; these in turn produce similar reactions in his victims who have by this time become infuriated to the point of desperation. Anal individuals (apart from their periodic sadism) may commonly be seen moving with calm dignity through the chaos they have thus created, demonstrating once again how superior they are to the poor fools around them. (Many of these characteristics were beautifully

73

portrayed by the fictional protagonists in the British television series, 'The Power Game'.)

Anal characters are easier to understand if we assume that they are fearful of their own anger; that they generalize their fear to all their emotions, and finally come to fear even the emotions of others. Spontaneity and lively feelings of any sort, and in anyone, are then regarded as direct threats to be crushed without pity. The expression of feelings in action must be controlled at all costs, and if possible paralysed completely. In his need to control everything (ultimately to the point of producing stasis in life and in himself) the anal character is saying 'as long as I can determine beforehand what I'll do, my own excitement won't let me do the things I'm afraid of'; and with others, 'I must make sure you don't do what I daren't do'. Many of his actions are performed merely to demonstrate, with the whole world as witness, how well he can control; hence, domination for its own sake. Any attempt to oppose this massive control system becomes a threat to him, so that he will (often cruelly) intensify his efforts to reinforce and extend his defences.

Thus, such people will often advance hair-splitting logic and reason against feelings; against actions they may set up barricades of constrictive rituals, which come eventually to be regarded as important and powerful in themselves. The ritual reflects the individual's fearful concern with *preparation* for action, for which it is both a substitute and a prophylaxis. Because he fears his own destructiveness, and cannot help creating situations in which it is legitimate to be destructive, he is compelled to build massive defences against his own tendency to express too much of it. Hence his chronic sense of shame, worthlessness, and impending disaster (see Table II).

The ordinary actions of other people tend to be interpreted by the anal character as either forgiveness or accusation. If, however, he is ever made to feel shame his penance will be formidable, involving both public expiation by suffering for himself ('hair-shirt' repentance), and a tremendous amount of inconvenience for everybody else. His defence system may show directly in anal form, as a fear of dirt (or 'dirty thoughts'), but if so the defence is always carefully exaggerated to the point where the 'dirt' shows through. Some of the Sunday newspapers are adept at expressing this tendency. They titillate their readers by dwelling pruriently and in great detail on sexual deviation, but do so under the guise of a crusade against vice. Similarly, the leagues of worthy ladies dedicated to purity and stamping out immorality excite themselves at weekly meetings by capping each other's reports (which must of course be written from data acquired by first-hand observation) about brothels and 'fallen women'.

It is hard to say to what extent these characteristics should be accommodated within the normal range. They represent not social values most sensible people would agree on, but caricatures or distortions of those values. In clinical terms, pathology begins when defences predominate in the life of the individual – when he is no longer striving for positive autonomy and self-esteem, but merely struggling against their negative form, i.e. shame and self-doubt, anal aggressiveness and anal dependency.

Two other forms of anal regression are represented by the so-called *passive-aggressive* and *passive-dependent* personality syndromes. These regressions, both of which are re-enactments of the unresolved aggressive-dependency dilemma of early childhood, are in fact two sides of the same coin. The passive-aggressive individual systematically frustrates (controls) others by his procrastination, by constant over-preparation for action, by criticism and negativism, and by his insistence on over-meticulous precision in all matters. When something has to be done he will neither do it himself nor let others do it. His anger is never full-blooded, but always has a waspish quality; it often shows as a constant sniping at everyone around him. He dominates by his thwarting of others in trivial matters. The passive-dependent individual, on the other hand, dominates through his apparent helplessness. He leaves things undone. He clings to others, making sure that they cannot make a move without hurting him. When they become angry he appeals to his own vulnerability, thus managing to thwart them doubly. Uriah Heep, in Dickens' *David Copperfield*, is the classic example of aggressive-dependent passivity.

Anal defences may be assessed not only in terms of their pervasiveness but also in terms of their obsessive or compulsive characteristics. Obsessions usually concern thoughts, ideas, or feelings, and compulsions concern actions; but both share the inability to discontinue, or shift from, a particular way of functioning. For example, it is normal to persevere at a task, and to refuse to be distracted by less important stimuli until it is completed; it is abnormal to 'perseverate', that is, to continue persevering when more important matters arise, when further effort is clearly fruitless, or when the task has been completed, i.e. when perseverance has become inappropriate. These distinctions help to differentiate between normal, borderline, or pathological anal characteristics. The borderline category, towards which all the above examples have approximated to an increasing degree, is usually called an *obsessive-compulsive personality*. Anal characteristics are an important feature of this personality, but they are sufficiently mild, or (if severe) sufficiently tolerated by society to be regarded as merely a typical life-style which does not prevent the individual from leading an ordinary life.

In order to clarify the distinction between borderline and pathological anality, let us look at a few examples of individuals whose defences do seem to show a certain obsessive or compulsive quality. Chronic risk-takers, for example, can be understood as people who are asserting their autonomy in a defiant, fearful, manner, and whose struggle for self-esteem entails a certain degree of despair.[4] This risk-taking may expose them to actual physical danger. For example, the drivers of racing cars constantly risk injury or death. Granted that the risk is always 'calculated' to some extent, it can never be 100 per cent so, simply because the drivers are racing and must have an inordinate degree of faith in the roadworthiness of their cars, the ability of other drivers in the race, and many other factors beyond their control. Many stunt-men are similarly forced to face situations so dangerous that a safe outcome is uncertain. When circus performers bring us to the edge of our seats with their daring on the trapeze or high-wire it is because we feel they have gone beyond the limit of safety, have left no margin for error, and must be in mortal danger. These people are all highly skilled, thoroughly trained, and extremely practised in their work, but when they repeatedly extend their activities beyond the point of personal safety they become chronic risk-takers in the sense implied above.

To clarify the anal psychodynamics of such individuals we can also look at people who risk not their own lives, but their money – which in our culture has come to be closely connected with self-esteem. This is the compulsive gambler – not the ordinary person who plays bridge for small stakes or occasionally has a flutter on the horses, but one who is so addicted to gambling that he will sacrifice practically everything else in his life to it. In risking his money, the compulsive gambler end-

4. We are not talking here of the youthful dare-devil who endangers his life and limb merely to show off to a girl friend, to test his own skill and nerve to the limit, or to express a sudden surge of healthy exuberance. This is just thoughtlessness. We are also excluding people who put themselves in a situation which seems dangerous but is not really so, in order to obtain a temporary thrill, e.g. a ride on the Big Dipper, Whirl-of-Death or Trip-to-the-Moon at the fairground.

lessly tries (tests) his luck. He contends with, and tries to control, not other people but fate or 'Providence'. Just as the young child seeks reassurance about his personal worth from his unpredictable mother, so the gambler attempts to propitiate 'Lady Luck'. To win, or to get something for nothing, which is the essence of gambling, is to be reassured that she is still there and still cares. The compulsive element, however, is apparent whether or not the gambler wins; if he does win, he is compelled to play his luck till it runs out, and when it does he is equally compelled to start all over again, in the desperate hope of 'better luck next time'.

It is significant that the gambler, usually a sophisticated statistician, knows he is facing odds which are, in the long run, hopeless. This self-defeating and hence depressive element in gambling is revealed when ill-luck becomes too constant, i.e. too humiliating to bear, so that his anger may turn against himself in the form of suicide. The deadly seriousness of the compulsive gambler, his endless attempts to win, his magic formulae, and his elaborate but trivial systems of betting, all bear witness to the urgency of his need to control his luck and to wrest from Providence the reassurance he has never achieved in real life.

There are of course degrees of compulsiveness. Presumably the croupier is a gambler who has stopped trying to beat fate and has joined forces with her instead. He settles for the percentages, which although small are always in his favour, and contents himself with watching other gamblers from his vantage point. Similarly the people who constantly take unnecessary physical risks may be graded in their degree of compulsiveness. It is as if these individuals are compelled to put themselves into situations so dangerous as to produce enough anxiety to offset their depression – they maintain a chronic neurotic balance. In general, the greater the element of unnecessary risk, the greater the degree of depression involved.

Most of the examples discussed so far imply a certain initiative, autonomy and self-esteem, which despite its poor quality does allow the individual to act. Even the deliberate placing of one's self in a dangerous situation requires some positive effort. There is another group of individuals who lack even this limited energy. Far from placing themselves in dangerous situations, they devote all their energies to keeping out of them. They do not tempt fate, they do their utmost to defend themselves against her. For them, all ordinary living is already filled with risk and danger, and fate is not unpredictable, but consistently and actively malevolent. They develop elaborate rites, rituals, and superstitions, which, if obeyed to the letter, will magically propitiate malignant Providence and ward off her powerful threat. The intense, diffuse apprehensiveness experienced daily by such individuals is really a dread of unknown forces of evil which, they are convinced, permeate their world. They see themselves not as dare-devils (far less tyrants) but as victims; without their charms and magic rituals they are helpless and vulnerable. In their desperate attempts to control threatening events, both their actions and feelings become constricted. Their energies are frozen or bound within their repetitive rituals. They may be beset by doubts about their own actions; for example, did they *really* lock the door, *really* turn off the gas, or wash their hands *really* clean, and so on. They feel compelled to repeat a particular action again and again, trying vainly to be absolutely certain that their environment is finally controlled. Or they may be distressed by their own ideas and images; these are often blasphemous, disgusting, or obscene. They may waste endless hours in interminable and inconclusive rumination on religious, metaphysical and philosophical questions.

Chronic fearfulness of this kind, whether obsessive or compulsive in form, may also focus on specific situations, such as being in any high place; or on particular objects, such as sharp instruments. Pathology begins when the fear becomes grossly exaggerated and the sense of danger immediate. For example, some people are so afraid of any open space that they are unable to leave their home and walk in the street; others are so afraid of enclosed spaces that they cannot bring themselves to enter a lift. In such case, anxiety is not generalized and 'free-floating' but is 'attached' to specific situations which in themselves cause no anxiety in normal people. Any ordinary, harmless situation or object may be invested with terror, usually because it is for them charged with symbolic meaning of a highly personalized and threatening kind. There is an almost infinite variety of such phobias.[5]

Although such fears seem unrealistic to the observer, they are extremely real to the person who experiences them. Bland reassurance that there is nothing to worry about is no help. The reason for this is that when the individual says, 'I fear something terrible may happen', he often means unconsciously, 'I fear *I* may do something terrible'. Unable to accept his own impulses, he projects them on to his environment, which then becomes threatening. If his rituals and repetitive stereotyped habits are understood as techniques which help him control not his surroundings, but himself, they often become much more understandable. He is trying to create a situation in which 'misbehaviour' and disgrace are impossible. The futility of such attempts becomes obvious when, in spite of (and sometimes even because of) his best efforts, he 'misbehaves' anyway.

Freud noted that there was often a religious element in the ritualism of obsessive-compulsive individuals, and actually

5. Many mild phobias (of snakes, for example), and minor rites of propitiation, are so common as to be normal, at least in the statistical sense. The person who hastily throws a pinch of spilled salt over his shoulder, feels uneasy when walking under a ladder, or touches wood when he has taken his luck too much for granted, is not neurotic until his life is stifled by such rituals.

referred to the compulsion neurosis as 'a private religion'. This is not to say that all forms of religious aspiration are nothing but obsessive-compulsive neuroses, but merely that the codes, rituals, and magic ceremonies of obsessive-compulsive people are very similar to the propitiatory, repetitive rites of many religious groups. The basic purpose, namely, to control destiny and to hope (or pray) that the question 'Who decides?' is settled finally is one's own favour, is identical. These analogies help us to understand the vehemence of certain moral and religious fanatics, who may in extreme cases be prepared to kill or be killed in their attempts to convert others to their faith. Such fanatics are naturally terrified and infuriated by the seemingly senseless foolhardiness of those who refuse to submit themselves to the same 'necessary' rules for self-protection. Their anger is of course expressed paradoxically; that is, it shows in their efforts to conceal it. We see this tendency in many well-meaning parents who force their children to conform to some restrictive religious practice – forgetting that they themselves may have given the children sufficient autonomy, self-esteem, self-confidence and sense of personal responsibility to enable them to do without the rituals.

The best defined example of anal regression incorporates nearly all the symptoms and traits discussed above. This is the *obsessive-compulsive neurotic*. Although the symptoms of the obsessive-compulsive neurotic are very similar to those of the obsessive-compulsive personalities already discussed, they represent more severe pathological impairment. Freud originally described the anal character as one who was excessively orderly, obstinate and parsimonious, particularly in matters involving money, time and affection. His affection, for example, is doled out sparingly to others, who are always made to feel ashamed (as the obsessive himself is ashamed) for not being more worthy or deserving of it. In money matters he is similarly unyielding and 'tight', always preferring to save rather than spend, demonstrating his control by the unimpeachable rectitude of his accounting system. Even where time is concerned he is parsimonious. Punctual to a fault, he is usually far too busy (i.e. too important) to allow others to 'waste' his time. He is in fact so busy being busy that anyone who wants to see him is inevitably kept waiting. A stickler for rules, he makes no exceptions, no concessions, no compromises, even when a reasonable degree of compromise might be to his advantage. Everything must be just so, and invariably in this particular sequence or at that particular tempo (i.e. *his* way).

What makes the obsessive-compulsive neurotic more severely impaired than the obsessive-compulsive personality is his rigidity. His personality is so constricted as to be socially crippling. He shows more of the severe anal symptoms, such as phobias, magic thinking and ritualism. His defence systems have extended over his whole life, and have become reaction formations (see Preface, p. xviii). His impairment is not merely behavioural but instinctual. Psychologists are now pretty well agreed that obsessive-compulsive neurosis involves not only aggression, but also sexuality, and that these two basic instincts appear to fuse together in the illness. The addition of sexuality changes anal aggression into sadism, in which the individual obtains a sexual satisfaction from inflicting pain; and it changes anal dependency to masochism, in which sexual satisfaction is obtained from suffering pain. The inextricability of these two basic instincts in obsessive-compulsive neurotics shows in their typical *sado-masochistic* tendencies. These impairments are almost impossible to reverse or even modify by means of psychotherapy, because the therapeutic process itself is incorporated into the patient's sado-masochistic system. At this level the obsessive-compulsive neurosis *is* the patient.

This acute form of obsessive-compulsive neurosis is rare, and is usually precipitated by severe emotional stress of some kind. The chronic form is much more common, and is usually progressive. If the obsessive-compulsive's massive defence systems become inadequate, because of age or extreme stress, he may break down into a *panic-reaction* (which is, in effect, the exact converse of his typically rigid control system); into a paranoid delusional system; or into more severe forms of psychosis.

SUMMARY

In this chapter we have outlined the biological, psychological and social changes which inevitably influence the young child and determine his main crises. We stressed the antithetical nature of these dilemmas, which centre largely around his need for autonomy and self-esteem, and discussed these in terms of 'holding on' and 'letting go'. Unsatisfactory resolutions of the crises were considered in their various behavioural forms of 'fighting' (aggression), 'fleeing' (dependency), and 'freezing' (chronic ambivalence); and in their affective form of shame and doubt.

In the section on anal regressions we again used responsiveness to advertising as an index of normal regression, then described various forms of anal character in order of increasing severity (persons who were predominantly contentious, snobbish, dominating, over-preoccupied with rules and regulations, pseudo-idealists, etc.), pausing at the borderline category of the obsessive–compulsive personality. We went on to consider the chronic risk-takers, for whom fate is unpredictable and must be constantly controlled by testing her benevolence; and the ritualists for whom fate is malevolent and must be controlled by endless propitiation. We considered also the more 'frozen' personalities such as phobic individuals, and the passive-aggressive and passive-dependent personalities. Finally we discussed the classic obsessive-compulsive neurotic as described by

Freud, towards which the other anal regressions approximate to a greater or lesser degree.

We stressed the extent to which anal characteristics pervade our everyday lives. We recognized that many of these characteristics are preferred and hence encouraged by society, so that individuals who exemplify them are often regarded as 'the salt of the earth', 'the backbone of society', or 'the pillars of the community'. We recognized also, however, that extreme forms of anal characteristics may cause very considerable psychological and social damage.

CHAPTER THREE

The Play Age (5–7 years)

Men deal with life as children with their play
COWPER, *Hope*

IN the play age, as in infancy and early childhood, the psychological preoccupations of the child are determined largely by the biological and psychosocial changes of his natural development. The capacity to walk, which was a major maturational achievement for the young child, becomes a largely unconscious ability for the child of four or five. Instead of having to concentrate on each single step, he takes it for granted. Already physically independent, he now becomes physically adventurous. In addition, he finds pleasure in locomotion as such: he *likes* to get around.

An equally important biological change occurs within the child's own body. His main physiological source of interest and pleasure, once his mouth and later his anal system, now changes to his genital organs. The child 'discovers' his genitals during this period. He becomes pleasurably preoccupied with comparisons between his own organs and those of other people, especially those of the opposite sex. Children of this age realize that little boys are different from little girls, and will 'play with themselves', 'play doctor' with each other, and show considerable interest in the genital equipment of adults.

There are also significant psychological changes. Between the ages of five and seven a genuinely cognitive, and not merely associational, mental development begins to take place. The child's intellectual functioning develops far beyond mere trial and error. His use of language develops to the point where 'he can ask about many things just enough to misunderstand them thoroughly' (Erikson, 1959). In addition, the development of fantasy thinking now allows him a vast range of pleasures that need not be real, but only anticipated in imagination. Indeed, so lively is his imagination that he sometimes has difficulty in distinguishing fantasy from reality. He may describe vividly to his mother how he fought off an enormous lion on his way home from school, offering some tiny scratch on his finger as evidence. This does not mean he is a pathological liar; it just shows his tendency to blur the distinction between what is real and what is wished-for. Most parents while gently tolerating these fantasies will help the child gradually to distinguish fiction from fact.

This period is often regarded as the age of play. Children take play seriously, so seriously that it has been described as the work of children. In play, the child moves from the known to the untried and unknown. Play involves risk, mastery by repetition and practice, and problem-solving. The child may use it as a vehicle for other feelings, such as self-assertion, the expression of otherwise forbidden impulses, and as a way of revealing his own nature. So far from being an idle pastime, play trains the child in social relationships.

In this period, the child's circle of significant social relationships widens considerably. His basic milieu changes from the one-person situation of infancy (where he interacted essentially with nobody but himself), through the two-person situation of early childhood, until now he is involved in an essentially three-person situation, consisting of himself and his two parents. This new social situation has such far-reaching effects on later psychological development that we should look here at its basic nature.

So far, our discussions of parental influences on the child

have focused mainly on the mother; and certainly the mother's influence is predominant during the child's earliest years. We should now recognize, however, the importance of the father. Even in infancy, when the child's needs are largely biological, the father is influential in more than one way. For example, the mother's attitudes towards her child depend to a very considerable extent on her relationship with her husband. Many experimental studies make specific reference to the mother's feelings for her husband, and regard these as a significant variable in the child's early rearing. Thus paternal influence may be felt by the child not only directly when the father is present but even indirectly when he is absent. The child of four or five understands absence. In earlier years an individual or an object not actually perceived by the child was simply non-existent; but by the age of four he knows that objects or persons may continue to exist when he is not actually with them. This mental development, convincingly demonstrated by Piaget and other investigators, confirms the earlier importance of the mother, who is most of the time physically present to the child, and the increasing subsequent importance of the father even when absent.

The significance of these changes is confirmed by a Home Office Research Unit Report (1961) on 'Delinquent Generations'. According to this study,

the peak excess criminality characterizes those born in the seven-year period of 1935–6 to 1941–2; the greatest crime proneness is found to be associated with that birth group who passed through their fifth year during the war. Whether this means that disturbed social conditions have their major impact on children between the age of four and five is not proven, but it is a likely hypothesis. A previous crime-prone group was born in the years 1926–7 and 1927–8. This birth group coincides with the worst part of the depression of the thirties. The concomitance of these two results seems unlikely to be due to chance. There appears to be something particularly significant in social disturbances occurring in the fourth or fifth year of a child's life. Perhaps the deprivation of mothers is important in very early life, and paternal deprivation later, say between four and five years of age.

This report highlights (1) the difference between the roles of the parents – mother important earlier and father later; (2) the importance of experiences during the fourth and fifth years; (3) the absence of the father (during the war, for instance) which tends to produce delinquency. These findings are in general accord with psychoanalytic theories about child development.

In considering the influence of parents on their children, we should make explicit certain general psychological assumptions about the parental roles. These will of course be considered more fully in later chapters, but here we shall describe, in terms of the broadest social stereotypes, the roles of the mother and the father.

To the child, the mother represents welfare. In infancy, the child's awareness and assessment of how good the world is will be largely determined by the kind of care and attention he receives from his mother. It is she who gratifies his most basic needs and does so without question; for the mother, it is enough that his need exists. The closeness of this physical and psychological bond, although essential for the child's survival in infancy, may, however, become a disadvantage for him if it persists too far beyond infancy. The real world will not gratify his needs merely because they occur, and this is something he has to learn.

It is here that the father becomes more prominent. If the mother, broadly speaking, represents welfare, the father, in an equally broad sense, represents law and order. If the mother represents how good the world is, the father represents how 'fair' it is. It is largely from the father that the child develops conscience, and comes to realize that gratifications are not always forthcoming with no questions asked; that they may be earned or deserved by his own efforts; and that only some gratifications are 'legitimate'. The father, ideally, is better equipped to guide the child in this respect because he is not, as it were, handicapped by mother love. He can step between mother and child in ways that are necessary and advantageous for the child's subsequent development. He does not deny or stifle the child's impulses, but merely helps him to set reasonable limits regarding their gratification. Unless children are given clear standards at this age they become very anxious, and will redouble their efforts to misbehave until they do find someone who will stop them, and reassure them that there are some limits somewhere. The successful imposition of law and order is facilitated if the child learns that he is not being excluded for ever but only until he is ready: 'You're getting to be a big boy now – and should be able to understand.'

These concepts of the warm, giving, 'conscience-less' mother and the strong, fair-minded, guiding father[1] are of course simply

1. These parental characteristics have been extended by some psychologists into much more global psychological principles. For example, when we see a father insisting that his child must 'do what he's told', while the mother keeps asking, 'But what good will it do?' – that is, when the father advocates obedience to a (family) law, while the mother is quite prepared to set aside any or all laws unless some tangible benefit can be demonstrated – we are said to be observing an example of the interaction between formal structured civilization (the male view) and 'free' unstructured nature (the female view). This extension, if accepted, certainly undermines the popular view of the relations between the sexes as being necessarily a battle. The principles are not antagonistic, but complementary to one another. The extreme maternal view (welfare at *any* price) leads to emotional anarchy, unless tempered with some law and order; the extreme paternal view (law enforcement at *any* price) leads to moralistic fascism, unless tempered with tenderness, a sense of humour, or, as we say, common humanity.

stereotypes. Other cultures have somewhat different stereotypes; and even our own culture has been profoundly influenced by the relatively recent emancipation of women. Many families do deviate in practice from the stereotype, in that the woman 'wears the pants', while the man is passive and henpecked. There is, however, ample clinical evidence that too great a departure from the ideal stereotypes above will eventually produce serious and predictable breakdowns in the personal relationships of the families concerned.

Both parents, then, are of paramount importance to us during this period. Their influence on our subsequent psychological development need not astonish us so long as we remember that our mother was the first woman, and our father the first man, in our lives. For all of us at this period the family situation was a three-person triangle, consisting of one female and two males, or one male and two females, thus:

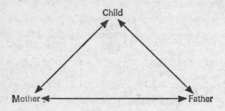

If there is more than one child, each one will of course become an apex in a series of triangles having a common parental base:

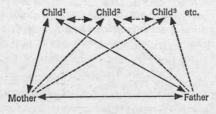

The second diagram reminds us that children within the same family interact with each other as well as with their parents. We confine ourselves meanwhile to emphasizing the essential triangularity of the parent–child relationship in this period, leaving the complexities of sibling relationships for discussion later in the chapter.

The child's awareness of those who are psychologically important to him is not confined to his parents and siblings, but extends to other adults and his peers. Around the age of five he has to go to school. This simple fact involves a tremendous and sudden widening of his mental, emotional and social horizons. He develops 'untiring curiosity about differences . . . in general, and sexual differences in particular. He tries to comprehend possible future roles or at any rate to understand what roles are worth imitating . . . he gradually enters into the infantile politics of nursery school, street corner, and barnyard' (Erikson, 1959).

PSYCHOLOGICAL CRISES IN THE PLAY AGE

In the play age the child is vigorously self-activating. He has a new sense of *initiative* (see Appendix, Table I) which appears in all his personal relationships. He is exuberantly energetic and active; he is suddenly aware of his widening personal and social boundaries – and often seems to be trying to leap (at least in his imagination) beyond those boundaries. He tries to conquer all that he surveys.

This conquest is attempted by boys and girls in different ways. Boys may be seen constantly asserting themselves by bursting into and bursting through everything in their environment, as if to say 'Look, everybody, see how big *I* am!' This is the age at which a boy, on his return home from school, crashes open the door, hurls his schoolbooks into a corner, flings his coat to the floor, and stamps through the house yelling, 'I'm going out to play cowboys and indians!' His initiative is intrusive; he intrudes 'into other people's ears and minds ... into the unknown by consuming curiosity' (Erikson, 1959). His efforts are directed towards conquest by force.

The initiative of girls is not so much intrusive as inclusive; the girl tries to make herself more endearing in order to attract people in her environment. In childish ways she takes pains with her personal appearance and grooming, practises a winning smile, develops social graces, and generally cultivates charm in ways which will ensure the attention of the maximum number of people. Her conquests are achieved not by force but by a more or less innocent seduction. These differences between the robust behaviour of boys and the more passive behaviour of girls, are of course heavily reinforced by society; we consistently encourage little boys to be manly, and little girls to be ladylike. However, initiative shows in both girls and boys as a determination to be always first and always best.

At this age children will compete vigorously with their parent of the same sex, and try to demonstrate how much better they themselves could look after the parent of the opposite sex. Boys strive to outdo their father in feats of strength, or even to outshine him as provider by going shopping for their mother and 'bringing home the bacon'. Girls dress up in their mother's clothes, use her make-up, and have their father's slippers ready warmed any time the mother is busy elsewhere. In all this there is no serious problem so long as the child merely wants to be *like* the parent of the same sex; but when imagination begins to distort reality the child may strive actually to be the parent, and act as such within the family. When these interactions in a family become over-intense they are described by psychoanalysts as *Oedipal*. This description is based on the Greek myth in which Oedipus unwittingly killed his father and married his mother; then, when he discovered what he had done, blinded himself.

The myth is certainly analogous to what goes on in families as part of normal development, but we may recognize the importance and pervasiveness of the Oedipal situation without committing ourselves to the view that the Greek tragedy is a literal description of what goes on in the daily life of a child of five. It is an observable fact that around this age a boy normally regards his father as a rival for the favour of his mother; but to say that the boy wants literally to murder his father and have sexual intercourse with his mother, then castrate himself, however symbolically, is to go far beyond the evidence. In addition, although the child's wishes and dreams do tend in an Oedipal direction, he is still too young to formulate his fantasies very clearly. Even if he could, his own physical immaturity would preclude his acting out such fantasies. The Oedipal myth, although it does in many ways illuminate the family situation in childhood, becomes adultomorphic when applied too literally. The child of four or five may be Oedipal, but he is not Oedipus.

It is clear nevertheless that the main psychological danger for the child of this age is that his initiative runs away with him. His imagination and energy often outstrip his judgement; so that instead of doing he finds himself over-doing. When this happens, his own imaginings begin to frighten him and his impulses get him into trouble. A boy may become not merely responsive but over-responsive to his mother; he may not simply identify but over-identify with his father. Similarly, a girl may become over-responsive to her father, and over-identify with her mother. Since both sons and daughters are pushed forward by their own dawning sexuality and initiative, and are simultaneously held back by their vague awareness that it will do them no good in the long run to persist, their feelings and actions often show conflict or ambivalence. Their psychological predicament here is not, however, quite the same as when they were struggling for autonomy. Then their attitude was an antithetical 'yes *or* no'; now it is (as we shall see) an ambivalent 'yes *and* no'.

For the normal child this crisis is resolved with help from two sources. To begin with, society will not let his initiative run wild. His environment constantly, and often in unspoken ways, curbs his exuberant imagination; it blocks, restrains, and re-directs his impulsive activity. For example, if he participates too enthusiastically in parental discussions he will eventually be encouraged to 'go away and play'.[2] If, after his play, he con-tinues to show inappropriate initiative, say, by tracking mud through the house, he may be encouraged even more vigorously to show some consideration for parental requirements.

When this type of situation is repeated often enough the child develops the capacity to *anticipate* the reactions of others. Instead of acting impulsively and waiting for external pro-hibitions and punishments he begins to realize that punishment may be forestalled if he first imposes the prohibition upon him-self. That is, he internalizes the value systems of the significant figures in his immediate environment. He may then feel guilty not only when he is found out, but also when he merely expects to be found out. He may feel guilty for deeds that nobody knows about, and even for vague thoughts, wishes and dreams existing only in his imagination.

The whole process, usually called introjection, is the psycho-logical basis of individual morality, or conscience. The prac-tical effect is that the child now begins to impose limits on himself, and to define his own legitimate goals. He begins to show a capacity for constructive cooperation with other chil-dren and adults instead of trying to boss and coerce them. He

2. If he is excluded too often, or too forcibly, from all parental interactions, he will of course begin to feel belittled – and may retaliate later by misbehaving or by conjuring up nightmares and waking his parents at night. He may even demand to sleep in their bed, prefer-ably between them.

learns not only to take care of himself but to care for younger children. Instead of competing vainly in the major league of the adult world he accepts, and then confidently develops, a satisfactory role in his own minor league of contemporaries. The games he plays become appropriate. Ideally, the introjective process will neither stifle nor over-stimulate the child's own initiative; he will neither swallow parental values in a wholesale and undiscriminating way, nor will he reject them totally. He will be able to govern his own natural initiative appropriately enough to avoid serious trouble.

What we have described above as normal for boys between the ages of four and seven may be applied also, *mutatis mutandis*, to girls of the same ages. Where the boy tended to rival his father for the mother's favour, the girl will tend to rival her mother for her father's favour.[3] However, although the same principles apply, the underlying psychodynamics are slightly more complicated for girls, or at least are less well formulated.

Like boys, girls are first influenced predominantly by their mother, and develop equally intense, positive feelings towards her. In the Oedipal stage, however, the boy's positive feelings towards the mother are retained, and indeed are considerably enhanced; while the girl's positive feelings may be lessened to some extent by the fact that her mother, besides continuing to be her mother, suddenly becomes an arch-rival as well. Any child's tie with its mother has deeper psychological roots (i.e. more unconscious and more biological) than the tie with its father. Boys tend to be less profoundly conflicted when *their* arch-rival, the father, gently indicates to them that the mother is already 'spoken for', and that they had better go and find a

3. The intensification of the girl's wish to rival her mother is usually described as the 'Electra situation', in analogy with the well-known Greek myth. Sometimes, however, the intra-familial situation is described as 'Oedipal' irrespective of the sex of the child.

girl-friend of their own age. This does not produce an internal conflict in their feelings for the mother. In contrast, girls whose Oedipal enthusiasm is quelled by their mothers may develop an ambivalent attitude towards her: 'She is still my mother, and I trust her – but perhaps not where men are concerned.'[4]

In discussing the child–parent relationships in the Oedipal stage it should be clear that the child's self-assertiveness involves more than his earlier anal contentiousness. Oedipal self-assertion always has a sexual component and is more specific, in that it is directed primarily at the parent of the same sex. It may be extended against anyone, and particularly siblings, who threaten the child's wish for a privileged position with the parent of the opposite sex. Hence the intense family rivalries and jealousies typical of children in this age group.

The birth of a brother or sister is always important to a child but it is perhaps most disturbing at the Oedipal stage. The child is suddenly forced to *share* the attention of his parents. His unique status is especially undermined if he is expected not only to stand aside, but actually to contribute to the family efforts regarding the newcomer. Parents may unwittingly increase the first child's resentment by insisting that he should have only positive attitudes to his younger sibling, and even by making unfavourable comparisons between them. Conflict in the child is inevitable here and it is unrealistic to expect to eliminate it altogether.

Parents are often astonished when two children of the same sex, of roughly comparable age, and reared under 'exactly the

4. The daughter's suspicions about the mother's motives regarding men may reappear more obviously in her teens, when the mother may captivate her daughter's adolescent boyfriends. Father–son rivalries are usually less intense here.

same' family conditions turn out to have very different personalities. Quite apart from genetic differences in psychological make-up, the simple explanation is of course that no two siblings *can* be brought up in exactly the same way. Their family environments are necessarily different. With the exception of twins, one child is always born before the other, so that the first child has a younger sibling while the second has an older one. This important difference in birth order leads to a difference in family status, which is not only recognized by the children themselves, but often heavily reinforced by the parents. For example, they usually expect more responsibility from the other child and less from the baby of the family. The younger child, having the older as a model, can learn faster from his mistakes; while the older child may feel uneasily that the younger child is forever liable to catch up with and even overtake him.

In a study of birth order and reaction to stress, it was found that early-born subjects were more anxious and frightened in standard anxiety-producing situations than were later-born subjects. When given a choice, first-born subjects chose to be with other subjects, while equally anxious later-born subjects did not do so. From these laboratory findings it was then hypothesized that anxious first borns would choose social means of coping with anxieties, while later-borns would seek non-social means.

Continuing this study in real-life situations, it was found that there were more later-born individuals and fewer first-borns among chronic alcoholics than would be expected by mere chance; that first-born and only children were more likely to seek help in psychotherapy and to continue in therapy longer than later-born individuals; and that among later-borns were more effective combat pilots than first-borns. To explain these findings, it was suggested that a mother is more worried and solicitous with a first child than with later children and would reduce anxiety more quickly and effectively. Thus, at an early age first-born and only children would learn to depend on the presence of others to reduce anxiety.

The child's psychological development is affected not only by his position in the family in terms of birth order, but also by the sex of the siblings. Boys with brothers have been found to be more 'masculine' (as measured by tests scores) than boys without brothers; girls with sisters were more 'feminine' than girls with no sisters; while siblings of the opposite sex produced no consistent influence on either boys or girls.

These studies, and many others, make it clear that at the play age the effect of family life on the growing child is extraordinarily complex. Some of the factors which complicate research in this area are: parental background, current family setting, the composition of the family, relationship between parents, personal characteristics of parents, parental attitudes towards children, overt parental patterns of behaviour, child's attitude towards parents and siblings, overt child behaviour towards other family members, personal characteristics of the child, and the child away from the family. We obviously cannot discuss all these in detail, but must confine ourselves to broad trends apparent in the Oedipal situation. In summary, therefore, the Oedipal child is psychologically successful when his initiative is not so exaggerated or intense as to result in guilt feelings, when he can establish his own sex role confidently and express his feelings adequately in the appropriate context of his own 'minor league' of contemporaries and siblings, and generally when he develops a firm, realistic sense of 'fair' play which is acceptable to his playmates, his parents, other adults, and himself.

DISTURBANCE IN THE PLAY AGE

The degree of success or failure for the child in the Oedipal stage depends almost entirely on two factors; first, how well the child resolves his own ambivalences; second, how he is helped by significant persons around him, in particular his mother and father. We shall take each of these in turn.

To understand how ambivalence occurs we should remember that the child is out for conquest, and is striving to obtain an exclusive position of privilege within his family and elsewhere. His arch-rival, namely the parent of the same sex, is as a matter of plain fact overwhelmingly superior to him, in size, competence, experience, power and everything else. The child's attempt to vanquish his parent is therefore doomed to failure. On the other hand, he cannot stop trying. Ambivalence naturally arises when he cannot help promoting situations in which he himself can foresee that he must fail.

Ambivalence arises also because the child who succeeds in supplanting the parent of the same sex simultaneously undermines the parenthood of that parent – and no child of this age is ready to cope with limitless independence. In addition, to vanquish the parent of the same sex would be to leave the way open to the parent of the opposite sex, and this also would be far too intense a relationship for the child to bear. The very thought of it (in wishes, dreams and fantasies) is terrifying to him. Furthermore, the child's own conscience is developing. Some of the prohibitions imposed by his parents are beginning to be imposed by the child himself. So a third source of ambivalence arises from his conflict between the tempting gratifications of Oedipal rivalry, and the guilt that this may produce.

Ambivalence may show in several ways and at different levels. Physically the child may be unable to settle firmly on his sexual identity. A boy, over-excited by normal penile erections and over-fearful of his own sexual fantasies, may well give up part of his masculine initiative, and become a 'sissy' or a 'nice boy'. In extreme cases this outcome can become the psychological basis for subsequent homosexuality. Girls, if they become too ambivalent in their attempts to attract others, may similarly give up their feminine initiative; they may try to imitate the boisterous intrusiveness of boys so successfully that they become tomboys.[5]

Thus the ambivalent child of this age oscillates between exaggerated initiative and, later, equally exaggerated guilt feelings. He constantly starts something he cannot finish, gets out of his depth, bites off more than he can chew, reaches beyond his grasp and generally rushes in where angels fear to tread. When his violent hyperactivity or heated imagination get him into trouble, he may overdo his reaction and become inhibited and passive; or he may rush frantically from his guilt into yet another exaggerated rivalry situation of his own promotion. Girls too, may overdo everything, and begin to grab at people who fail to be attracted. Much of this over-possessive behaviour is of the sort often described as 'bitchy'. Extreme forms of these tendencies can show as exhibitionism, which represents in the child a guilty but determined desire to be noticed at all costs.

Purely psychological forms of ambivalence occur in the child's inner life. 'The child indulges in fantasies of being a giant and a tiger but in his dreams he runs for dear life' (Erikson, 1951). His fears of being small, powerless or inadequate, when confirmed by external events such as parental criticism or scorn, produce in him a keen sense of *belittlement*. If this persists too long he may regress to an anal type of anger and shame.

If anger predominates, the child may over-compensate by seeking the limelight wherever he goes; 'he will put up a great show of spontaneity and tireless initiative, as if his worth as an individual consisted not in what he is, or even in what he is doing, but only in what he is going to do next' (Erikson, 1950). If shame predominates, he may start up a vicious circle of

5. Psychoanalysts have explained these difficulties in terms of the child's possession or lack of a penis. We may, however, recognize sex-role ambivalence without taking literally all the psychoanalytic theories regarding 'penis-envy' and 'masculine protest'.

fantasy and guilt. Outwardly he will begin to go through life apologetically, as if afraid to be seen or heard, though he will try to get away with things when unseen, resorting to cheating and lying instead of developing genuine initiative. He may also try to gain a quick, easy, and temporary prestige by discovering (or manufacturing) 'secrets', with which he can tantalize others and thus hold their attention.

Such children are never really sure what they feel, who they are, or what they may become. Hence the false identity typical of the child troubled in this period of his life. He is always acting a part, pretending to himself as well as to others, until he begins to lose (more permanently) the distinction between fact and fantasy.

Earlier in this chapter we described Oedipal rivalry as more specific in its focus (i.e. on the parent of the same sex) and as more sexual in its content, than anal contentiousness. We should now emphasize that the Oedipal child's attempt to demonstrate his superiority over one parent is made in order to impress the other parent. This brings us to the second main factor in the child's resolution of his Oedipal crisis, namely the extent to which, and the ways in which, he is influenced by his parents.[6] The classic Oedipal situation arises for the child when the parental roles are, in effect, reversed; that is, when the father 'goes soft' and comes to represent welfare more than law and order, and the mother 'goes hard', and comes to represent law and order more than welfare. Since these reversals involve a change of parental role but not a change of parental sex, they inevitably produce confusion in the child searching for genuine

6. Children are not influenced *only* by members of their family, but during the Oedipal phase they are *predominantly* influenced by family, and particularly parents; i.e. although the child also has a tendency to identify with adults outside the family (teachers, or anyone whose role is clear-cut and relatively unemotional), these are secondary identifications.

and useful identifications.[7] The effects of parental role-reversal are more clearly seen in later life, and will therefore be discussed in detail in the next section as regressions to this age. In general, however, just as parents may fail to include (without frightening) the child in the emotional intimacies of family life, and exclude (without belittling) him from them, so they themselves may fail to approximate closely enough to their natural parental role, and as a result may not interact in a complementary fashion appropriate for their child's Oedipal needs. All the psychological difficulties described above represent different outcomes to the child's Oedipal ambivalence produced by his over-intense wish to rival his parent of the same sex and gain an exclusive prestige with his parent of the opposite sex.

If the child's ambivalences are severe and remain unresolved too long, he may regress to earlier forms of behaviour, and show symptoms in which guilt, anger, and shame seem to fuse together. That is, if he falls short (see Appendix, Table II) too often, his sense of belittlement may become chronic and he may come to feel that people do not love him because he is essentially unlovable. To feel unloved often produces anger; to feel unlovable produces depression. In its direct form the child may show anal or oral-dependent features, for instance, whining, petulant behaviour demanding love and attention from the

7. Obviously, Oedipal problems may stem from many other distortions of parental roles. These roles may become directly exaggerated rather than reversed (both parents too strict or too indulgent); or one parent's natural influence may predominate too much over the other; and so on. We will confine ourselves here to parental role-reversals because the resulting problems are more Oedipal in their nature, i.e. they arise from the child's natural preoccupations with initiative, conscience, phallic sexuality etc. Also, the psychodynamics described within this context may be extended to cover those children who have actually (and not psychologically) lost one or other parent and who consequently must work through their Oedipal conflicts partly in fantasy and with parent substitutes.

parents. Sometimes, however, the depression is covered up with anal or oral forms of defiance. Such children may be obedient, but their obedience contains a good deal of spite.

Mild forms of spiteful obedience are of course quite common in normal children of this age. To take an everyday example: suppose the parents have told their young daughter that she must brush her teeth as part of her morning toilet, and have issued this dictum like a royal command; next morning they may well find that they are unable to get into the bathroom for an hour or so – the daughter is brushing her teeth, and brushing her teeth, and brushing her teeth . . . as she was told.

Regressions in children at this stage of development may show also as phobias (see Chapter 2), the commonest one being the so-called 'school phobia', which may arise when the child is 'expelled' from his family into school. Ambivalence here is present not only in the child but in the parents as well, particularly the mother. If a mother, herself ambivalent about relinquishing her child, insists (*a*) that he go to school but (*b*) that he needn't go if he feels ill, the child will soon develop a variety of complaints and become a genuine patient. 'School phobia' is different from separation anxiety as seen in younger children, because of its ambivalence. The younger child suffering from separation anxiety is not ambivalent; he wants to be back with his mother. The Oedipal child suffering from 'school phobia' both does and does not want to discontinue his specially privileged relationship with his mother. To resolve the crisis by becoming a patient gives him the advantage of neither alternative and the disadvantage of both.

REGRESSIONS TO THE PLAY AGE

Since everybody had a mother and a father, and lived through the play age, it is to be expected that unresolved Oedipal conflicts, and persisting Oedipal tendencies, should appear in the ordinary life patterns of normal people. And so they do. In fact, we must make an allowance for normal Oedipal regressions, as we did in Chapter 2 for anal regressions, and in Chapter 1 for oral regressions.

There are many Oedipal promises in modern advertisements. The psychological basis of the whole 'glamour' market in advertising is, very largely, the Oedipal child's preoccupation with conquest, and his tendency to sexualize all his interests. In advertisements we are offered unrealistically easy sexual conquests. We are sold techniques on how to become irresistible to the opposite sex, how to obtain the dreamed-of prize without earning it, and generally, how to be first and best without even trying. Men may become Casanovas and conquer *all* women, merely by using a particular hair cream; women may become *femmes fatales* and conquer *all* men, merely by using a particular perfume (some of which are so frankly aphrodisiac that the customer is advised never to use it 'unless you really mean it').

It is important to notice that what is being sold is not actual sexual satisfaction, but merely sexual excitement. What the customer buys is attractiveness and its related fantasies, not 'the real thing'. The emphasis is on romance, idealized perfection, and glamour – on promise rather than fulfilment. This means that there is unlimited scope for dreaming and wishing, with no harsh reality to contradict or spoil things. Our lingering resentment that nobody really pays us enough attention, or treats us with the ever-loving kindness that we really deserve, is diminished by advertisements that promise to make us lovable with no effort on our part. So we are offered an antidote for the sexual belittlement we all experienced to some extent in the Oedipal stage. We are encouraged to believe that we can capture the attention of all persons of the opposite sex, to the eternal confusion of all persons of the same sex. In addition, there is probably an underlying psychological message to the effect that 'it's quite all right' to be sexually intrusive or inclusive; the advertisement reassures us and, as it were, gives us permission to act on our Oedipal initiative.

The essential triangularity (two males and one female, or two females and one male) of the Oedipal situation is also emphasized in many forms of art. The most popular theme in fiction is the triangular love-story, in which boy-meets-girl-plus-one-other. The heroine becomes involved with two men or the hero with two women; and the three-way Oedipal interactions maintain our interest until the resolution, in which the favoured pair are seen approaching the altar or walking off together into the sunset, leaving the 'other' permanently excluded. Very often the theme is more directly Oedipal, as when the 'other woman' or the 'other man' explicitly belongs to someone else. There is usually an underlying theme of rescue, as when the male earns the female by overthrowing his competitor and taking the heroine 'away from all this', i.e. possessing her exclusively; or when the female saves the male from the clutches of the other woman, who is of course quite 'unsuitable', that is to say, less worthy. Such triangular situations have held our interest since the days of the early troubadours and storytellers; they are now consistently exploited by big business, as in the dream factories of Hollywood.

Although love-stories are read more by women, there is a male counterpart of female Oedipal fantasies in fiction, namely, the Western story. As we might expect, there is a good deal of obsessional contention (see Chapter 2) here, with its climax of the shoot-out between the goodies and the baddies, and at first sight this might appear to be more anal than Oedipal. But in the Western there is the same element of idealized romanticism.[8] There is a constant theme of masculine penis-

8. The authentic West was never as portrayed in fiction. For example, the famous Colt .45 had such a kick that the user could hardly expect to hit a barn door at ten paces, far less disarm his adversary at thirty paces by grazing the knuckles of his gun hand.

measuring, an endless preoccupation with the question 'Who is the fastest, and hence the most feared?' i.e. who is first and best? In Western fiction guns are used not merely as reasonable and necessary weapons of defence against real danger, but as symbols of masculine display and rivalry. The prowess of the professional gunman and the tricks he can play with his equipment are often exaggerated to the point of caricaturing masculinity.

Women in Western fiction tend to be unreal, exaggerated sexual stereotypes – incredibly good women representing the ideals of chastity, innocence, and purity (to be saved only); incredibly bad women such as the saloon girls (to be used only); or tomboys behaving more like men than women. They are cardboard, two-dimensional figures who could only have been dreamed up by men and who are always forced to take second place in a setting in which intrusive male action is the only important value. The naïvely over-simplified ethic or code of the West, the emphasis on limitless horizons ('Don't fence me in'), and the scope for super-initiative ('Where never is heard a discouraging word'), all bear witness to a continuing phallic boyishness that most men never entirely relinquish. There is of course no need to classify such mild Oedipal tendencies as abnormal until the escapist fiction, dreaming, idealization, fantasy and play-acting become a substitute for reality. On the whole, our interest and pleasure in the Oedipal manoeuvrings of fictional characters remain vicarious.

Many Oedipal tendencies are regarded as normal even in real life. Ambivalent intrusive-inclusive reactions are liable to be triggered off whenever an individual feels neglected or belittled by someone who is psychologically or sexually important to them. Some people, smarting because nobody is paying enough attention, force attention by disturbing others and generally 'stirring things up'. What they do is less important than the end result of being noticed. The typical gambit is to arouse others by being unnecessarily provocative in a sexual way. We are not talking here of a genuine sexual overture, but only of teasing, flirtatious behaviour which is pseudo-sexual in that it implies a promise but no genuine intention of fulfilment. The ambivalence in such pseudo-seductive coquettish titillation is usually quite apparent. Women who wish merely to 'collect scalps', and no more, may do so in a wide variety of ways, encouraging their victim to come closer by a meaningful glance, an air of mystery, a flutter of the eyelids, a suggestive posture; any male who responds to this as if it were a genuine invitation is immediately discouraged – the woman simulates outrage ('What kind of a girl do you take me for?', or 'I've never been so insulted in all my life', or even 'Why do you want to *spoil* things between us?', and so forth). If she overdoes her rebuff, the male, crestfallen, may try to withdraw, thus depriving her of his attention; and she then has to encourage him again ('Well, I suppose it *was* a kind of compliment'). This advanced gambit not only re-encourages the victim, it indicates that he may regain credit only by means of sustained, fulsome flattery; and of course it also promotes a cosy, safe relationship based on the sharing of a guilty secret. The woman has in the end manu- factured a situation in which she is 'special'. Should she then wish to keep her victim, i.e. play with him, she may have to entice him on to a sexual tightrope of ambivalence, using an impressive repertoire of vague temptations, secret smiles, half-hearted reproofs and baffling inconsistencies, all of which are designed to make the bewildered male feel that if only he could find the key to all this, say the right word, do the right thing, he would finally conquer. Meantime, of course, he is conquered.

Although these mild Oedipal ambivalences may be observed at any cocktail party, their essential triangularity is not always immediately apparent. When the person who arouses others, or the person being aroused, belongs to someone else (is already married, perhaps, or otherwise attached), the triangularity is obvious. But even when the two parties concerned are free and unattached there is always a third party nearby. Oedipal teasing is instigated mainly to impress a 'someone else' who, although perhaps not present at the time, is certain to become jealously interested later on. The teasing female may not have any genuine sexual interest in her victim, and may not even like him. This does not stop her from perpetually testing his interest in her, either by making overtures to yet another man, or by pushing other women in his path. She always deals with people in groups of three.

Oedipal ambivalence is of course not confined to women. In men it shows in obtrusive attention-getting behaviour which may take equally varied forms. Often it involves a narcissistic courtship display, a kind of perpetual muscle-flexing, an ostentatious self-assertion, as if to say 'See how big and strong *I* am'. Young athletes turning somersaults on the beach may be merely practising, but when in the process they also kick sand over the girls and noisily thrust themselves on their attention they proclaim their need for an admiring audience. Less robust forms of Oedipal initiative may show as mind – rather than muscle – flexing. Universities are filled with professors who have never stopped making endless sibling-rivalry comparisons in terms of size: 'Who has the longest string of letters after his name?' or 'Who has the longest list of publications?' Such individuals are of course prone to tease and belittle their students' academic qualifications and give incomprehensible lectures, as if to say 'See how clever *I* am'. They do to their younger students what was once, they think, done to them.

Oedipal childishness is better tolerated in women than in men. In our social culture there is a strong expectation that men should be single-minded, decisive, not given to play-acting, and indeed slightly obsessional; women on the other hand are given the eternal right (and in fact are often encouraged) to change their minds whenever they feel like it, or even for no reason at all.[9] A certain demure provocativeness is, however, easily aroused in both sexes. It may be observed whenever a male enters a room full of females, or when a female enters a room full of males. The immediate change in atmosphere, the surreptitious universal preening, derive basically from the multiple triangles and rivalries which have suddenly sprung into existence.

There are many careers in which Oedipal needs may be expressed and gratified in ways that are socially acceptable. For example, the need to be noticed may find an outlet in careers which consist essentially of being looked at and admired, e.g. 'show biz'. We refer here not so much to the artistes who have devoted years of hard work to developing some unique talent (although for these, too, fame is the spur) as to the much less talented individuals who depend merely on their appearance, and will do almost anything to obtain publicity. There are obviously degrees of 'showing off'. For example, fashion parades and beauty contests are 'exhibitions', but the contestants do not 'make exhibitions of themselves'. Even those who pose for pinup photographs vary in the degree to which they are prepared to exhibit themselves. The professional strippers probably take their need for display one step further. In our society only the classic sexual exhibitionists (almost all of whom are male) behave in ways that we regard clinically as abnormal.

Similarly, the Oedipal tendency to act a part may be expressed quite legitimately a stage career. Professional acting

9. Goethe's 'eternal feminine' may have been no more than the socially permissible female Oedipal ambivalence of his day. So far, no poet has sung 'the eternal masculine'. In so far as this might involve the vain attempt to control the eternal feminine, it would presumably derive from socially permissible male anal obsessiveness. Perhaps these are the stereotypes to which we appeal when we demand, 'Isn't that just like a woman?' – or a man, as the case may be.

demands of the actor that he be able to adopt different roles, and sometimes this training may threaten the actor's own sense of personal identity, his sense of who he really is. If this happens, the actor may find it hard to drop his current stage role, or may even come to identify himself with the histrionic image created for him by his agent. That is, he may come to believe, and try to live up to, the exaggerated identity in his own publicity.

In some careers Oedipal identity seems to be exaggerated to the point of caricature. Modern all-in wrestlers, for example, are publicized as men who are irresistibly masculine, incredibly potent, and so tough as to be immune to physical pain. Similarly, the Hollywood female sex symbols are presented to the public as women in a chronic state of extreme libidinal arousal and near-nymphomanic availability. Most actors will of course recognize the unreality of their public roles, simply because they are themselves 'behind the scenes' in the play-acting.

Many of the more severe forms of Oedipal behaviour are still not classified formally as pathological, but are extravagant enough to cause social disruption and distress. When this happens the individual is no longer content merely to indulge in Oedipal fantasies, but tries to act them out in real life. The bored housewife, for example, dissatisfied with her dull marriage and neglectful husband, does not think that his neglect may be the result of her own unattractiveness. She 'proves' her attractiveness by teasing the milkman into making a pass at her, then makes sure that her husband gets to hear about it. If he is not immediately outraged, that is, inspired to become a rival with the milkman for the prize of his own wife, she may redouble her ambivalent teasing of the milkman, investing him imaginatively with all kinds of desirable qualities which he does not in fact possess, and, when she has aroused both herself and him into a guilty frenzy of ardour, may run off with him — this time taking care to leave their forwarding address on the farewell note to her husband. This may produce the desired effect of galvanizing her husband into activity, and he may follow and retrieve his wife before she gets herself into more serious trouble. If so, she has of course succeeded in obtaining his attention.

Of course, the husband might not respond in this way. He might have Oedipal fantasies of his own, say, about his secretary. When his wife runs off with the milkman, he might defiantly take his secretary out to dinner. This might do no real harm, unless of course his secretary has had comparable Oedipal fantasies about him – so that *they* find themselves running off together, and so on. Oedipal love very quickly becomes 'a many-splendoured thing', involving triads of people in geometric progression.

The problem here is that behaviour comes to be determined not by reality but fantasy. The housewife described above never settles down, never deals with the here-and-now practical situation, and never tries to develop her initiative in constructive ways. Instead she dreams of a life of unimaginable bliss. To face her own problems would require too much effort and might even involve accepting responsibility for them. Therefore she dreams, preferring to convince herself that 'love is just around the corner'. Acting on these dreams, she abandons her own man and runs off with somebody else's, hoping that he will somehow (magically, as in the other fairy stories) turn out to be the long-awaited knight in shining armour. (It never occurs to her to ask why such glorious specimens of male humanity should choose her.)

Very few of these other men will in fact turn out to be the Lochinvar she searches for. She herself ensures this, by demanding such impossibly high standards. When she attributes heroic qualities to unheroic men she is in fact guaranteeing that in the long run they will fail to satisfy her requirements. To put someone on a pedestal and insist that he never steps down from it is a typically Oedipal form of ambivalence. And the ambivalence is communicated. That is, she may entice her chosen hero into a domestic triangle by pseudo-sexual promises, but then she makes it crystal clear that since she is giving him her all he for his part had better be worth the sacrifice. The men may be flattered at first, but they will soon become very anxious when they realize what they have let themselves in for; nor are they likely to be reassured when they realize also that their idealization has been achieved at someone else's expense.

There is of course a male counterpart for female psychodynamics of this sort. Some men show precisely the same Hollywoodish, dream-like qualities in their relationships with women. They protest their masculinity and talk a great deal of sex, but rarely do much about it. Their preoccupation is with sexual excitement, suggestive jokes, flattery, and novelty. When they do tease themselves into making a pass at a woman they usually flee the consequences. Their behaviour is generally more of an attention-getting device than a meaningful sexual overture. Like their female counterparts, such men often become involved in relationships of great intimacy, in deep secrets and innumerable confidences, so creating false and exaggerated responsibilities which they are usually unable to meet when called upon. They interfere tirelessly in the affairs of others, showing insatiable curiosity, trying to solve everybody's problems but their own, and always causing more trouble in the end.

In their pseudo-sexual adventures they usually involve a woman who belongs to someone else, because for them sexuality is exciting only when it is forbidden. What they seek is an ambivalent, guilty thrill, which of course derives from their Oedipal fear that they may be caught. In setting up such sexually dangerous situations, they are in effect 'daring' their own conscience, and often try to increase the thrill artificially by imaginatively exaggerating the fearsomeness of the forbidding authority. Like the woman described above, such men seldom find thrills within their own marriage, only within the marriages of others; they threaten marriages, whether their own or those of others, by promoting romantic extra-marital affairs. In all this there is a constant posture of naughty-little-boyishness, comparable to the naughty-little-girlishness of their female counterpart; and an equal inability to accept any responsibility for the trouble they cause. It is hardly surprising that whereas the female tends to look for a 'sugar-daddy', the male searches for a 'sugar-mummy' – a girl-friend with her own flat, her own car, and enough money to keep them both well supplied with cigarettes, drinks, and expensive presents.

The relationships of the Oedipal male with other males are equally predictable. He tends to accuse them of preventing him from achieving anything and, because of his over-sensitivity to belittlement, is constantly worried about his status. He struggles constantly to steal the other fellow's job, and to usurp (often by cheating) the prestige and privileges of other men. He becomes shrilly competitive in all things important or trivial. He cannot bear any rivals for the limelight. On the other hand, although his continual preoccupation with (i.e. doubts about) his own masculinity forces him to keep on proving himself, his essential ambivalence often compels him to throw away his success by some insensate folly or other (for instance, getting drunk and insulting his boss); in this way he can start proving himself all over again. Actual success is in fact frightening to such people because they never feel well enough equipped to deal with the responsibilities they hanker after. They feel that their success is undeserved, and that they are impostors whose credentials have been obtained only by dishonesty, their achievements only by illegitimate shortcuts, and their social position by their manipulation of others. Although always active, they are disinclined for hard work.

In general, then, the Oedipal male wants women to be

mothers to him, and to contribute nothing himself to the relationship. He will not tolerate any feminine demands, or any interference with his masculine plans. Women are to be 'used' or idealized; men are to be 'shown up' publicly, for his own relative aggrandizement, and are to be blindly opposed whenever they might steal the centre of the stage. Like his female counterpart, he cannot bear rivalry, even from his own children (whom he regards as competitors for the favours of his wife-mother); and when unable to outshine other males he is liable to show a childish, petulant reaction.

These exaggerated Oedipal tendencies, whether in men or women, have the same roots in the early family triangle, in which the father is weak and the mother strong. A son who sees that his father is unable to impose order on the domestic situation becomes ambivalent about competing with him; he fears not losing but winning. His problem may then be increased by the dominant mother if she, disappointed and contemptuous of her weak husband, confirms his weakness to the son. She may invite her son to secret tête-à-têtes, often late at night, and always when the father is absent and unable to stand up for himself. The usual line is, 'Your father never really understood me, my dear. He's a lazy, good-for-nothing brute . . .' (copious details of the husband's perfidy, insensitivity and general uselessness) '. . . but *you* understand me, don't you? You'll take care of your mother when you grow up, won't you? You're big and strong . . .' and so on.

In such encounters the son has, in effect, been seduced by the mother into believing that he is to be the first and best male in the family. In his excitement at being taken behind the parental scenes he does not notice that he is now in league with his mother against his father, committed to filling his father's shoes long before he is ready. Thereafter his ambivalence is inevitably increased by the mother, who if the son does try to assert his Oedipal primacy, must welsh on the deal – if he ever gets 'too big for his boots' she must (for her own sake) cut him down to size again.

People, whether male or female, who have all these characteristics are not difficult to understand solely in terms of the Oedipal situation. Their lives are almost literal re-enactments, with different dramatis personae, of play-age conflicts. Despite the social turmoil created by people like this, the basic triangularity, rivalry, fantasy, and need to be noticed can always be detected in their relationships with others. In attempting to convince themselves of their own phallic adequacy they are forever teasing someone into forming a three-person situation, trying to cut one person out, then creating another three-person situation, and so on *ad infinitum*. So long as the people involved can be kept on tenterhooks, wondering what will happen next, they will give their undivided attention to whoever has stirred them up.

When the degree of Oedipal exaggeration reaches this level of impairment, we begin to describe the individual as a *hysterical personality*. This is usually regarded as a condition on the borderline between the 'normal' Oedipal regressions already described, and the Oedipal regressions which are really pathological.

We should emphasize here that in any Oedipal personality any one of the typical Oedipal characteristics may become predominant. Consider, for example, the astonishing ability of hysterical personalities to 'forget' (i.e. repress) their own part in the uproar and disturbance they have caused. Their bland denial of responsibility, a kind of amnesia for their guilt, may be no more than an exaggerated tendency to prefer fantasy to reality or, as one writer has described it, a 'wishing away of an undesired piece of the world'. But sometimes the amnesia is more severe and involuntary, to a point where the individual is 'dissociated'; that is, his symptomatic behaviour is completely severed from his awareness of its meaning and significance. He may then be in *fugue state*, a kind of sleep-walking by day in which he continues to live an ordinary life, but completely forgets large areas of his past. As the label suggests, these states are usually interpreted as involuntary flights from guilt.

Similarly, Oedipal *identity* problems may become predominant. Hysterical personalities are never sure which of their many imagined selves is really them. They may play at personal relationships until they come to regard their whole life as a game, one in which winning is possible only by secret cheating. The more they 'get away with it', the more guilt is accumulated, so that any social triumph becomes also a personal disaster. Success in hoodwinking others may come to be seen as a demonstration that dishonesty is the best policy; it usually produces a contempt for those who are too stupid to see through the deception; but it also confirms the doubt as to 'who is the *real* me?' (This perpetual game-playing is of course essentially a 'playing safe', a technique for avoiding personal relationships in which they may be hurt or belittled by being 'shown up', and thus having their doubts about themselves confirmed.) If such identity problems are severe, the hysterical personality may become fragmented, and end up as a *multiple or dissociated personality*.

Although these people are severely disturbed, their symptoms may nevertheless be regarded as exaggerated Oedipal (or play-age) failures. As in the hysterical personality *per se*, the fugues, somnabulisms, and dissociated or multiple personalities may be regarded as lying on the borderline between normal Oedipal regressions, and the pathological ones. These include *hysteria* proper (often involving phobias, hypochondriasis, and psychosomatic symptoms), *conversion hysteria*, and *anorexia nervosa*. What makes these conditions pathological is the increasing severity of the Oedipal disturbance (e.g. more depression than anxiety), the growing predominance of physical over psychological features, and the increasing involvement of pre-Oedipal levels of regression. Let us look at these illnesses briefly in turn.

Since we are now beginning to use the word 'hysterical' to describe more serious Oedipal regressions we should say a word or two about hysteria as such. Hysteria was for a long time considered to be an ailment peculiar to women.[10] This view may have originated from the word's Greek derivation, from such social stereotypes as those outlined earlier, or even from the fact that most psychological investigators have been men. In any event, female hysterics seem to have succeeded in arousing most writers in psychology. The literature on hysterics abounds in descriptions by doctors who seem to have been irritated out of their very professionalism. One group of researchers compiled a list of epithets which have been applied to hysterics by different authors. Here are some of them:

(1) egotistic, vain, self-indulgent

(2) exhibitionistic, dramatic, lying, exaggerating, play-acting, stimulating

(3) irrational, capricious, excitable, inconsistent, affectively labile and unbridled

(4) emotionally shallow, fraudulent

(5) lascivious, coquettish, provocative, sexualizing all non-sexual situations

(6) immature, apprehensive, sexually frigid

(7) demanding, dependent.

They add wryly that 'number 8 should obviously be a Thurber drawing of a predatory female bearing down on a timorous male psychiatrist.'

10. By discussing male as well as female hysterical tendencies throughout this section, we are of course discountenancing this point of view.

From this we may perhaps deduce that while the normal teasing female merely arouses male interest (with perhaps a certain pleasurable sense of insecurity and challenge), and the borderline hysterical personality merely stimulates males into behaving foolishly, the full-blown female hysteric will ultimately arouse anxiety, guilt, anger, and a desire to retaliate. To understand this, we need to take a closer look at the original Oedipal triangle.

Hysteria essentially arises when the child's feelings towards both his parents become exaggerated and over-intense, when the parents over-respond or under-respond to his needs, and particularly when the parental roles are reversed. Thus the female finds her mother dominant and cold, while her father is relatively weak and indulgent. We are of course referring to the parents as they appear to the child, not as they may appear to other people outside the family. The mother may be renowned as a charming social hostess, and the father as an industrial potentate; but if they fail to meet the (perhaps exaggerated) Oedipal needs of their daughter, they are in her eyes psychological nonentities and disasters. With such parents, no child can ever develop genuine initiative and a realistic conscience.

Her relationships with the opposite sex will in fact be determined by her Oedipal situation. If she has been coerced into accepting law and order by her arch-rival, her mother, she will never forgive her father for his weakness. In addition, his inability to impose reasonable limits on family relationships allows excessive scope for her natural Oedipal attraction towards her father. In failing to help her resolve this ambivalence her father has, in effect, let her down. She becomes resentful and angry, has increased feelings of ambivalence, becomes too dependent on fantasy and idealized masculine stereotypes, and may well spend the rest of her life searching vengefully for men who will not let her down. Her search, however, involves too much vengeance ever to be successful; she makes sure that the men she finds *will* let her down, simply by demanding the impossible from them. Their failure to meet her exalted standards justifies her in becoming a contemptuous 'man-hater' and in using her sexuality as a weapon.

The core of the hysteric's problem is her exaggerated ambivalence. If she finds a 'strong' man she then tries to undermine (test) his strength, by tempting him into triangular relationships, by introducing rivals for him to outdo for her sake, or by teasing or flattering him into attempting some task utterly beyond his powers. Paradoxically, she demands a strong man whom she can nevertheless dominate. It is hardly surprising that, in spite of her need for a strong man, she ends up with a weak boy. If she finds a weak boy, she immediately feels compelled to try to invigorate him, by despising him in public ('why don't you *do* something?'), and by comparing him unfavourably with his rivals for her approval. That is, she demands, paradoxically, a weak boy who will sweep her off her feet. So her interpersonal aspirations, whether with strong or weak men, are inherently self-defeating.

The apparent sexuality of the hysteric is really a false sexuality. In clinical terms, it is phallic rather than genital. She may talk constantly of 'love' and 'passion', or show so much frenetic restlessness (her substitute for genuine initiative) with the opposite sex that she appears to be promiscuous, but in fact hysterics tend to be sexually frigid. Her frigidity of course derives from her early fears of paternal tenderness, which has become generalized to male tenderness as such; but strictly speaking, what frightens her is her guilt concerning her own exaggerated responsiveness to tenderness. Hysterics often have fantasies and dreams of men who are not merely strong, but brutal and aggressive. To be overpowered and raped is to be guiltless. Typical also are the hysteric's chronic doubts about her own sexual identity. ('Am I really a chaste Madonna, or am I *really* a prostitute?')[11]

The pseudo-promiscuity of hysterics may also become 'legalized' and take the form of frequent multiple marriages. These marital adventures do not imply an insatiable need for sex, but only the desperate hope that 'perhaps this will be the one' who can resolve Oedipal ambivalences; they represent a despairing attempt to impress everyone that the parent of the opposite sex is no longer an Oedipal problem. To the outside observer such partners often seem indistinguishable from one another, and indeed the hysteric usually chooses a man who she feels resembles (or is the psychological converse of) the parent who caused the trouble in the first place.

The other extreme, of choosing not promiscuity but complete celibacy and chastity, is attractive to many people with unresolved Oedipal problems. We cannot, however, infer that all such persons are psychological failures. Some religious orders seem to offer sufficient compensations to allow the individual to sublimate his sexuality – although recent schisms within such orders on the point of celibacy suggest that the compensations are becoming less satisfying than they were in earlier years.

As we might expect, hysterics do not often get on well with

11. One resolution of such severe Oedipal problems is to become a prostitute in fact. Contrary to old-fashioned popular opinion, prostitutes are not man-crazy or sex-mad; they seldom become genuinely involved in genital sexuality or love relationships, and indeed usually have a good deal of contempt for their customers. The male Oedipal counterpart of the prostitute, the gigolo, similarly preys on the opposite sex (often women old enough to be his mother) and achieves little sexual satisfaction in the process. A good many prostitutes, because of their weakly developed heterosexual initiative, may therefore have lesbian or homosexual tendencies as well. Their way of life is hardly a satisfactory resolution of their Oedipal conflicts, so that many of them become severely depressed and are liable eventually to commit suicide.

women, although they sometimes appear to. Since the early rivalry with a dominant mother remains unresolved, the hysteric (in so far as she does not give up her own femininity and become an asexual tomboy) will forever rival and attempt to outdo all other women. The underlying anger and need to control women drives some hysterics into high-powered female organizations, where indeed they may become the president, and hence, the first and best clubwoman. They may extend their activities into big business, dominating their male competitors, and becoming terrors in the boardroom. This is the classic, power-hungry, 'castrating' female who creates so much anxiety in the average North American male.

At this point we may begin to suspect that the pseudo-sexuality of the typical hysteric conceals an underlying anal tendency, i.e. a need to control and dominate. Female hysterics never let their men get away from them. Initiative in a man threatens neglect and consequently belittlement to the hysteric. Hence her virulent jealousy, her tendency to baffle and bewilder, and her twenty-four-hours-a-day watchfulness. If her man foolishly ignores her insatiable demands for attention (say, by trying to live a quiet life of his own) she interprets this as intolerable opposition, and will cause him endless trouble until he capitulates once more. It is always when the hysteric feels belittled or neglected that the trouble starts, and her underlying venom and implacability stand revealed.[12]

The effects of expressing anal aggression are usually disastrous to the hysteric herself, so that in time she may come to see herself as a bad person who is cursed, and has within herself a magic malevolence which will destroy everything she touches. She may develop *phobias* (see Chapter 2) which prevent further

12. Although we have used the example of the female hysteric, the same psychodynamics occur in male hysterics; the hero of Osborne's *Look Back in Anger* was the precise male counterpart of the female hysteric described above.

'evil-doing' on her part, and at the same time inhibit and control those around her. For example, she may be unable to go out alone. She may express her anxiety about herself not in psychological terms but in exaggerated physical preoccupations, such as *hypochondriasis*.

It is around this point of regression that we begin to include not merely an anal component, but oral features as well. Oral features show in both psychosocial and physical ways.The hysteric's anal domination is attempted essentially in order to wrest supplies of love from her victim – 'You *must* love me, no matter what I do'. Such demands, often showing an infantile vindictiveness, are usually concealed by the hysteric's tendency to proclaim herself as extremely vulnerable and helpless. Such an attitude is of course depressive, and it derives from her chronic doubts as to whether or not she is lovable. Only massive, sustained, indeed never-ending, supplies of love and welfare will reassure such people, and if these are not forthcoming there is likely to be continuing regression.

One typical reaction of the depressed hysteric is the so-called *suicidal gesture*, in which she makes as if to take her own life but does not really intend to. She takes a large but not fatal overdose of pills, or cuts her wrists when she is sure to be discovered in time, and so on. The message is, 'Look what you have brought me to with your neglect'; and is delivered with the maximum of screaming, weeping, fighting and general public disturbance. To ignore such attempts because of the 'grand opera' component is most dangerous. The hysteric's chronic ambivalence and her carelessness in practical matters often lead to miscalculation; and of course inadvertent suicide is no less final than deliberate suicide. Similarly, to disregard such warnings is exceedingly dangerous. The popular belief that 'those who talk about it never do it' is completely false.

Denial of the hysteric's oral needs may also lead to the development of physical symptoms, often of the *psychosomatic* variety. Generally, the more marked the physical component, the closer the individual approximates to the classic condition known as *conversion hysteria*. These physical symptoms are different from ordinary ones in that they have no discoverable organic basis, and may in fact affect the body in ways which are inconsistent with known patterns of the nervous system. They are usually attributed to 'blockages' in the higher levels of the nervous system, and may be muscular (e.g. hysterical paralysis) or sensory (e.g. hysterical anaesthesia). They usually involve secondary gain for the patient – although they are genuinely distressing, they also serve to prevent the patient from doing something difficult or unpleasant.

Symptoms in conversion hysteria can seldom be alleviated by giving the patients insight into their causes. This may produce a pattern of shifting symptoms which become progressively diffuse and generalized, or alternatively focus and 'petrify' in a particular area of the body. This is a common point of surgical intervention. If such regression continues, however, the whole body function may be affected; as in *anorexia nervosa* where the patients may refuse to eat or sleep, and may progressively waste away, even to the point of death. Thus, in some cases, the oral need to be recognized as 'poor little me' may be pushed to its logical extreme at appalling cost.

This by no means exhausts the possible variety of hysterical regressions. The persistence of Oedipal conflicts in adults takes so many forms that its detailed description would require a great deal of space. The examples we have listed do no more than suggest some of the more typical complexities involved in Oedipal regressions in order of their increasing severity.

It should be emphasized that although the milder forms of neurotic illness are often accepted by society, they nevertheless involve some suffering to the person concerned sooner or later. For instance, in many normal marriages the male may be slightly obsessional, asserting himself more often than he should; while the female may be slightly hysterical, being unnecessarily inconsequential and flighty. So long as these tendencies remain mild, the couple may seem at first to get on quite well with one another; they appear complementary, in that his dominant control prevents her extravagances, while her liveliness lightens his pomposity.[13] Nevertheless, although neither partner suffers greatly, they would both obviously find much more satisfaction in each other if they were to give up the obsessional-hysterical elements in their relationship. The trouble is that they cannot bring themselves to do so, and hence continue to suffer to that extent.

The degree of suffering, both for the patients and for those who interact with them, of course increases with the severity of the illness. For example, severe obsessionality in a husband and severe hysteria in a wife results in the 'immovable object and irresistible force' situation, so that the marriage eventually becomes a state of holy deadlock. Typically, the obsessive tries to impose not merely control but an iron, constipated blight on his wife's butterfly restlessness and disorganized spontaneity. Typically, if she defiantly flirts with other men ('I'll show him') he responds only with a dignified martyrdom, intended to demonstrate to his poor fool of a wife that he is superior to all such nonsense. In doing so he is of course belittling her, and thus promotes even more acting out on her part. She may become unfaithful in fact, and 'let it slip' to her husband afterwards. If he is implacable, or responds with an imperious aloofness, she may embark on a series of highly publicized outrages ('I'll show everybody') designed and timed to cause her

13. When the neurotic tendencies do not complement but reinforce one another (as when both partners are obsessive, or hysteric), the prognosis for the marriage is considerably worse. Similarly, when the psychological tendencies conflict with accepted social stereotypes (as when the female is obsessive and the male hysterical) there is a fair possibility of marital disaster, either between the partners themselves, or, later, in the children of the marriage.

husband the maximum of concern and trouble, e.g. promiscuity, suicidal attempts, or taking to drink or drugs. The problems of each partner reinforce those of the other. As we sometimes say, 'They seem to bring out the worst in each other'.

SUMMARY

In the introduction to this chapter we described the developmental changes in the child, his adventurousness and imaginativeness, his increasingly intensive and extensive social relationships, and his awareness of changes in his own body, all of which contributed to his so-called Oedipal situation.

We outlined this crisis in terms of 'initiative', suggesting how this showed as a need for conquest, a desire to be competitive, a tendency to overdo things, and a danger of becoming ambivalent in all enterprises. We stressed rivalry with siblings, and the essentially Oedipal tendency to compete with the parent of the same sex in order to impress the parent of the opposite sex, and mentioned the additional complexities for girls in the triangular family situation. We discussed the normal resolution of 'intrusiveness' and 'inclusiveness', referring to social limits and the development of the child's own conscience.

Illness in children we described as deriving mainly from an exaggerated ambivalence. This might show physically, in weakly developed sex roles; psychologically, in such features as guilt, shame, false identity, distorted values, etc.; or socially, in maladaptive behaviour such as cheating, manufacturing secrets, limelight seeking, exaggerated initiative, defiance and spiteful obedience. We noted also that children might regress from the Oedipal stage and develop phobias or physical symptoms.

In considering regressions to the Oedipal stage we first estimated *normal* regression in terms of our response to advertisements, the popularity of certain kinds of literature, our typical behaviour in some social situations, and the legitimate expression of Oedipal needs in some careers. We then considered the 'hysterical personality' as a borderline Oedipal regression, and included in this category some sexual extremes (prostitution, homosexuality) and some dissociated states (fugues, somnambulisms, multiple personality). Clearly *pathological* regressions were listed as: hysteria proper (often involving phobias, suicidal gestures, hypochondriasis, or psychosomatic symptoms); the classic conversion hysteria; and the very severe *anorexia nervosa*. We graded the severity of these forms of hysteria in terms of how many pre-Oedipal features – anal and oral (including physiological) features – were incorporated in the illness.

We concluded by emphasizing some of the basic differences between hysteria and pre-Oedipal regressions such as obsessionality.

CHAPTER FOUR

The School Age (6–12 years)

But good gracious, you've got to educate him first.
You can't expect a boy to be vicious till he's been to
a good school.

SAKI (H. H. MUNRO), *The Baker's Dozen*

AT this point in our developmental outline we begin to expand
our time scale. Where each previous growth stage covered
roughly two years, this stage covers six years.

We are also making an important shift in emphasis. In discussing previous stages we focused more on biological and
psychological factors in the child's development, concentrating
as it were on his inner life. Here we shall be giving more weight
to external, social influences. The reason for this shift is that the
school age, unlike preceding stages, is not heralded by major or
abrupt changes in biological and psychological growth. In fact,
the child's basic instincts seem to lie fallow during this period,
showing (as Freud suggested in 1936) a certain latency. The
child therefore does not try to change the environment to suit
his own needs. On the contrary, he accepts his environment,
wants to master its problems, and tries hard to fulfil its
demands. He becomes preoccupied with externals.

This transition from Oedipal to school-age preoccupations is
usually fairly smooth. As Erikson (1959) describes it:

While all children at times need to be left alone in solitary play
... they all, sooner or later, become dissatisfied and disgruntled
without a sense of being useful ... The child can become an
eager and absorbed unit of a production situation. To bring a
productive situation to completion is an aim which gradually

supersedes the whims and wishes of his idiosyncratic drives and personal disappointments.

Again,

Children at this stage do like to be mildly but firmly coerced into the adventure of finding out that one can learn to accomplish things which one would never have thought of oneself, things which owe their attractiveness to the very fact that they are not the product of fantasy but the product of reality, practicability, and logic; things which thus provide a token sense of participation in the real world of adults. [ibid.]

The child therefore is probably as amenable at this stage as he is ever likely to be. He is ready to learn, in the formal sense of learning, and to be directed by others.

The increasing importance of social and environmental influences has been discernible in the first three developmental phases. The achievement of trust, autonomy, and initiative in turn necessarily involve the child with increasing numbers of other people. By going to school, however, his social sphere is extended tremendously. He begins to interact not merely with parents but with teachers and other adults, not merely with brothers and sisters but with other children of his own age.

The child's ability to come to terms with these new demands depends of course to some extent on how well his family life has prepared him for school life. In leaving home he may feel that he has suffered certain losses. Within his own family he may have enjoyed special status, and been given a certain inalienable consideration simply because he was part of the family. In school, where there is (at least to begin with) no preferential treatment, he will lose this status, and will not regain it automatically. In addition, he may feel he has lost a good deal of his independence. It is made very clear to him that in school he must often adapt and conform to the group, even at the expense of his own individuality. Above all, he has no say regarding the value, method and aims of his school work. He is in the hands of professionals – experts – namely, his teachers. Much will depend on how adequately school fulfils the promises implicit in his early family experiences.

Although the child of school age is eminently teachable, his willingness to do what he is told becomes considerably modified as he moves through school. Piaget found that children of seven or eight are only incipiently cooperative, both in their games and in their personal relationships generally. By the age of eleven they do achieve genuine cooperation, but only within their own age group. In their games, rules are obeyed strictly, or changed only by consent of the players; there is no appeal to external authority. As Piaget has shown, the child passes gradually from a stage where he accepts adult authority as the only source of moral control, to a stage where he feels that his own group has moral autonomy. If children submit to authority in the later phases of this period, it is generally to an authority found to be mutually acceptable.

This does not mean that the child inevitably exchanges his dependence on adult authority for dependence on peer group authority. His own individuality may continue to be expressed, for example in terms of his personal conscience, whose dictates may not coincide exactly with the codes of either his adult mentors or his peer group. Piaget, when he asked children what they would do if another child punched them, found that the majority of nine-to-twelve-year-olds would punch back, and that boys in particular would give back the same number of blows that they had received. But many individual children, especially girls, saw beyond the principle of simple retaliation, and justified their view with both practical and abstract reasons. A ten-year-old girl said, 'I'd hit him back less, because if I hit him back the same or more, he begins again.' A boy of ten objected to revenge, because 'there is no end to it'. Thus, if the child's personal morality is learned within the family, it seems that his social morality is learned in school.

PSYCHOLOGICAL CRISES IN THE SCHOOL AGE

Erikson (1950, 1959) used the concept of 'industry' to describe the child's central concern at this stage. Industry involves learning 'how to'[1] and has two main aspects: acquiring practical skills, and adapting socially. Erikson emphasized only the first of these, but it seems clear that learning how to fit in socially, and how to get on with others, is no less important for the school child than developing competence in practical matters. One writer described school as 'a ten or twelve year rehearsal of how the child is expected to behave when he grows up', and emphasized its importance as a principal means of learning social adaptation. In discussing the influence of school on the child, therefore, we shall consider not only its educational, but its social importance as well.

In taking over the child's training from his parents, the school leaves the child in no doubt as to where he stands. From the beginning, when he is assigned to a 'grade', his degree of achievement is continuously assessed by teachers, peers, parents, etc. in tests and examinations whose results are periodically proclaimed in 'reports'. The school evaluates his merit clearly

1. The subordination of the child's emotional and instinctive needs to his cognitive and intellectual interests may be exemplified in terms of his new attitudes to sex. Although schoolchildren are probably as fascinated by sex in school as they were in the Oedipal stage, their interest here is not so much in the personal sensations as in the practical technique. It is usually in school that children learn 'how to do it'. Lacking the appropriate emotions, however, (and perhaps in defence against the sudden realization that their own parents must 'do it') they tend to be impressed only with the ridiculous and undignified features of sexuality, and consequently express their interest in smutty jokes, poems, and graffiti.

in percentages, sometimes refining its judgements to the nearest half or even quarter mark. His degree of success is indicated
by his position in his class. Similarly, his school play is evaluated – at least, insofar as his games are officially formalized. He
is told what games to play, how to play them, and even in what
spirit he must play them. It is these achievements in school play
and school work which largely determine his status in school
society. And, if he achieves any special status, he may then be
awarded special privileges or given special responsibilities,
such as being class leader, prefect, or captain; or, he may not.

The child spends the greater part of his waking life in school,
and even in his leisure times school values continue to influence
him indirectly. His homework reminds him that his domestic
efforts will be evaluated in school; the games he plays at home
are often school games, played in school ways, and played as
practice to do better in school teams. His leisure reading often
consists mainly of books or comics whose values are school
values. (One possible exception to the child's general sus-
ceptibility to school standards is his tendency to take up individualistic hobbies.)

In most cultures there is a tendency to organize the school-
age child's leisure activities for him, and to systematically encourage his practical skills and social achievements. For
example, much of our national, officially-sponsored youth
groups are specifically concerned with individual training, e.g.
how to light a fire without using matches; or with teamwork,
e.g. parades, group gymnastics, etc. Here again the child is
given carefully graded tests, and is eventually identified as one
who has passed those tests by his display of an impressive array
of badges and certificates. (Some Boy Scouts accumulate so
many badges that there is scarcely enough uniform to accommodate them.) In all this learning, the child is usually given
guidance by some older child who has already learned, a big
brother such as a Scout troop leader or a big sister such as the

Guides' Brown Owl (by implication, the repository of all practical and social wisdom).[2]

It would be astonishing indeed if all the sustained, systematic school influences to which the child is exposed at his most amenable age did not show their effects far into his adult life. We cannot discuss all these effects in detail, but we can group them into two broad categories; that is, we shall consider how the school experience of endless evaluation and comparison makes the child aware of both *differences* and *similarities* between himself and his contemporaries.

In learning 'how to', the child soon realizes that children differ in their learning capacity. A few schools, perhaps overimpressed with democratic principles, assume complete equality of capacity in their children and base their policies on this false premise; but most schools, in practice if not in theory, recognize the differences in native endowment. In such schools, one effect of continuous grading is to provide the child with a general framework or scale for making critical comparisons himself. He is of course always liable to apply these scales in ways not intended by the school. For instance, his own placing of children may differ considerably from that of the teachers. Sociometric studies have repeatedly shown that the correlation between gradings by children and teachers may be zero, or in many cases have a negative value. That is, the 'best' child in the eyes of the adults may be 'worst' in the eyes of the children, and vice versa. The clever boy favoured by his teachers in the class-

2. Although both learning how to do practical things and fitting into some group are central preoccupations for the child of school age, we do not imply that the two activities are necessarily connected. A child may be academically brilliant and pass all his examinations, yet be an unpopular misfit in all non-academic areas of his school life; or he may be the most popular child in school, yet fail every class test. Nevertheless, the achievement of practical competence on the one hand, and social adaptation on the other, usually do go hand in hand in most children.

room may be taunted unmercifully as a swot by his schoolmates in the playground; while the class dunce, hated by his teacher as a troublemaker, may be hero-worshipped by the pupils because he once openly defied the headmaster. Children also grade their teachers; that is, they learn to assess their assessors. Ideally, the child gradually accommodates these multiple value systems and learns to use them appropriately, but in general the school's constant emphasis on individual differences between children means that the school experience is by no means the same for every child.

Individual differences of a biological sort, such as differences in growth rate, become more significant in school. It has been found that boys whose physical maturation was early rather than late (big boys) showed significant differences in their motivation, their relationships with other people, and their conception of themselves. The mere size of a child may affect his whole school life, sometimes in adverse ways. When physical or personal characteristics are unique or deviate significantly from the norm, they may provoke severe and even savage penalties from other schoolchildren. If a child has an odd name, speaks with an unusual accent, has a speech impediment, a physical blemish or deformity, has a father whose job is 'unacceptable', or is himself too good or too bad at some school activity, he may be teased mercilessly or ostracized for failing to conform to the standards of the majority of middle-range achievers. Most of us have either suffered, or helped to administer, such punishments.

Individual differences in the capacity to learn 'how to' are sometimes equated by the school with differences in social class. Teachers are often heard saying, 'What can you expect from a child with his home background?' Indeed, it is often in school that the child himself first becomes aware of differences in social class. Just as he assumes that everybody of his own age is similar to himself in capacity, aptitude, and intelligence, so he takes it for granted that everybody else's family has the same social values and habits. These beliefs may be violently contradicted when he enters school and finds that all differences, academic, personal, and social, are heavily emphasized and ostentatiously measured.

It is important to realize that, for the schoolchild at least, such categories are not natural but artificial. They do not arise spontaneously and inevitably from within the individual, but are imposed on him from outside, and often as a matter of deliberate policy. Children themselves see no important difference between eating meals with silverware and using a tablecloth of Irish linen, and eating with their fingers and using yesterday's newspaper; but adults will soon make them aware of the difference. Similarly in school, children will associate with anyone with whom they get on well; but adults will soon make a distinction for them between those who are all right and those who are not. Thus the source of social values is not in children themselves, but in the adults who are their caretakers during the school period – and who of course have been through the mill themselves in earlier years. The system tends to be self-perpetuating.

McNeil (1966) pointed out that schools themselves are fundamentally determined by an important class factor. He suggested that school represents 'an opportunity to train oneself in the skills that bring rewards valued by the middle class; namely, social position and status, individual success and comfort'. He pointed out that lower-class families tend not to stress upward mobility and achievement as important social values; they lay less emphasis on controlling spontaneous impulses, and tend not to familiarize the child with books and ideas. To this extent the lower-class child is handicapped and may in fact be unable to meet the essentially middle-class demands of school.

There is a good deal of evidence to support McNeil's contention. A group of psychologists recently investigated the social mobility of middle-class as opposed to working-class schoolchildren, concentrating on the degree of anxiety, the degree of conflict between home and school values, and the teachers' behaviour towards the two groups. They found that middle-class children were better integrated in school, had their homework and other activities more closely supervised by their families, had higher educational and vocational aspirations, and, although they were much more concerned about their progress at school, were not more anxious or tense. (They also showed relatively less interest in the opposite sex, had a more rigid system of values, and believed more strongly in punishment.)

Among the working-class boys, those who were socially mobile upwards came from homes in which the parents over-conformed to *middle-class* values. Yet, despite massive pressure and support from home, these boys were less well-integrated in school, and subscribed less to the school ethos. It was considered that the crucial factor here was the attitudes of teachers. In selecting their 'best' pupils, teachers almost invariably chose middle-class children, and saw them as better mannered, more mature, more responsible, and also as more popular. The children's own attitudes showed no such preferences. It was remarked that the teachers who said most often that the current educational system allowed 'the wrong type of child' into grammar schools tended to be more authoritarian and to have been upwardly mobile themselves.

Since school is compulsory in our culture, we shall probably never know whether the sense of class difference inculcated by schools would arise in children if they were left to themselves, free from adult influence. Class differences as such probably derive essentially from differences in family and social habits, which derive in turn from differences in income established either in the current or preceding generations. Just as intellectual and personal differences must be accepted as a fact of life, so presumably must class differences be accepted (at least meantime) as an important factor in social living. Whether or not we condone or disparage class differences, we must at least recognize their existence and their influence – especially when they are formally codified by some governments in such official publications as the Social Class Register.

Although the school fosters the child's awareness of differences (physical, psychological, or social) between himself and others, it simultaneously encourages his recognition of certain similarities. If these do not exist, they may be manufactured by the school. That is, the school demands a high degree of conformity. Thus, within any school class academic and personal differences are emphasized, but the class itself is regarded as an integrated unit with a unified allegiance to its teacher. Similarly, differences between school classes or 'grades' are emphasized, but the school itself is a unified whole, with co-ordinated allegiance to its headmaster. He represents the general values and policies peculiar to the school, which in turn are differentiated from the values and policies of other schools – and so on. In some countries, schools emphasize both their internal unity and their distinctiveness from other schools by establishing a special school uniform, which of course then facilitates the necessary regimentation of the children.

Here again we are forced to recognize the profound social effects of school on a child's attitudes. It is easy to see how his personal relationships may be directly influenced by his school peer group. For example, school friends, school idols and their admirers, school bullies and their victims, often find in later years that they still have the same feelings for one another, quite apart from their respective achievements as adults. But on the wider scale of school influence, the essentially juvenile attitude of unquestioning loyalty towards 'house' or school is very easily transferred later to college or university, business firm, club or regiment, to the local community or to the nation to which one belongs. It may indeed be psychologically true that adult patriotism stems from school training, or, to put it more popularly, that the battle of Waterloo was won on the playing fields of Eton.

To discuss whether or not the school's insistence on conformity and group-joining is a good thing would take us far beyond the domain of psychology proper. We should perhaps suggest, however, that conformity tends to become a bad thing when it leaves no room whatever for individuality or personal idiosyncrasy. In social adaptation at its best, the child learns to cooperate with others, to compete without rancour, and to enjoy teamwork in projects which might be impossible for the isolated individual. In social adaptation at its worst, the child may become merely indoctrinated and brainwashed, have all his native originality stifled forever, and come to believe that the aim of schooling is to make all children average for the sake of administrative convenience. Such an over-emphasis on the similarities between children is probably less damaging where the school subject is itself technical, and deals with matters of fact (mathematics, for instance); but in more liberal subjects which deal with matters of value judgement, a demand for conformity may have disastrous and irreversible effects on the child's mind.

Besides the group to which the school may allocate a child without consulting him, there are of course groups which he may join voluntarily and into which he himself may try to fit. Psychologists have expended much effort and research on the schoolchild's voluntary relationships with his contemporaries, but the findings are anything but clear, perhaps because they are influenced by the involuntary relationships discussed above. Some psychologists have gone so far as to suggest that there may be a need in the child for social affiliation (rather like the old-fashioned herd instinct), but if such a need exists it has never been clearly defined; nor has it been clearly distinguished from other needs. Investigators have in fact tended to define affiliation in different ways. Taking the concept of social affiliation at face value, as the child's need to be a member of a group, it seems clear that the urgency of the need will vary from child to child. Some children (and some adults, for that matter) will affiliate with any group for which they are eligible; others resist joining groups; others again join groups although they have no affiliative need whatever, e.g. psychopaths. Furthermore, two people may have the same degree of need, but express it differently. Shy people often have strong needs of this kind which may never be expressed, and may in fact be contradicted by their overt behaviour. And so on.

In summary, then, the successful school child learns how to win recognition for himself in new ways. He learns to perform given tasks, to complete work, to produce things, and how to do these well. He develops a growing sense of his own practical competence, begins to enjoy his own industry, and feel confident of his own usefulness. In learning how to fit in and get along with others he also develops a firm sense of 'belonging'.

ILLNESS IN THE SCHOOL AGE

Most children entering school have *some* psychological problems. For example, when Wolff (1967) compared schoolchildren who were referred to a psychiatric clinic with those who were not, she found that there was no significant difference between them concerning such symptoms as 'recklessness, timidity, over-compliance, shyness, physical complaints, overconcern with illness, obsessionality, nail-biting, overeating, and food fads'. Clinical symptoms have also been noted in normal groups of children in other studies. These findings suggest that we should make some general allowance for symptoms in children who are entering school before we begin to regard them as psychologically ill.

Another important finding by Wolff was that the psychiatric referral of children tends to be determined not so much by the severity of the child's symptoms as by the attitudes of the adults involved. Children's reports of their own illness may be quite different from what their mothers say, especially regarding the more subjective symptoms. In addition, adults themselves often disagree. Agreement between assessors (including the children themselves) is common only on the most obvious and 'objective' disturbances, such as stammering, soiling, bedwetting, stealing and truancy. Wolff emphasizes that 'quite apart from the fact that certain forms of behaviour can be observed only at home or only at school, in other areas of behaviour observable in both settings the child may react differently in the two situations.'[3]

In general, psychological disorders in schoolchildren may derive from stresses originating from within school, from conflicts about being away from their familiar home surroundings, or from their own tendency to regress to earlier forms of behaviour. Some typical forms of disturbance are obviously and directly connected with the child's current problem; for example, truancy from school, or running away from home. The child may also become destructive, quarrelsome, and perpetually involved in fights. More chronic problems may show as near-delinquent behaviour, such as unnecessary stealing, lying, cheating or sexual acting-out. Further regressive tendencies may involve phobias, or some of the more physio-

3. Another difficulty in assessing psychological illness in children is that so far we have no system of diagnostic classification apart from the one used for adults. An attempt has been made to group children's illnesses in terms of their typical behavioural characteristics, but this is hardly adequate.

logical forms of anal difficulties such as soiling (see Chapters 2 and 3).[4]

Within the school setting the child is mainly concerned with two things; acquiring practical competence and skills, and achieving a legitimate status among his peers and supervisors. The schoolchild who fails in these goals (see Appendix, Table II) will become afraid that he is incapable of learning 'how to'; he will begin to feel that no matter how hard he tries he will never be any good at anything; he will suffer a pervading sense of his own uselessness and will gradually come to accept his role as a perpetual social misfit. This constellation of negative feelings about one's self is usually described as an *inferiority complex* (Adler, 1927a, 1927b, 1930).[5]

4. All these disorders were found to be typical of children referred to psychiatric clinics; they occurred very rarely in children not referred (Wolff, 1967).

5. In Adler's view psychological maladjustment has to do with the individual's role and mode of functioning in society. He emphasized the importance of the here-and-now current life situation and was less concerned with reconstructing the past, or with making the unconscious conscious. According to Adler, human beings strive constantly to move from an inferior (or 'minus') life situation to a superior (or 'plus') situation. The term 'inferiority complex' referred originally to the individual's awareness of *differences* between himself and others, which then came to be interpreted as evidence of inferiority. Thus for Adler, inferiority involves the individual's own assessment of his failure to achieve his goals. Such goals might or might not be realistic, and society might or might not agree with the individual's self-assessment. Adler's theory is of course a general one, and may be regarded as complementary to the other depth psychologies of Freud and Jung; it is, however, particularly helpful in explaining the specific psychosocial situation of the school child.

In recent years there has been more interest in Adler's theory. 'Ego-psychologist' investigators, such as Kris, Federn, and Erikson; 'self-actualization' investigators, such as Maslow; and even the experimental investigators of aspiration level: all reflect this interest. One investigator who has borrowed heavily from Adler, and whose re-

Inferiority feelings may cause the school child not only to develop a false industry but also to adopt a false role. He may over-conform to the school system, and work hard only in trying to ingratiate himself as the teacher's pet. (Some teachers reinforce such overtures and create favourites.) He may try to buy friends with sweets or money. Alternatively, the child unable to earn a legitimate status in the school group may defiantly oppose its values – he may under-conform and adopt the role of rebel, outsider, or outcast. In such cases a vicious circle of reciprocal antagonism develops in which the child can only be the loser. The child who never learns how to be taken seriously may settle for the role of class clown, and gain a precarious status by keeping others amused instead of seeking their cooperation. Or he may adopt the role of impostor, denying his inferiority feelings and over-compensating for them by boasting and bragging; this kind of forced and hollow 'superiority' is usually exposed very quickly by classmates. Finally, the child who finds these unsatisfactory roles *too* unsatisfactory may revert to earlier family roles. 'He may still want his mummy more than knowledge; he may still rather be the baby at home than the big child at school' (Erikson, 1959).

REGRESSIONS TO THE SCHOOL AGE

Since our culture is highly technological and puts a premium on practical 'know-how' in adults, there is a sense in which we

---

formulation of his concepts are particularly relevant to the stage of development we are considering, is White (1959), whose studies of the need for competence has been fruitful both for theoretical and empirical research. Part of the general need for competence, which White believes is apparent at all ages but which probably becomes predominant during the school age, shows as the need to manipulate objects and gain mastery over them.

are not allowed by society to give up the preoccupations of our school age. Schooling continues far beyond the age of twelve, in the form of secondary school, apprenticeship and higher education. In some careers, formal training may continue even to the age of thirty. The social obligation to fit in with our neighbours continues in effect for the rest of our lives. We must therefore make a correspondingly large allowance for normal regressions to school age. Indeed, many of the schoolchild's preoccupations are regarded as quite normal in adults.

Advertisements which appeal to school-age needs focus mainly on how to learn without tears. The do-it-yourself kit in which instructions are not conveyed directly by a more competent big brother but are written on the container; the 'how to play the piano in seven days or your money back' kind of advertisement; all arouse the wish to be more able technically. Similarly, the 'how to win friends and influence people' type of advertisement offers techniques for fitting in socially with a minimum expenditure of effort.

Many socially acceptable careers are open to those who continue to be preoccupied with school-age problems. Inferiority feelings about their capacity to learn, if confirmed afterwards by the real world outside, may drive some people back into school. Some may re-enter the ivory towers to become perpetual students and exam-passers, qualifying themselves endlessly for yet more training and believing devoutly that personal excellence is measurable only in public and official certificates of merit. They continue their learning merely to obtain additional prizes. Other fugitives from adult reality may seek sanctuary in schools, not by continuing as pupils, but by becoming teachers themselves. (Those who enter that difficult and honourable profession often become the worst teachers because they cannot bear to leave school.) Having failed to apply what they have learned, they can only teach others to learn, enforcing school codes and values, awarding marks and conferring degrees, until they come to believe that these scholastic tokens represent ultimate and absolute values in themselves. In effect, having failed to beat the school system at the appropriate time they join it afterwards. Such people are often greatly preoccupied with the differences between 'first-class' and 'second-class' minds and eventually come to regard themselves as uniquely qualified to make the distinction. To them, becoming a teacher is proof that they themselves have no more to learn. Others again may perpetuate their schooldays by becoming neither a pupil nor a teacher, but an 'educationist'. They preoccupy themselves not with course content but with timetables; not with teaching but with technique; not with fundamentals but with fashions. They do not encourage learning, but merely 'inspect' teachers. The educationists who show such regressive tendencies were neatly described in George Bernard Shaw's aphorism: 'those who can, do; those who can't, teach; those who can't teach, teach teachers'.

Some people perpetuate in their lives not the standards and aims of school work but those of the school value-system. The over-conformity of such individuals tends to be both intense and limited in scope; that is, they can fit in only with those who think as they do. In seaside boarding-houses, for example, ageing spinsters may often be heard proclaiming the 'jolly hockey stick' point of view, while elderly gentlemen sign themselves 'mens sana in corpore sano' in their outraged letters to *The Times*. Juvenile codes are perpetuated in some adult clubs, where trivial kinds of behaviour are regarded as either obligatory on the one hand, or intolerable on the other. Beneath such sanctions there is often more than a trace of class distinction. To be 'not a scholar' is often regarded as forgivable and indeed may be in some clubs a mark of distinction; but to be neither a scholar nor a gentleman is to be beyond the pale.[6]

6. It is perhaps too easy to sneer at the triviality and juvenility of these school value-systems, and certainly in recent years there has been

An adult who continues to live his life according to school values may do so because his own school values were so satisfying that even after graduation he cannot bear to relinquish them. The universally popular school captain, the champion school athlete, or the brilliant exam-passer may find that school prowess and popularity dwindle to nothing in the context of adult value-systems. If such individuals are unable to wean themselves away from their past glory they may spend the rest of their lives in wistful nostalgia, bewilderment, or a state of aggrieved petulance at the world's strange indifference to their youthful achievements.

More commonly, however, school roles which come to be perpetuated in adults are the ones which they originally found unsatisfactory. The child who was afraid of being too different from the majority of his peers may develop an over-intense need to conform, and spend his life anxiously trying to 'keep up with the Joneses', and inhibiting his own tastes and preferences for fear of 'what the neighbours might think'. A more extreme example of exaggerated loyalty to the *status quo* is perhaps the militant patriot, prepared to fight with anyone who questions his belief in 'my country, right or wrong'. (E. M. Forster went

no shortage of willing iconoclasts. We should remember, however, that codes of behaviour do have certain positive values, not merely in school but even in later life. Many people are not capable of developing a code of their own, and yet have shown themselves capable of fine action as adults simply because they could not bring themselves to behave in a way which might disgrace 'the Alma Mater'.

A sensitive and able analysis of what it meant, and what it means now, to be a 'gentleman' will be found in *The English Gentleman* by Simon Raven – who admits openly that he himself was a bounder and a cad. We are here merely categorizing these school systems as regressions insofar as they may be inappropriate as standards of value for mature adults. Nor do we imply that the underlying class distinction is unique to the English public school system and its products. Class distinction is usually discernible at all levels of social living, and in all countries, despite loud public protestations to the contrary.

to the other extreme when he wrote: 'if I had to choose between betraying my country and betraying my friend I hope I should have the guts to betray my country.')

Some adults find themselves unable to fit in to their society because they are unable to give up specific false roles adopted in school. The child unable to get on in school life without currying favour with the teacher becomes the employee unable to get on in his job without ingratiating himself with the boss; that is, the teacher's pet becomes the industrial toady. The class tell-tale becomes the police informer. The class rebel becomes an angry young man. The class clown becomes a professional comedian. The class outsider becomes a professional outcast, ostentatiously protesting by dropping out of society's value-system. The class impostor maintains a precarious existence on the fringe of society, staying one jump ahead of the law. The less intelligent child, who got by in school only by following every trivial rule, feels secure as an adult only when he goes by the book in his job. The schoolchild who had to buy friends (and sometimes stole to obtain the necessary pocket money) becomes a compulsive party-giver living beyond his income (and sometimes going bankrupt in the process). And so on.

It is probably unwise to categorize all these forms of regression to school age as clinically pathological. Many of the individuals described do find a place in society, and, if not well liked, are at least well accepted. Even when they are thought limited or juvenile in their attitudes, they are not regarded as sick. In addition, success (even by school-age standards) includes *both* vocational competence *and* social adaptation. Many adults achieve a one-sided success. They may be triumphant vocationally but inept socially, e.g. the big business tycoon, hated and feared by his colleagues, employees and family; or vice-versa – the vocational mediocrity unable to achieve promotion, but nevertheless the cornerstone of domestic security and happiness in his home.

One-sidedness shows also in those people who find they can do well only in their private hobby, and make the hobby a way of life to which all other values are subordinated. Similarly, a false industry may be achieved by becoming an expert at some trivial occupation where the competition is extremely limited, a tendency which has been satirized by the newspaper columnist, Beachcomber, who used to report on a world champion 'pea-pusher-with-his-nose'.

Not all forms of one-sidedness are regressive in the eyes of society. Many adults, such as artists, musicians, craftsmen and athletes, devote their entire lives to cultivating one special taste or talent, and these people are often the reverse of 'inferior'.

Here we must recognize that in assessing the degree of pathology of those who have regressed to the school-age level of development, we are in danger of becoming involved in value-systems which are not really within the domain of psychology proper. Nevertheless it is relevant to point out that our technological society does tend to admire 'industry' and 'fitting in' as such; that our schools reflect this tendency; and that we ourselves are the products of our schools in this respect. The term of greatest opprobrium that a teacher can use against a pupil is that he is lazy. We are trained in the belief that work is always a good thing in itself; that our adaptation to society is an unquestioned requirement; that our games and pastimes should be organized into competitions; that musing, daydreaming, or even contemplation should always be sacrificed to hard-driving effort; and in general that everything we do should count towards something else.

Thus we feel compelled to keep busy to the point where we find it difficult to relax; we may even come to loathe holidays and rush back to work with a sigh of relief or, worse, degenerate to the ultimate horror of the business lunch where we cannot stop working even to eat. In our social living we may find ourselves enmeshed in reciprocal entertaining, working away at the catering instead of enjoying the company of friends. Our leisure, unless filled with productivity and achievement, may actually make us feel guilty or inferior. If we want to sit quietly on a river bank watching the patterns of sunlight on the water, we feel obliged to disguise our purpose with elaborate fishing tackle. Or we may encumber ourselves with fourteen heavy golf clubs and strive to beat par. Golf has been defined as 'a good walk spoiled'. When we *must* do these things we seem to have learned too well our schoolteacher's lesson that loafing must always mean laziness.

In considering regressions to the school age we are probably on safer ground when we consider them from a psychological rather than a social point of view. We are then confining ourselves to those people who suffer from the classic inferiority complex. This may show as exaggeration of any of the tendencies already described in social terms, but essentially the inferiority complex derives from the failure to achieve a sense of industry in Erikson's sense. In such cases the sense of inadequacy is generalized and intense; the individual feels that he will never learn, never be good for anything; he feels that he will be forever useless and a failure.

Feelings of inferiority, while they predominate in those who have regressed to the school age, may of course occur in any illness, and it has been suggested that they are in fact part of all illnesses. That is, merely to be a patient is to be idle, to be out of ordinary society, and (often) to be discouraged and to have low self-esteem. This view is implicitly supported by those hospitals with occupational therapy departments. The central purpose of such departments is to help and encourage patients, irrespective of their diagnosis, to be active and to re-learn how to manage their practical and social affairs during convalescence. The various rehabilitation training schemes, sheltered workshops, trade instruction in prisons, and 'half-way houses', all serve much the same purpose.

We should, however, distinguish the self-esteem obtained by school-age industry and social adaptation from the self-esteem achieved in the anal stage of early childhood (see Chapter 2). Although both are social, and derive largely from the consistent attitudes of others, the earlier form of self-esteem is the more fundamental. It is determined principally by the child's mother and, as time passes, becomes much less conscious. In contrast, the origins of school-age self-esteem (the attitudes of peers, authority figures, and 'experts') are usually quite apparent to the individual, both at the time and later. It is much easier to recall psychological problems in school than trauma or conflict in the anal stage. Within our developmental framework, adults who regress only to the school age are by definition much less seriously disturbed than those who regress to earlier stages.

Schooldays are popularly regarded as the happiest days of our lives; and for a certain few, or those who are disappointed in their later lives, they may be. It is also possible that most of us hanker after schooldays because they were 'dear old golden rule days': that is, when our lives were systematically regulated, when our goals and aspirations were clearer, more tangible, and more simply obtained; and when we were being spoon-fed by those who took all our decisions and most of our responsibilities on their shoulders.

SUMMARY

In this chapter we have encompassed a larger unit of time. We concentrated more on social than psycho-biological determinants of the school-age crises, and suggested that the child's need to learn 'how to' involved both industry (the acquisition of practical skills) and social adaptation (getting along with others).

We stressed the pervasiveness of school influences on the child, the importance of individual differences (some of which tend to be equated with differences in social class), and the school's systematic attempts to emphasize similarities, and thus encourage conformity, in children.

In discussing illness we made allowance for normal difficulties experienced by children in making the transition from home to school, then described the 'inferiority complex' as it shows in children who fail to achieve industry or social adaptation.

Regressions to school age were difficult to pinpoint, since in most cultures the perpetuation of many school-age attitudes is encouraged by society. We attempted to discuss some forms of school-age preoccupations which at least limited, without necessarily making ill, the individuals who continued them into adult life. We regarded only the classic inferiority complex as a true regression to school-age conflicts, but recognized its occurrence in many other forms of illness.

We concluded by distinguishing school-age self-esteem from the more basic self-esteem derived from the anal stage of development.

CHAPTER FIVE

Adolescence (13–19 years)

'I just don't know what to do with myself'
(*Pop Song, featured by Miss Dusty Springfield*)

ALTHOUGH teenagers have always been with us, their existence as a specific group, with unique psychological characteristics, has been recognized by society only recently.
Until the eighteenth century teenagers were not distinguished
from children. In the Victorian era they were regarded as either
overgrown children or undergrown adults, and in any case they
were expected to be seen and not heard. Thirty years ago the
teenager was still being described (by the late Judy Garland,
herself a teenager) as 'just an in-between, too old for toys, too
young for boys'. Nowadays, however, adolescents have become
identified as a separate social group, and indeed may have
become a specially privileged group.

The emergence of adolescents as a recognizable group probably dates from the early 1940s. At that time, when parents
were either absent or distracted by their 'war efforts', adolescents found themselves with new freedoms and responsibilities. It is unlikely that this factor alone caused the teenage
group to emerge as a new social unit, but teenagers in the early
1940s also found a group leader who provided a focus for their
values and offered them a vehicle for their self-expression. This
was Frank Sinatra.[1]

Adults, on the whole, tended to resent Sinatra. They criticized his rather nondescript appearance, describing him as 'a

[1]. And, very soon afterwards, Elvis Presley.

rag, a bone, and a hank of hair'; they compared his singing voice unfavourably with the mellow tones of Bing Crosby; and generally they regarded him as an upstart, totally unable to live up to his advance publicity, and impertinently trying to supplant old favourites in the musical world.

These negative reactions from older generations probably enhanced Sinatra's appeal for the younger generation. The fact that he was not much to look at, and could not sing very well, mattered nothing to teenagers. If his appearance was nondescript and his voice mediocre – well, so were theirs. Thus Sinatra ('The Voice') soon became *their* voice, the voice of teenagers everywhere.[2]

It is hardly surprising that adolescents, in the process of identifying themselves as a group, also developed their own esoteric catch phrases. At first these referred directly to their music and dancing, e.g. 'jive', 'jitterbug', etc. Later, however, the connotations of teenage jargon, such as 'hep', 'cool', 'with it', 'fab', 'gear', and so on, began to expand beyond teenage music; they began to refer to specific personal experiences, to exclusive social values and patterns, and eventually to a way of life that was unique to the teenager. These jargon words are of

2. In any culture, music is one of the most direct forms of emotional communication. In our culture, pop music has come to represent direct emotional communication for adolescents, and indeed may be the clearest social expression of adolescent psychodynamics available to us. (A more detailed discussion of this possibility will be found later in this chapter.) There is of course a commercial element in the selection of pop music for the Hit Parade, the Top Twenty, and the Boss Forty; but the records selected will not sell well if adolescents do not obtain satisfaction from them. It is adolescents who buy them, and Tin Pan Alley dare not stray too far from genuine adolescent specifications. Similarly, the extravagant swooning response of teenagers to Sinatra may at first have been contrived by his publicity agents, but soon became involuntary (or voluntary) reactions which adolescents continue to show to this day.

course never clearly defined by teenagers: they understand them.

Along with the adolescent verbal code came the adolescent uniform. The early 1940s, it may be remembered, was the era of the bobby-soxer. Nowadays, although teenage styles and clothing show more variety, all have remained unmistakably adolescent.[3] As well as clothes styles, adolescents have developed their own hair styles, art forms, literature, T.V. programmes, and so on. Adolescent values have been given an inordinate amount of publicity, and have of course been exploited commercially. The whole process has had the effect of slowly confirming, clarifying, and elaborating the adolescents' value-systems.

THE PSYCHOLOGICAL CRISES OF ADOLESCENCE

Until Erikson (1950, 1959) formulated his concept of *identity*, psychologists had found it extremely difficult to explain, or even to understand, the psychological preoccupations of adolescence. We have referred to 'identity' in earlier sections (see Preface and Chapter 1), but only insofar as it was a basic, general feature of our lives, apparent in one form or another at all developmental stages. We have also suggested, following D. C. Levin (1963), that in clinical illness 'identity *pathology*' may be regarded as a 'psychiatric primitive', a feature in one form or another of all disturbed psychological conditions. What we are suggesting here, again following Erikson, is that during adolescence identity, in both its healthy and pathological aspects, becomes predominant. It is identity which is first disrupted in early adolescence, gradually becomes reintegrated

3. Any attempt by adults to imitate teenage trends is a signal to teenagers that their fashion has become old-fashioned, and so precipitates an immediate change.

during mid-adolescence, and finally stabilizes in late adolescence or early adulthood.

Identity is most obviously disrupted in adolescence by biological changes which are not only extreme and profound, but are in many ways inconsistent. The skeleton, muscles, internal organs, and especially the reproductive system, show a growth spurt; on the other hand, neural tissue stops growing and lymphatic tissue atrophies. The growth of different body tissues at different rates is common to all adolescents.

Puberty is not a clear-cut phenomenon and is defined in different ways by different investigators. Douglas, for example, found that if puberty in girls was defined by the first menstrual period the mean age of puberty was about thirteen years; if, however, wider physical criteria were used, 17 per cent of the girls surveyed were sexually mature at the age of eleven. Puberty, depending on how it is defined, may begin between nine and sixteen years, and end anywhere between thirteen and twenty, with girls reaching puberty about two years earlier than boys.

The puberty of Western Europeans has shown a slow evolutionary change between 1830 and 1960. During this period puberty has started four months earlier every ten years, and there is no evidence to suggest that the trend has stopped. It has also been found that adolescents are taller today than they were a hundred years ago, the increase being about 2.5 centimetres per decade. It has been suggested that these trends are produced by improved nutrition and less illness in Western Europe during the period surveyed, but whatever the reason, the effect is that adolescence is starting earlier.

Biological changes, whenever they occur, always have important psychological consequences. The mere fact that the muscles of boys become nearly twice as large between the ages of twelve and sixteen makes them more energetic and expansive, and gives them greater self-confidence in competing with adults; boys may find their physical strength equal, or even superior, to that of their fathers. The attitudes of both adults and contemporaries towards an adolescent depend to some extent on his physical maturity, and it has been suggested that one's permanent pattern of social behaviour may be determined by the timing of maturation and the extent to which the adolescent is in or out of phase with his contemporaries rather than his final pattern of physical maturity.

Biological changes will of course also affect the adolescent's conception of himself. His 'body-image' is disturbed by puberty, and although he may be secretive about his anxiety regarding physique, he often spends hours in front of a mirror, as if he were trying to stabilize his body-image by visual inspection, checking constantly to see that his appearance has not changed in grotesque ways. Later, instead of looking at himself, he may talk to himself, either literally or indirectly in the form of keeping a diary in which he records all his movements. Sometimes adolescent diaries are banal ('Went downtown, saw Fred, went to cinema, came home at 10.30, went to bed . . .' etc.). Nevertheless such record-keeping expresses the adolescent's attempt to reassure himself about his identity. He may feel that his experiences and movements are important enough to be shared by posterity, but more often the diary merely helps him to place himself in space and time, and is discontinued when he no longer needs to do so. Throughout adolescence there is always some consciousness of self, or 'self-consciousness'.

The glandular changes of adolescence produce new and turbulent sexual feelings which are usually strange and disturbing when first experienced, and indeed may change drastically the adolescent's attitude towards half the population of the world, namely, the opposite sex. Anxious parents often make more of adolescent sexuality than the facts warrant.[4] Granted that

4. The readers' letters section in women's magazines usually provides a good cross-section of the normal adolescent's sexual pre-

sexual identity, sexual urges, and sexual limits and boundaries constitute an important preoccupation among adolescents, these are often approached and investigated as part of identity generally. That is, the question is not 'What are the actual opportunities for sexual behaviour?' so much as 'What kind of person am I sexually?' Adolescents, especially in their earlier years, spend more time discussing and clarifying their sexual nature than acting it out in behaviour. Their actual behaviour, which is in any case inhibited by the contradictory nature of their impulses, tends eventually to be determined by the standards of the peer group within which they find themselves. If the adolescent's friends are sexually permissive and 'go the whole way', or alternatively are strict, with prohibitive moral standards, then he himself will be very likely to follow their example in practice.

When considering sexual preoccupations in adolescence, we should perhaps subdivide them into early, middle and late teenages. In early adolescence the individual's need for companionship is usually satisfied mainly by a member of the same sex, who is more important than any adult or any member of the opposite sex. There is then usually a phase of multiple and almost interchangeable heterosexual friends with an increase in the number of friends of the same sex. Later the numbers are usually reduced to a few intimate friends, and 'going steady' with one person of the opposite sex, who may nevertheless be changed fairly frequently for some time afterwards. Recently, between 1942 and 1963, the heterosexual interests of

---

occupations, and the standard adult advice for dealing with them. When 'Worried Blue Eyes' asks how to cope with her boyfriend's sexual importunities, she is usually encouraged to join a youth club. This is of course perfectly sensible advice for a young teenager who is not yet ready for intensely sexualized relationships with one male. Multiple relationships, such as those formed in youth clubs, diffuse the intensity, so that indeed there is 'safety in numbers'.

adolescents seem to have increased. Members of the opposite sex are now preferred more often as companions for such things as going to the cinema. The trend is more marked with boys, but for both sexes the frequencies increase with increasing age. This would seem to be one behavioural example of the earlier maturation of adolescents nowadays.

Identity in adolescence is affected not only by biological changes within the individual himself, but also by the social expectations and opportunities he meets. In western society, the transition from childhood to adulthood is not the same for all adolescents. The adolescent may determine his economic and social status by entering 'an educational steeplechase in which a series of tests and examinations progressively restrict the vocational choice of the majority ... these selection procedures represent the real *rites de passage* of this society by dramatically focussing the stresses of mobility on the moments of evaluation through which individuals are said to find their own level' (Irvine and Brown, 1966). But, depending on the individual's social class, educational ability, or opportunity, the transition from student to worker, or from the educational to the productive social system, may occur at sixteen, or in the mid-twenties. We should remember also that for most adolescents the period of education has been extended. Thus, as the school-leaving age has risen, the adolescent has had to cope with an extension of his period of dependency, and with a prolongation of his continuous control by adults.

It is ironic that, just at the time when he is beginning to become confused by his own dawning adolescence, adult society begins to make new demands on him. Adults, perhaps in anxious reaction to the growing instability they see in their children, encourage them to choose careers, and generally to make up their minds what they intend to be, in early adolescence. From the adolescent's point of view, a worse time could hardly be selected for this. To add to the confusion, adult society is still in considerable doubt as to what it may legitimately expect from teenagers.

Consider, for example, society's changing attitudes towards the responsibility for criminal actions. In England the age of legal responsibility has crept upwards gradually from the age of eight to seventeen. In the United States it has risen from seven to sixteen, to eighteen, and in some states is now fixed at twenty-one. The adolescent in modern society still lacks clear values and stable institutions which he can claim as his own. Indeed, society's lack of accepted norms for adolescent behaviour places the teenager in a kind of social limbo, in which his natural adolescent tensions may become exacerbated. In contrast, many primitive societies do have clear, unambiguous *rites de passage* that help to make adolescent roles explicit.

The combined effect of the physical and social changes outlined above is often *psychologically* devastating to the adolescent. The stability, control, balance, and consistency that he acquired in his earlier school years may be shattered. His increase in energy may make him awkward and clumsy, and the clamorous demands of those around him may do little but increase his confusion. He himself is bewildered by his exaggerated changes in mood and inconsistencies in behaviour. He 'just doesn't know what to do with himself'.

Thus the psychological problem in adolescence is that 'deep down you are not sure that you are a man (or a woman), that you will ever grow together again and be attractive, that you will ever master your drives, that you really know who you are, that you know what you want to be, that you know what you look like to others, and that you will know how to make the right decision without once and for all committing yourself to the wrong friend, sexual partner, leader or career' (Erikson, 1959).[5]

5. According to Winnicott (1964) the adolescent is 'engaged in trying to find the self to be true to'.

Having outlined in rather abstract fashion the various biological, social and psychological aspects of the adolescent's identity crisis, we should attempt also to give some practical and concrete examples of the adolescent in action, as it were. Granted that he finds puberty bewildering and spends his teens searching for a new identity, how does he go about it? What may we actually see him doing? And how may we recognize the adolescent who is successful?

The teenager, searching for signposts towards a new identity, looking for some way to make sense of his experiences, and trying to reconcile his inner promptings and impulses with what his environment will allow, cannot easily find solutions by simple introspection. His inner feelings are too unfamiliar, turbulent, transient, and ambivalent for him to make sense of them. So he tends to search 'out there' in the world, externalizing his problems and acting out (really living out) his conflicts. When perplexed by the question 'Who am I, *really*?', he tends to formulate it in terms of 'Who can I be like?' or 'What do others think I am like?', or 'How do I appear to others?'.

Adolescents clarify their identity by interacting with other people, mingling in groups, and by engaging in endless conversations. Such conversations are not really techniques for communicating information but merely another means of redefining identity. The typical content of these colloquies is 'here's what I think of myself, of you, of others, of life in general; what do you think of yourself, of others, of life in general? What do you believe others think of themselves, of us, of life in general?' etc. Personal and social values, interpersonal relationships and boundaries of all sorts are gradually confirmed and clarified by these interminable sessions.

Here we should remember that between the ages of eleven and fifteen, there is a profound change in our intellectual structure. In adolescence a youth's mode of thinking develops from the 'concrete' to the 'hypothetical-deductive' level, and he begins to use propositional logic (see Table I). Where before he perceived mainly though his senses he can now use abstract concepts and work out complex relationships as well; and in effect he ends by applying the laws of formal thinking and reason to everything in his experience. This developmental and cognitive change helps to explain the adolescent's marked interest in discussions. He becomes fascinated by scientific, philosophical, artistic, political, and social issues. Adults often forget that what is for them a reiteration of old and stale problems is for the adolescent an exciting and delightful discovery. In trying out new opinions, paradoxes, heterodoxies and sophistries (and in gauging their value by the extent to which they shock, impress, or convince others) the adolescent is really exploring new possibilities of identity for himself. He is forever clarifying by redefinition.

This increase in intellectual enterprise does not in any way diminish the adolescent's emotional impulses. In every area of psychological functioning he lives 'at the pitch of his voice'. In fact his sensuality (his awareness of sensory or emotional events) is probably at its peak during his adolescence. As most readers will remember, it is in the teens that agonies and ecstasies are experienced most intensely.

On the other hand we should remember that adolescent self-consciousness may show emotionally as well as intellectually. The teenager tends to revel in emotion, any emotion, and enjoy the experience for its own sake. He watches very carefully to see how others (and himself, for that matter) are responding to his emotional reactions. The extreme of such self-consciousness occurs when the teenager spoofs his own feelings and value-systems, as if to forestall criticism by others. It does not do, therefore, always to take teenagers more seriously than they take themselves.

We have suggested that the adolescent attempts to clarify his identity mainly by interacting with others. It is important to realize, however, that he often interacts with others not as persons but as models, or types with whom he may identify. He tends to regard other people as examples of what he himself may become. The identities of these models are, as it were, 'tried on for size'. By continually asking himself 'Am I like this person or this one, or this other . . . ?' he gradually becomes clearer in his own mind about his identity. It is as if he uses other people as mirrors in which he tries to see some part of himself.

The models selected by the adolescent are, as we might expect, many and varied. He may choose older people, whose identity is already established, and who represent some specific type of person. Alternatively, he may choose another adolescent, especially if the latter seems to exemplify some characteristic whose value he is exploring at the time. If he cannot find models to serve his purpose he may construct some, either by investing real people with the qualities he requires, or by a purely imaginative effort which creates idealized fantasy figures in his own mind.

Here we see that to a considerable extent the adolescent exaggerates or invents qualities in others with whom he wants to identify. Since his search for identity is urgent, he needs models that are stark and clearly defined. To make models larger than life, so that they can be seen at a glance, leads to greater ease of identification. In a sense, what the adolescent requires is not merely people, but heroes and heroines. These of course have always been supplied in a never-ending stream by Hollywood film producers, in the form of stars with a clearly defined public image. Nowadays the pop stars provide the adolescent with heroes and heroines directly, from his own age group.

Adolescent identifications are sometimes so intense as to be called over-identification. This, after all, is the age of the 'crush'. Adults who are unkind, or who have forgotten their own adolescence, tend to deride the teenager who moons around the house in despair because the object of his 'crush' has slighted him in some way; or become irritated when the teenager is wildly exuberant because the idol has at last recognized his existence. (Here readers are asked to recall their own crushes – their breathless excitement on awakening in the morning when on that very day they would actually see 'the person', the palpitating anxiety with which they approached the fateful encounter, and the ecstasy, or agony, or both, when the confrontation occurred.) There is of course a good deal of idealization in such attachments. Indeed, they usually continue only so long as the adolescent and the person on whom he has a crush maintain a certain distance from one another. Idols are not to be touched, only worshipped from afar.

Adolescent over-identifications are usually brief and temporary. The crush comes to a sudden end, almost literally overnight, the scales fall from the adolescent's eyes, and he wonders 'what he ever saw in her'. All that has happened is that his attention is now drawn to some other aspect of his identity. This may lead to another crush, or, if the required value is non-sexual (e.g. intellectual), he may enter a misogynistic phase while he pursues some philosophical ideal. The transience and complexity of adolescent over-identifications is of course even more noticeable when the object is another teenager who is simultaneously attempting to clarify his own identity.

Identity is not merely a process of identifying and accepting, but also one of excluding and repudiating. The adolescent wants an answer not only to the question, 'Who am I?' but also the question, 'Who am I *not*?' As well as heroes, he needs villains. Hence his sudden, intense, transient identification with (eventually followed by equally sudden rejection of) models who are, at least in the eyes of anxious parents, 'quite unsuitable'. Again, if there are no actual villains available, the adolescent will create them. He is especially liable to appoint some well-meaning and relatively harmless older person, such as a parent. (We shall discuss this in more detail in the next section.) Generally, the teenager's repudiation of negative models is as vigorous as his identification with positive ones. The same model may be used at different times as both hero and villain, depending on the needs of the adolescent, e.g. whether he is concerned about his own saintliness on the one hand, or his devilishness on the other. These violent swings between extremes may show not only in emotional ways, but also in purely intellectual ones, for example in idealistic conservatism versus free-wheeling anarchism.

The contradictoriness and transience of adolescent identifications suggest that they are not really complete and total, only partial. At any one time the adolescent requires a multiplicity of models, each of which may be used as a separate peg on which to hang a different fragment of his own rather incohesive personality. Indeed, the more models, the more detailed the adolescent's delineation and definition of his ego boundaries will be. Hence his dislike of intense one-to-one relationships in which his own weak ego might become overwhelmed and swamped; and his preference for groups where the relationship is one-to-as-many-as-possible. Kaleidoscopic personalities require multiple mirrors.

In referring to the biological, social and psychological aspects of adolescents we have suggested that the adolescent's identity goes through a process of fairly sudden disruption, fragmentation, and subsequent gradual reintegration. We need not expect, therefore, that adolescents, especially in the earlier stages of this process, will be particularly stable. Their feelings, thinking, behaviour and personal relationships are not consistent and patterned, but transitory, diffuse, and almost infinitely variable.

These contradictions can only partly be explained by bio-

psycho-social influences, and the adolescent's struggle to reconcile his strange new inner promptings with the expectations
of his environment. The contradiction may make more sense to
us if we consider his need to define his world, his society, and
himself in terms of our developmental framework – that is, if
we think of him not merely as 'defining' but 'redefining'. He is
redefining everything and everybody in his world; trying to re-
evaluate all his past psychological achievements, re-examine
his previous relationships, re-establish some sense of continuity
in his life, and reintegrate his own identity. The contradictions
arise because he is trying to redefine all these things simultaneously.

There is in fact considerable agreement among psychologists
that adolescence is a period of recapitulation (see Chapter 1), in
which all previous psychological crises are reawakened, and are
worked through or 're-worked' at the same time. For example,
Chess suggests that in adolescence

problems characteristic of earlier stages may seem to drop out
altogether, but in reality persist with changed characteristics ...
behaviour problems that have not been resolved in childhood are
likely to appear in intensified form in adolescence ... childhood
attributes of ingratiation, exploitation, arrogance and conceit,
feelings of unworthiness, and other personality traits, are carried
over into adolescent life, where their expression may have more
serious, far-reaching effects than in childhood.

Fenichel puts it the other way round:

... the return of infantile impulses is caused by the child's fear of
the new forms of his drives, which makes him regress to the old
and familiar forms. Thus the ascetism of puberty may be
understood as a sign of fear of sexuality, and indeed a defense
against it.

Here we see that the contradictions in adolescent psychology
become less contradictory, or at least more ordered, if we think

of them in terms of regression to various earlier levels of development. The adolescent's predominant preoccupation will vary according to which earlier crisis is currently being reactivated. If he is concerned with infantile dependency problems (Stage I) he may become over-trusting or over-cynical in his attitude to authority figures. If his sense of autonomy and self-esteem is undermined (Stage II) he may become negativistic in his behaviour, antithetical in his thinking, and ashamed or doubtful about his own capacities. His Oedipal battles (Stage III) have to be re-fought because his sexual impulses are resurgent in adolescence. The competence and confidence he acquired in school years (Stage IV), may disintegrate to the point where he suffers mild inferiority feelings, and may refuse even to try to fit in with his contemporaries. And so on. If even normal adolescents have to resolve all their reactivated crises of trust, autonomy, initiative, and industry during their teens it is little wonder that they show such 'consistent inconsistency' in everything they do. When the turbulence of their lives is considered in terms of a wholesale developmental recapitulation, their contradictoriness becomes much less bewildering.

To sum up, 'success' for the adolescent really entails a series of interrelated successes in the teen years. In early adolescence he has to accommodate the sudden increase in sexual and aggressive drives, and adapt to the changes in size, shape, function, and appearance of his body. In mid-adolescence he has to find suitable ways of satisfying his new needs for responsibility and independence; here his developing identity is confirmed both by the educational or training qualifications he acquires, and by the social rites of his contemporaries. In late adolescence he will have settled on some appropriate career, achieved a mature sexual identity, and integrated his own ethical standards with those of his society. That is, his identity will be a stable one if he knows who he is, where he stands, where he's going, and (perhaps) who is going with him. That this is success for the adolescent will be more apparent after we have considered some of the ways he may fail to resolve his adolescent identity crisis.[6]

ILLNESS IN ADOLESCENCE

In one sense the normal adolescent has very little chance of resolving his crisis smoothly. It could even be said that adolescence is the stage of development at which it is normal to be unstable. As Anna Freud (1965) points out, 'Adolescence produces its own symptomatology which, in the more severe cases, is of a quasi-dissocial, quasi-psychotic, borderline order.' She adds, 'This pathology also disappears when adolescence has run its course.' To the extent that this is true, adolescents are diagnostically unique.

The ordinary techniques of research, psychotherapy, and psychological testing tend not to work when applied to adolescents. Most psychological tests provide conflicting, or misleading findings when their norms are applied directly and without artificial 'smoothing' to adolescents. It has been suggested, on the evidence of psychological test manuals themselves, that adolescents are too inconstant in their psychological functioning to be assessed with any degree of scientific accuracy.

6. Erikson pointed out that one sub-group of adolescents is not required by society to establish their identity by the end of their teens – those who go on to higher education in colleges and universities. Society offers such students a moratorium, or delayed payment, in allowing their adolescence to be artificially prolonged into adulthood, perhaps with the implicit expectation that their contribution will be correspondingly greater afterwards. Students often get away with behaviour that would be regarded as socially intolerable or punishable in non-students, so that minor crimes are often condoned as student 'rags'. On the other hand, society does not take students very seriously until they become workers and earners.

It seems to be extraordinarily difficult for adults (including many psychologists) simply to accept the fact that adolescents do not fit neatly into categories. Adult society is of course composed of individuals who have passed through and resolved their own identity crisis. Thus some adults, although they now recognize adolescence, are not yet willing to admit adolescents as full members of the socio-developmental hierarchy. It may even be true, as Margaret Mead suggested, that adolescents inspire a vague sense of danger and threat in adults. 'We prescribe no ritual, the girl continues on her round of school or work, but she is constantly confronted by a mysterious apprehensiveness in her parents and guardians ... the society in which she lives has all of the tensity of a room full of people who expect the latest arrival to throw a bomb' (Mead, 1930).

The great danger, therefore, is that adults, whether parents, guardians, or mental health 'experts', will attempt to force adolescents into diagnostic or social classifications which they do not fit. Erikson emphasized that the adolescent's greatest need, and often his only solution, 'is the refusal on the part of older friends and advisers and judiciary personnel to type him further by pat diagnosis and social judgement which ignore the special diagnostic conditions of adolescence'. Adults do tend to bear down on the passing foibles of adolescents as if they were irreversible personality traits. Clinicians in particular are liable to misdiagnose the transient features of youth as indications of serious underlying disorders.

Although the diagnosis of illness in adolescence must be heavily qualified, this does not mean that adolescents are never ill. Adolescents may always be deviant by adult (or childhood) standards; but some are deviant even by adolescent standards and may therefore be considered genuinely ill. The behaviour of such adolescents is significantly more extravagant than that of their peers, and the severity of their psychological disturbance does not diminish as they near the end of their teens.

Erikson (1950) subsumed adolescent disorders under the general concept of 'identity diffusion'. This is not merely a condition in which the adolescent attempts to reintegrate his identity, but is, strictly speaking, a condition in which he *fails* to do so. He *remains* confused and unpredictable. To the end of his teens, and often beyond, he is unable to reconcile the contradictory expectations of others, his own contradictory ego-functions and ideals, and his earlier identifications and social stereotypes (see Table II). He continues to be, as adolescents themselves used to describe it, 'mixed up'.

Identity diffusion takes such a variety of forms that a comprehensive list would take us far beyond the confines of our developmental outline. We will describe briefly some forms of adolescent psychopathology considered (*a*) as regressions to earlier levels of behaviour, and (*b*) as failure to resolve current identity crises.

We saw in the last section that normal adolescents were recapitulating earlier crises, and were working through them all more or less at the same time. Unsuccessful adolescents, although they too are recapitulating, cannot work through their reactivated earlier conflicts, nor can they reconcile them within the framework of a redefined identity. They may show the same features as normal adolescents, but in more severe and much less flexible forms. These features may be ordered developmentally as follows. A minor adolescent regression (to Stage IV) may show as consistent feelings of inferiority, a prevailing sense of helpless incompetence, and a chronic inability to achieve any acceptable social or vocational role. Slightly more severe adolescent regressions (to Stage III) might take Oedipal forms, such as grossly theatrical behaviour, severe conflicts with parents and siblings (or their substitutes), extreme confusion about sexuality and sex role, guilt feelings, or wildly distorted moral attitudes. Further regressions (to Stage II) would probably involve anal conflicts, in which the adolescent might suffer endless doubts about his own worth as a person, show implacable obstinacy and meanness, or become cruel, disorderly, or destructive. These different constellations are usually transient in the normal adolescent,[7] but when any one of them becomes predominant and lasts for a considerable period of time we begin to think in terms of *adolescent neurosis*.[8]

Some adolescents regress beyond neurosis to *characterological* (psychopathic) or *borderline-psychotic* levels, in which case the disorder usually has the features described in Chapter 1. Most of the so-called behaviour disorders of adolescents involve active delinquency, in which case the adolescent is liable to be diagnosed as psychopathic. In classifying an adolescent as psychopathic, however, we should remember that delinquency is not in itself an illness; it only means that the youngster has been caught by the law. Many adolescents break the law and are not caught. A further qualification is that the same delinquent behaviour may involve different

7. For example, the typical teenage weakness in maintaining sexual identity is often misinterpreted as homosexuality. But although many youths have long hair, dress effeminately and have mannerisms which are more girlish than the female adolescents who favour short, boyish haircuts, and wear trousers or jeans rather than skirts, such 'symptoms' are seldom retained into subsequent adulthood. It is therefore harmful to the normal adolescent when these are invalidly confirmed as homosexuality by insensitive (and forgetful) adults.

8. Few clinicians use standard diagnostic labels to differentiate these various neurotic regressions in adolescents (e.g. adolescent inferiority complex, adolescent hysteria, adolescent obsessive-compulsive personality and so on), but some use the general label of 'adolescent adjustment reaction' or 'situational adjustment reaction in adolescence'. Such descriptions do not really differentiate one adolescent neurosis from another, but merely emphasize the social aspect of the disorder.

motivations, and have different meanings, for different adolescents. In general, delinquent adolescents cannot justifiably be regarded as clinically psychopathic so long as they remain well-adapted to some social group, even if this is only their own age group, or even a gang. (The tendency of adolescents to be responsible and socially adapted at least to their fellow adolescents was encouraged recently by one judge in Dallas, Texas, who regularly called on teenagers to act as jurors in trials of adolescent delinquents.) Most delinquent adolescents, although they may be similar to psychopaths in that they are impulsive and threaten adult values in society, are in fact loyal and devoted to other members of their own group.

All adolescents experiment with, and try to upset, everything that savours of the *status quo*. After all, when one's own psychological 'establishment' has been forcibly and suddenly disrupted, one is not likely to have many scruples about over-throwing the Establishment. A healthy rebelliousness is part of normal adolescence. Nevertheless, the distinction between those adolescents who rebel against, and those who attempt to destroy generally accepted social values remains a real one. There is a considerable difference between protest marches and sit-ins on the one hand, and slashing railway carriages, smashing telephone kiosks, and assaulting innocent citizens on the other.

Oral or Stage I regressions in adolescents are usually serious in their consequences, even when they take the form of dependent rather than aggressive behaviour. One severe form of oral-dependency occurs in those adolescents who take drugs and become addicted. Many teenagers try drugs merely to become accepted by their peer group, for kicks, or in order to experience psychedelic or consciousness-expanding sensations. In a way, this is no more than the typical adolescent inability to evaluate some sensations as being worth more than others. Nevertheless, although the wish for kicks may be a fairly predictable form of adolescent sensuality, the resultant addiction is always dangerous (See Chapter 1).[9]

Adolescents who regress almost entirely to Stage I may become extremely moody (even by adolescent standards), withdrawn, and 'autistic'. When these features are accompanied by, for example, a gross deterioration in personal habits, and severe intellectual irregularities, clinicians tend to think in terms of *adolescent schizophrenia*, or what used to be called *dementia praecox*. Here again, however, we must make certain distinctions. Many of the apparently schizophrenic symptoms which show in adolescents are in fact pseudo-psychotic; that is, they may be infantile recapitulations in process of being worked through, rather than infantile regressions within which the adolescent is helplessly fixated. Apparently 'autistic' withdrawals in adolescence may be merely fantasy and daydreaming, which, according to all available evidence (see summary in Lowe, 1969) are very much more pronounced in adolescents than at any other period of development. Adolescents who become schizophrenic have usually shown psychological, intellectual, and educational deterioration prior to puberty, and continue to show psychotic symptoms (marked withdrawal, gross lack of sexual interest, etc.) in their subsequent adulthood.

In general then, adolescents who recapitulate in the normal way will, in the process of redefining all their earlier and their current relationships, show a good deal of behaviour that would certainly be described as sick if it occurred in anybody else.

9. The wide publicity given recently to the problem of teenage addiction (which has done little except draw attention to the shortage of facts and the extreme difficulty in treating addictive conditions) has also encouraged the expression of opinions which are dangerous when voiced by laymen, and criminally irresponsible when voiced by professionals. Of these opinions, the most pernicious is probably the one which advocates that adolescents (and presumably adolescent adults) should be allowed or even encouraged to take drugs.

Even those adolescents who regress rather than merely re-capitulate are liable to be misdiagnosed. And to misdiagnose an adolescent forces on him a false clinical identity, to avoid which he may react violently and ruthlessly. As Erikson (1959) put it: 'If the environment tries to deprive him too radically of all the forms of expression which permit him to develop and to integrate the next step in his ego identity, he will resist with the astonishing strength encountered in animals who are suddenly forced to defend their lives.' Thus, in many cases of turbulent teenage acting-out – when an adolescent is furiously leaving school, changing jobs, staying out all night, withdrawing into bizarre, inaccessible moods, or causing management problems on the hospital wards – he may merely be repudiating some false identity which is being thrust upon him.[10]

Adolescent illnesses may be regarded not only as regressions to earlier conflicts but also as failures to resolve current conflicts. The easiest way to do this is to consider the main feature of adolescent illness, namely identity diffusion, in terms of anxiety and depression. As shown in Table II, adolescent anxiety is a fear of failure to master new and conflicting inner drives; and adolescent depression is the feeling that the world is not good enough. These symptoms can be related to the typical interpersonal relationships of adolescents.

There is a sense in which the adolescent's psychological turbulence generally centres round his parents, for until adulthood

---

10. By this time it will be apparent to the reader that a patient's diagnosis is liable to be determined, or at least coloured, not only by the level to which he has regressed but also by his age. For example, a regression to Stage II which involved both destructiveness and hypochondriacal features might be labelled 'obsessive-compulsiveness' if the patient were adult, delinquency or sociopathy or psychopathy if he were adolescent, 'school phobia' if he were of school age, or 'hyperactivity' if he were a six-year-old child. In this way a developmental framework may be used to help clarify the current chaos in standard psychiatric classification.

his mother and father continue to be the most significant figures in his life. Thus, in the normal teenager's search for models, his obvious first choice will be his parents. At the beginning of adolescence he tends to idealize his parents, and to attribute to them qualities of perfection which they do not possess. (Those who are themselves parents will not require to be reminded that this is a very brief period indeed.) This initial idealization comes to an end simply because no parent can be as perfect as the adolescent would have them be.

In addition, parents are always too few in number to meet the complex and multitudinous needs of the adolescent. He therefore goes out of his family circle into a wider social group of peers and other adults. (Any adolescent who is unable to do this will become increasingly aware that he has over-identified with his parents; and his attachment will become more and more inappropriate as his teens continue.) The adolescent never does things by half. He does not turn quietly from his parents and leave them. He revolts against them with a vigour that often catapults him out of the family. He does not merely change his mind about parental values. He becomes outraged at parental pretension and hypocrisy, and vehemently repudiates his parents as stuffy, boring, old-fashioned frauds whom he has at last, thank God, 'seen through'.

The normal outcome of this process is of course that the adolescent, avoiding the danger of having his identity overwhelmed by those of his parents, begins to develop independence and to fashion a life of his own. He usually retains some tendency to become irritated by his parents; alternatively he may accept their shortcomings, and treat them, in the kindest possible way (i.e. with insufferable condescension) as rather dim-witted children who need a good deal of guidance.

For some adolescents, however, the process of forcible self-weaning may cost too dear or, when achieved, leave them still unable to develop an identity of their own. Such adolescents are not mildly but bitterly disappointed and resentful of their parents. These feelings are usually directed mainly against the father, or father-substitutes such as authority figures, institutions, or ideals representing law and order. The resentment may be many-sided. For example, it often focuses on the new demands of society which the adolescent is afraid he may be unable to satisfy. Here the adolescent's anxiety often shows in vociferous protestations that 'it's not fair!', or in vehement demands for instant world reform. If his anxiety becomes chronic, he may never find out what he wants of society, or what society expects of him; he knows only that he never wants what seems to be available. Anxiety thus leads to increased confusion, resentment, and ineptitude, until the adolescent, suffering agonies of mortification, comes to believe that he is his own worst enemy, and can no longer refrain from acting-out in ways which others (and he himself) cannot stand. Behind adolescent anxiety, therefore, there is often a good deal of self-directed resentment. The adolescent cannot forgive himself for being unable to change the unfair world to suit his needs. If his own inner drives nevertheless continue to trouble him, his anxiety will increase; that is, he becomes afraid of his own impulse to change things too violently. Hence his fear of the failure to master new and conflicting inner drives (see Appendix, Table II). Generally, those adolescents who become anxious yet do not act out are more afraid of their confused impulses than they are of the environment which confuses and frustrates them.

Adolescents who are not so much resentful as disappointed in their parents may become depressed. Depression, like anxiety, is of course noticeable in all adolescents. In the process of achieving independence of his parents, the adolescent first idealizes, then repudiates them, finally 'getting rid of them' altogether. The greater the initial idealization, the more intense the final rejection. (Parents bewildered by an adolescent who has suddenly changed from loving and admiring them to hating and despising them may take some consolation.) It is when the idealization has been too extreme, and the repudiation too complete, that the adolescent becomes depressed. Adolescent independence is a fine thing, but it often means losing those on whom he may still wish to depend.

The basis of adolescent depression is a sense of loss. Those who can accommodate the loss may experience only mild and transient depression, a gentle melancholy, or a vague nostalgia for things past. For some, however, adolescence may become almost entirely a period of mourning. For them, the psychological weaning process, even when self-initiated, is more than they can bear – usually because it reactivates infantile conflicts as well. (In extreme cases, adolescent depression can lead to suicidal attempts.) Depressed adolescents come to feel that their parents (and their mother in particular) are lost to them for ever. This feeling becomes generalized into the sad conviction that the world is not good enough (Table II), and that it never will be.

In discussing the adolescent's failure to resolve his current crises we have of course been following the parental stereotypes outlined earlier (Chapter 3), according to which the mother represented 'welfare' and the father 'law and order'. That is, the adolescent who loses (i.e. repudiates) his mother will feel that the world is not good enough; while the one who similarly loses his father will think that the world is not fair enough. Adolescent depression and anxiety, however, are essentially facets of the main problem in adolescence, namely identity diffusion. We can clarify the relationships here by recognizing that when adolescents are unable to externalize their conflicts of anxiety and depression they may give up, and escape into their inner world of fantasy. This is not the normal adolescent tendency to day-dream; nor is it the severe withdrawal from reality seen in adolescent schizophrenics; but something in between, where fantasy becomes a neurotic defence mechanism. For example, the adolescent who feels he is losing his parents may interpret this as abandonment by his parents. If he is unable to hold on to them in overtly aggressive or dependent ways, he may try to alleviate his fears by creating imaginary and idealized parent-substitutes which he uses as a basis for fantasy. This is another source of adolescent over-identification. In extreme cases such fantasy models (because they are entirely under the adolescent's control and can therefore never get away) may come to be preferred to the real models who provide only disillusionment. So the adolescent's problem, although promoted by his inability to deal with anxiety and depression, usually presents itself in the end as an identity problem of one kind or another.

In this way the adolescent who fails to resolve his identity crisis may continue to interact neurotically with his parents. He keeps on searching for 'better' parents, constantly and unsuccessfully over-identifying with all kinds of parent-substitutes. The eventual fruitlessness of such a quest is of course inevitable, for as the adolescent passes through adulthood there will come a point where there are no 'parents' left for him, whether 'better' or otherwise.

The healthy or successful adolescent, although he begins by searching for better parents, eventually resolves his identity crisis by becoming a better parent himself. He usually enters adulthood proclaiming that when he becomes a parent he won't make the same mistakes that his parents did – and then brings up his children in ways which they will criticize in their turn when *they* reach adolescence.

ADOLESCENCE AND POP MUSIC

It is interesting to approach the psychology of adolescents through their music. If it is true, as suggested earlier, that adolescent preoccupations are reflected in pop, we should be able to draw certain parallels between adolescent psychodynamics and the Hit Parade. Although the tunes on the Hit Parade change rapidly (as indeed we might expect) the content of the lyrics, and the form of the music itself, remain fairly constant.

In one form of pop music what predominates is the beat; the beat is often intensified and exaggerated, as indeed are the biological drives of the young teenager. Such music seldom has memorable lyrics, but usually consists of a series of rhythmic yells to which the adolescent keeps time by throwing himself about and thus working off his surplus energy. The yells are usually assertive – 'Yeah!', 'All right!', 'Come on!', 'Twist and Shout!', etc. Some adults consider such music discordant. Some have even gone so far as to liken it to the noise made by a bomb hitting a guitar factory. But we should surely accept that when biological drives are both urgent and conflicted, their expression in music is bound to be jangled also. Certainly teenagers themselves enjoy loud, clashing, rhythmical noises, and indeed will do everything they can to enhance the effect by means of electronic amplifiers. Occasionally they prefer the quieter rhythm, where the words become nonsense syllables such as 'do wah dum diddy dum diddy dum', or merely 'la, la, la'. Generally, rhythmic pop music tends to express adolescent exuberance and enjoyment, often accompanied by an unabashed sensuality.

The adolescent's bewilderment, sense of strangeness, and need for redefinition, are expressed in songs describing the failure to understand what life is all about, the inability to make sense of experience, and the feeling of not being understood by others. Adolescent depression shows in pop songs which express a dim nostalgia, a vague sadness, or in blues where the singer has been abandoned by some loved person. (The word 'baby', which recurs over and over again in such songs, is of considerable psychological interest; the song seldom makes it clear who is to be baby to whom.) When depression is mixed with adolescent anxiety and resentment at the unfair complexity of the world, we hear the pop songs with pseudo-philosophical themes, in which the singer indulges in rather helpless tirades against current social values. Adolescent self-consciousness shows occasionally in the songs which 'take off' his own values. Day-dreaming is of course well tolerated in the Hit Parade, where it is accepted as a perfectly adequate substitute for practical and constructive action.

Of all pop groups, the Beatles and the Rolling Stones have made the greatest impact on the 'teen scene'. If we oversimplify a little, we may regard these groups as representatives of the successful adolescent on the one hand, and the unsuccessful adolescent on the other. The Beatles, quite apart from the fact that their music seems to be of a higher quality and shows greater imagination, cover a wide spectrum of teenage and older values, and indeed often suggest teenage solutions, as if pointing the way to young adulthood. They nearly always express the exuberance and enjoyment of life which typifies the successful teenager. Their later music goes far beyond the teen scene, and often shows a mature, poetic quality. The Rolling Stones, on the other hand, although equally popular, seem to represent teenage values which are predominantly negative.

Many of the lesser stars and pop groups appear to have chosen names which unwittingly reflect teenage identity problems. Some seem to protest their maturity too much, like Manfred Mann or The Supremes. Some claim a premature identity, like the Mamas and the Papas. Some frankly admit their identity difficulty – the Who, The Shadows, The Marmalade, etc. Some settle for a safe, undemanding identity, for instance, the Zombies. Some imply that social withdrawal is the answer to teenage problems (the Hermits) and some merely get angry (Billy Fury) . . . and so on.

It is of course easy to read too much into the Hit Parade. Certainly adolescents themselves do not make any such analysis of their music, but perhaps this is because they are too busy responding to it. Most of the adolescent characteristics described in the earlier part of this chapter do find expression again and again in pop music. To this extent at least they may be regarded as valid, stable indicators of the basic preoccupations of teenagers working through their adolescent identity crisis.

REGRESSIONS TO ADOLESCENCE

Some forms of regression to adolescence are impossible for adults, as some aspects of identity are settled in the very process of completing adolescence – this happens simply with the passage of time. For example, our biological drives inevitably stabilize to some extent. They may of course remain conflicted, but they become less turbulent; and they are less disturbing simply because they are no longer unfamiliar. Adults (even young adults) cannot feel as they did when they were adolescents.

Some aspects of identity are also inevitably settled, for better or for worse, by society itself. That part of identity which we call marital status, for instance, is settled when the adolescent reaches marriageable age in young adulthood; that is, he marries, or he remains single. Although there is a fairly powerful social expectation in favour of marriage (see Chapter 6), either alternative confirms part of the young adult's identity. Similarly, the need to earn a living in effect forces some kind of a vocational identity.[14] Our inability to retain a wholesale ident-

14. The exception here is again the individual who goes on to higher education, and thus enjoys a moratorium. Most college students are more than ready to establish and confirm their identities, but are prevented from doing so by their unique circumstances. In this situation, where dependence and independence are in uneasy conflict, it is perhaps hardly surprising that students sometimes develop a certain assertive stridency of manner, or alternatively show a certain intellectualized priggishness in their dealings with others.

ity diffusion into adulthood is therefore to some extent a fact of life rather than a specific psychological achievement on our part. Some clarification of our identity is thrust upon us merely by our growing older.

Thus, although some adults do regress to adolescence, they cannot be said to be showing a generalized identity diffusion *per se*, but only some aspects of it. For example, they may have developed false or superficial identities, or adopted some specific adolescent defences, or symptoms. Their regression is necessarily partial. Indeed it may be said that adults who regress to adolescence have merely grown older, but, in some respects, not grown up. They are not so much ill as immature.

We should also make certain allowances, as in previous chapters, for normal or socially tolerated regressions to adolescence. Many advertisements nowadays are slanted directly at the adolescent group, and use adolescent language to describe their products. Many offer novelty as an inducement, sufficient in itself as a reason for buying; and some stress the excitement of specific new sensations available to those who try the product. The whole advertising market nowadays is based on 'planned obsolescence'. That is, products which are essentially good for years of serviceable use are given new packages, styles and dressings, and the customer is told that to continue to own a last year's model is to be derisorily out of date ('Your 1970 dazzle is dying'). The addiction of adults to trends and fashions seems to be proof against the clearest evidence that old fashions will become new if one merely waits long enough, and that the real trend-setter is often the person who has enough individuality (or personal identity) to refrain from following the crowd and go his own way with what he knows suits him. Adults hankering after novelty are now sufficiently numerous to be regarded as normal, in the sense that they exemplify a relatively harmless feature of adolescence which can be expected to persist (largely because it is encouraged to persist) into adulthood. The tendency may also reflect the direct influence of adolescents on older age groups. Few adults are immune to the adolescent demand that everybody should be 'with it'.

There are of course more specific, and slightly more severe, ways in which an adult may regress to adolescence. He may, for example, adopt a false identity. A surprising number of adults settle for an identity that is not individual but merely vocational. The 'organization man' who sells his soul, and sometimes the souls of his family as well, to the company he works for, is one example of false identity. Anyone who always, invariably, and without question subordinates himself to the dictates of some political, social, or other group has in effect given up the attempt to establish an identity of his own. Such an individual is not really an individual; he exists only as an example of a set of principles or policies, lacking which he would become disintegrated and purposeless. Sometimes the over-identification is more personal, e.g. the person who forever stands in the shadow of some selected hero or other. Sometimes identity does not develop because it is, as it were, spread too thinly, for instance in someone who has only multiple relationships, and ends by having dozens of acquaintances but no real friends. Anyone who needs to lose himself in someone else's, or something else's, identity achieves only a false or partial identity for himself.

Some adults regress by trying to become adolescent again. They insist on being buddies with adolescents, adopting their slang and dress, and hovering wherever they congregate. They may even appoint themselves leaders or trend-setters for adolescents in an attempt to bolster their own identity by overshadowing those who have not yet achieved one. Since, however, adolescents require adults to be adults (in order to see more clearly what they may identify with or rebel against), the regressed adult is usually rejected both as a model and as a friend.

Another regressive role is the one adopted by the adult who insists on remaining 'one of the boys'. Many adults who over-identify with their own sex do so because they have identity problems in their relationships with the opposite sex. They prefer the boys because they have never learned how to get on with the girls. Some can tolerate heterosexual relationships only if the partner is adolescent. Many such individuals do not even act out this tendency, but merely dream about it, as in the 'Lolita' fantasies of some older men. Regressive adolescent day-dreaming is often typical of such people. An extreme example is Thurber's Walter Mitty, whose secret life, in which he compensated for the shortcomings of his own identity, was an adolescent substitute for reality.

Another specific adolescent symptom (or defence) is seen in the adult who is always 'agin the government', perpetually criticizing the status quo merely because it is the status quo. This is not the chronically contentious individual described in Chapter 2, whose way of life is more malignant and de-structive; nor is it the adult cynicism of one who has been genuinely embittered by real adversity in his life. It is adolescent cynicism (really adolescent idealism turned sour) and is usually so diffuse as to be completely ineffective. This kind of person prefers to grumble, to be disillusioned and misanthropic, or affect a *fin de siècle* ennui, while taking full advantage of the system he criticizes; he will never overthrow the Establish-ment.

A more active form of this type of regression is shown by the individual who forces wild-cat strikes even when the majority of his work-mates try to dissuade him. This adolescent rebel-liousness tends to become chronic. The same tendency shows in some of the more extremist college students who come to prefer protesting, sitting in, and destroying property in the univer-sities, even when the authorities are willing to negotiate peace-fully.

Many adults, perhaps over-impressed or traumatized by their own puberty rites in adolescence, regress by perpetuating those rites. In our society there are many highly ritualistic initiation ceremonies for would-be members of certain fraternities. In many adult institutions there are rites, oaths, secrecies, vows, pageantries, magical punishments, and mystical mumbo-jumbo, the object of which is to impress the novitiate with the importance of being identified as belonging to the group, and of course with his own insignificance until he has been so identified. These are often adult perpetuations of adolescent puberty rites.

A final example of adult regression to adolescence is perhaps the increasingly common attitude that everything is equally valuable, and that nothing is any better or any worse than anything else. The basis of the view is of course an adolescent difficulty in evaluating different types of human achievement, in recognizing that some activities are superior to others, some sensations more valuable, some experiences more illuminating, some ideas more enlightened, and some viewpoints more civilized than others.

Although the regressions of adults to adolescence are sometimes quite difficult to distinguish from regressions to earlier stages, closer inspection usually confirms the disorder as an adolescent or recapitulated form of the earlier conflict. Adult regressions to adolescence are always much less malignant in their pathology and indeed are seldom treated clinically.

SUMMARY

We introduced this chapter with a brief historical and sociological note, describing the emergence of the adolescent group as a unique social entity.

We discussed the adolescent crisis almost entirely in terms of Erikson's concept of identity. We stressed the importance of new biological and social influences in producing a psychological identity diffusion in adolescents. We suggested that adolescence is a period in which identity is gradually re-integrated, in a turbulent and largely externalized process of recapitulation. That is, as the adolescent searches for models and clear boundaries he is simultaneously re-working all his earlier crises and identifications. The end result of this process was described as successful when the adolescent achieved a firm sense of personal, social, and vocational identity, retained a considerable degree of energetic exuberance, weaned himself away from his parents without too much psychological disruption on either side, and generally saw his way clear into the impending crisis of young adulthood as an independent individual.

Illness in adolescence was regarded as a continuance of identity diffusion which might show as getting stuck, as it were, in one of the earlier conflicts being recapitulated (i.e. regressions *from* adolescence), or alternatively as a straight-forward failure to resolve current stresses in the adolescent crisis itself. We emphasized the danger of diagnosing, or forcing a false identity upon, the adolescent who was temporarily regressing. We discussed adolescent failure to resolve current identity crises in terms of anxiety and depression, and attempted to use these as reference points in explaining adolescent anger, sense of loss, tendency to fantasize, and the tendency to continue searching for 'better' parents.

We added a note on the Hit Parade, suggesting that in pop music, with its ever-changing content but relatively constant form, we might have a continuous reflection or externalization of the psychological preoccupations of adolescents.

We recognized that the regressions of adults to adolescence were necessarily partial. Advertisements which appealed to adolescent needs were again used as an indicator of the allowance we made for 'normal' regressions. More marked regressions were discussed in terms of the adult's adoption of a false identity ('the organization man', 'one of the boys', or other over-identifications with groups, ideas, rites, etc.); or as the adult's continuing dependence on adolescent defences such as fantasy, diffuse protesting, pop values for living, and an inability to assert his own individuality against the current trends. It was recognized that adult regressions to adolescence are not usually regarded as pathological in the clinical sense, but merely as immature behaviour.

CHAPTER SIX

Young Adulthood (20–30 years)

Come live with me and be my love
And we will all the pleasures prove
MARLOWE, *The Passionate Shepherd to his Love*

UNLIKE adolescence, young adulthood is not heralded by any major physical changes. On the other hand, certain new social influences begin to exert powerful pressures; it is expected that the young adult will begin to earn a living, that he will choose a mate, and so on. Many of these social expectations could of course have been fulfilled during adolescence, but in our society such early fulfilment is fairly consistently discouraged.

The psycho-social crises of any young adult will obviously be determined to a considerable extent by the social values which happen to be preferred in his society. Social standards also vary of course from society to society, and indeed between different groups within one society at any given time. Nevertheless, in discussing the psychological crises of young adults we shall emphasize common factors more than individual differences, and basic psychological traits more than variations in social value-systems.

THE PSYCHOLOGICAL CRISES OF YOUNG ADULTHOOD

Erikson called the goal of early adulthood 'intimacy'. Intimacy takes different forms in different situations, but it invariably requires a willingness on the part of the young adult to surrender part of his hard-won identity. Although the adolescent emerges from his teens with a firm sense of personal identity (and thus is naturally 'self-centred'), as a young adult he is confronted with many situations in which too strident an assertion of his identity would be inappropriate. In such situations he requires not only the capacity to assert his identity, but in addition a certain capacity for 'self-abandonment'. These situations arise in relation to, and in fact are determined by, his particular preoccupations during this period: his work or his study for a career; his personal and social relationships, particularly with the opposite sex; and his marriage.[1] In each of these areas he should ideally achieve 'intimacy through self-abandon'.

The prime example of a situation where intimacy is impossible without self-abandon is of course sexual union, but in fact any close relationship with others requires that the young adult surrender, at least temporarily and partially, his adolescent identity. The ability to recognize, and sometimes to act on, the views of others; and the willingness to listen to, to read, to work for and work with, or even to be inspired by others, involve a similar yielding. The young adult must also allow himself now and again to be guided by his own promptings, i.e. to achieve the kind of self-abandon where he can comfortably trust himself as well as others. The surer he is of himself the greater his capacity for intimacy in sex, love, marriage, friendship, and apprenticeship; and in situations involving cooperation, competition, leadership, and inspiration.

For the young adult these relationships are all somewhat paradoxical. Although they seem to require an initial surrender, a loss of identity, and an abandonment of self, their successful achievement leads to a subsequent extension of identity, an expansion or enhancement of self, without which further

1. Parenthood and child-rearing, as distinct from marriage, are more the central preoccupations of older adults rather than young, and will therefore be discussed in subsequent chapters.

psychological development is less likely to occur. There are no technical terms for these extensions. The process seems to entail something like 'commitment' in the existential sense, or perhaps the Biblical idea of losing one's soul in order to save it. An additional paradoxical element in intimacy is that it involves not a goal to be striven for but a goal which can be reached only by relaxing into self-abandonment. These features of intimacy make it difficult to describe simply. The difficulty is increased by the fact that intimacy seems to depend on highly subjective factors, not well described in most of the psychological literature.

We will begin by considering the sex, love, and marriage relationships of young adults. Although these forms of intimacy are all closely connected, and their successful achievement requires self-abandon, the connection between them is probably not a necessary one. An adult may achieve partial intimacy only – he may develop self-abandon in one or more of these relationships, but not in the other. We shall therefore consider each relationship separately.

Sexual intimacy in young adults is particularly difficult to describe. To begin with, it does not always or necessarily occur whenever sexual behaviour such as coitus or physiological climax, has occurred. Sexual intercourse may occur without climax, and climax may occur without orgasm. Sexual intimacy, in Erikson's sense, requires orgasm as the minimum physiological condition of its occurrence. On this view any sexual behaviour, or physiological change, less than full orgasm, limits the eventual sexual intimacy possible.

Even orgasm is not a sufficient condition. Sexual intimacy requires more than behavioural and organic effects; it requires also that certain pleasurable, sensual, and emotional (i.e. highly subjective) experiences should occur concomitantly. These subjective experiences are even more difficult to describe than the physiological changes; they involve a deep satisfaction, a sense of completeness and joy, with no negative emotion such as irritability, moodiness, or sense of loss. We may for convenience refer to these experiences as 'satisfaction'. Thus, sexual intimacy necessarily involves both physiological orgasm and psychological satisfaction.

We must recognize that for sexual intimacy, so defined, psychologists still lack basic data. A moment's reflection will make it clear why this should be so. Sexuality is practised in private. In addition, those whose sexuality has led to sexual intimacy are usually the very people least likely to talk about it – except perhaps to each other. This reticence is due neither to prudishness nor shyness. In addition, the subjective elements of sexual intimacy are exceedingly difficult to communicate. The problem can be seen at its most acute when the subjective elements have to be communicated to someone whose own sexual experience may be limited. How can orgasm, with its concomitant psychological satisfactions, be described to someone who is still sexually virgin? Indeed, how can orgasm be described to someone who, although no longer virgin, has experience only of limited climax? In the first situation we are trying to describe colour to a blind man. In the second, we are trying to describe colour to a myopic, convinced that he can see normally. Thus, while those who have never experienced orgasm will never understand sexual intimacy until they have experienced it; some of those who *have* experienced orgasm often think erroneously (because they have had intercourse or limited climax) that they have experienced sexual intimacy.

Sexual intimacy, once achieved and maintained, is not only private but personal as well. It is in fact liable to be diminished, or even destroyed, by too much public analysis and detailed dissection. The self-abandon required for sexual intimacy, because it is spontaneous, involuntary, and unconscious, may wither and be made less by 'scientific' formulation and over-meticulous explanation on the part of those who have achieved it. Sexual intimacy may, in effect, be talked away.

Many intense and largely subjective human experiences are of this order. To force someone to explain precisely and in great detail just why he laughed at a joke, why he enjoyed a piece of music, why he found a painting satisfying, why he was deeply moved by a spring sunrise, or why he responded with warmth to the kind action of a friend, is effectively to kill the original experience. So, with sexual intimacy, the explanation itself requires a degree of enforced self-consciousness which can inhibit and may prevent a spontaneous recurrence of the experience. The more elaborate, detailed and comprehensive the description, the *less* accurately, truthfully and meaningfully the experience is communicated. It may be that subtle human experiences in general, and sexual intimacy in particular, are simply not amenable to scientific investigation and description by psychology. Certainly many of the most important and profound human experiences are at present described most inadequately by psychologists. The novelists and poets do much better – but then, very few psychologists are also poets.

On the whole, then, we cannot expect basic data on sexual intimacy to be obtainable by simple and direct report from those best qualified to provide it, namely, those who have experienced it. The basic data we do possess, and in some profusion, refers not to sexual intimacy, but to its purely physiological aspects or to its abnormal psychological forms. Social surveys on sexuality tend to be mere head-counting exercises, using subjects who are prepared to talk about the intimate details of their personal life; and some of these surveys use such restricted criteria for sexual experience that they end not by describing sexual intimacy but merely the variety and prevalence of inadequate, partial, or abnormal sexuality. There are of course many instruction books on sex, but many of these are mines of misinformation which do little except prove that sexual intimacy is not so easily described. We do not claim to have described it well here.

It is often assumed that sexual intimacy or 'genitality' is the sole criterion for health in young adults. As Erikson put it, 'Many people have become convinced, or have wished to convince themselves, that before God and man they have only one obligation: to have good orgasms, with a fitting "object", and that regularly.' He also pointed out that this assumption is not true. He emphasized that although a healthy young adult should be able, at least potentially,[2] to accomplish mutual orgasm and hence sexual intimacy, 'he should also be so constituted as to bear frustration in the matter without undue regression, whenever considerations of reality and loyalty call for it'. Freud himself extended the goal of adulthood beyond genitality; his answer to the question, 'What should a normal adult be able to do well?' was *Lieben und arbeiten* (to love and to work). In Freud's view sexual intimacy alone was not enough.[3] As Lowen (1966) also pointed out, mere orgasm (although central to sexual intimacy) is never in itself a means to a complete

2. In some healthy young adults the capacity for sexual intimacy may, through circumstances or even from choice, remain potential and never in fact become actualized. Not all of these individuals who remain virgin throughout their lives can be regarded as abnormal. Insofar as the psychological crisis of young adults is based on biological development, heterosexual intimacy is a natural experience and anyone who does not have the experience must remain unfulfilled in that respect. There is no direct equivalent for sexual experience, despite the Victorian belief that sexual impulses could be abolished by cold showers or diminished by vigorous exercise. Substitute activities remain substitute activities. Even sublimations can express sexuality only partially, indirectly, and with less eventual satisfaction than 'the real thing'. This still does not mean that to be a virgin is necessarily pathological. It means only that he or she has missed something important in human experience. It certainly does not preclude love, nor does it prevent psychological success in many subsequent adjustments of later life.

3. We might wish that Freud had extended his terse formulation even further, for example, to include 'play'.

life, or manhood, or womanhood: on the contrary, it is the result of these.

So far we have attempted to discuss sexual intimacy without reference to the intimacy in love. The two forms of intimacy often occur simultaneously, but they are certainly capable of being distinguished from one another also. Sex can occur without love, and love without sex.

The usual objection to any description of love (or sex, for that matter) is that it will always be rendered invalid by cultural variations; that is, what is regarded as healthy or normal in one society may be regarded as deviant and abnormal in another. Lowen, however, distinguished love from sex in a way that helps to avoid this objection: he pointed out that sex is a biological drive that is largely unconscious and non-discriminating, while love has a greater conscious component, is selective, and focuses sexual feeling on some specific individual. Sex, as a pure instinctive drive, obeys the pleasure principle. It demands instant and complete gratification without thought of circumstances or consequences. Anyone will do. Love involves conscious factors as well, because selectivity and discrimination necessarily involve choice, and the preference for one person over others. It often entails voluntary and temporary self-restraint, and the need to consider reality factors which are accepted for the sake of greater pleasure in the long run.

Thus, individual differences and cultural variations in intimacy decrease when the biological and unconscious aspects predominate (when there is more sex than love), but increase when psychological and more conscious aspects predominate (when there is more love than sex). This means that orgasm and purely sensual satisfactions are much less variable cross-culturally than specific learned techniques of love-making, or social preferences for particular kinds of people as being especially 'love-worthy'.

The development of love from sex depends to some extent on certain physiological factors. Affectionate or loving behaviour is shown only amongst animals who are physically intimate, and whose mating involves actual contact, penetration, and the internal deposit of sperm cells in the female. Thus love may develop only where the physical contact of blood-rich erotogenic body zones is an essential part of mating. It has been suggested that the evolutionary change in coital position from the rear approach to the frontal may have enhanced the human tendency to experience love in the sexual act. The frontal position involves more contact of the sensitive areas of the body, and an increase of personal awareness and perception of the other person's feelings and reactions.

We should recognize, too, that some of the differences between males and females in their love relationships, and indeed in their basic attitudes to sex, may have a biological basis. Presumably the 'body images' of males and females are influenced by the fact that the genital organs are respectively outside and inside the body, and that the one penetrates and ejaculates while the other is penetrated and receives. Differences in attitude may arise also from the fact that sexual arousal is both faster and less stable in men as compared with women.

There is a close connection between intimacy in sex and intimacy in love. Erikson suggests that sexual gratification resolves many of the psychological tensions inherent in ordinary living and which otherwise would prevent love relationships from developing. 'The experience of the climactic mutuality of orgasm provides a supreme example of the mutual regulation of complicated patterns, and in some way appeases the potential rages caused by the daily evidence of the oppositeness of male and female, of fact and fancy, of love and hate, of work and play.'[4] Erikson goes on to suggest that 'satisfactory sex re-

4. These basic oppositional tendencies have been dramatically portrayed by D. H. Lawrence and other novelists.

lations makes sex less obsessive, overcompensation less necessary, and sadistic control superfluous.'

Lowen relates sex to love by suggesting that love increases the tension of sexual attraction by creating a psychic distance between the lovers. The distance is created because each individual has a heightened consciousness of the loved person. It is this which separates the partners, because it emphasizes their individuality. Certainly a loved person is always regarded as unique and irreplaceable. Thus, the greater the love, the greater the distance is felt to be. Sex has the effect of eliminating distance, discharging tension, and causing pleasure. As Freud suggested, pleasure varies with the amount of initial tension, so that the more love, the greater the tension, and the greater the pleasure from sexual union.

To suggest that love is more selective and involves a higher degree of consciousness than sex, is not to say that the two are always clearly distinguishable. Both sex and love tend to be spontaneous and unreasoning, and to entail the total absorption of each partner in the other. In addition, love is determined to *some* extent by unconscious factors. When people in love are asked why they love each other, they often give reasons that appear trivial or totally irrelevant to the outside observer. For example, one woman, obviously deeply devoted to her man, stated seriously that she found him irresistible because of the way his hair grew around his ears. Other reasons given for loving are more understandable in that they are related to sexual satisfaction: 'Whenever he comes near me my heart seems to turn over, and I seem to melt inside.' Although this thrilling sensation of warm, trusting, breathless vulnerability is more typical of the earlier stages of the love relationship, it is often still discernible in the intimacy of some couples after many years of domesticity. The helplessness is often more apparent than real; it involves not a loss of individuality but an extension or enhancement of it. The partners experience a shared unity. If sex is predominantly physical, and love predominantly psychological, it may be that what we describe as 'passion' represents the psycho-physical overlap between sex and love when we experience these simultaneously.

As for the more conscious elements of love, it is still a mystery why two people should fall in love only with each other, and not with other people equally available at the time. It may be true, as the cynics tell us, that love is merely an illusory exaggeration of the difference between one woman (or man) and another. But even so, we still cannot explain why this illusion should occur at all, or why one person should be favoured over all others. Love is probably determined not only by the unconscious factors mentioned above but also by external and environmental factors such as learning, imitation, social example, and culturally preferred stereotypes of allegedly 'ideal' partners (Hollywood has even specified the ideal vital statistics). This of course is not to say, with Larochefoucauld, that 'nobody would ever fall in love if they had never read about it', but merely to recognize that love is influenced by external as well as internal factors. Whether it is determined more by the one than the other, there are more individual differences in love relationships than in sex relationships. Personal needs, conscious attitudes, and social norms regarding love may all conflict with one another, and what each couple finally does will represent, as it were, the 'resultant' of these opposing forces. In practice, most couples will behave towards each other, with mutual consent, in ways which enhance their pleasure and satisfaction, and further develop the degree of intimacy they have already achieved.

If there is such a thing as equality, as distinct from complementariness of the sexes, it probably occurs in its most meaningful form in sex and love relationships. Before sexual intimacy can arise each partner must recognize the individuality of the other; that is, the basic differences are fully accepted, and each regards the other as a person, not merely as an object or a means to their own gratification. Intimacy and loving requires more; as well as desire there must be tenderness. As Lowen puts it: 'the man respects the woman as a woman, and the woman respects the man as a man'.[5]

In particular, neither is trying to 'prove' anything; there is nothing to prove. If intimacy is to develop, mutuality in all aspects of the relationship is essential. Mutuality does not produce blandness or placidity in the relationship; on the contrary, it is quite compatible with vigour and passion. Yet neither partner need *strive* to be dominant or submissive, to use sex as a means of proclaiming masculinity or femininity, to publicize his or her own attractiveness, or otherwise to trade on the partner's love. Each partner wants to be wanted, not to be used or taken by the other; each wants to give to the other; so that the relationship is *both* self-centred *and* other-centred at the same time. Thus, for the healthy young adult, sex–love intimacy derives, to a very considerable extent, from 'doing what comes naturally'. It will be a spontaneous achievement which will be taken for granted unless something goes wrong with it. And it will tend to be diminished if self-centredness (or other-centredness) becomes too predominant.

So far we have said nothing about intimacy in marriage. Marital intimacy is different from either sexual or love intimacies, in that it is based essentially on domesticity, i.e. the relatively permanent sharing of daily chores, material comforts, and practical household affairs generally. Although domestic matters are usually settled by mutual consent of the partners, this need not involve in any way their feelings of sex or love. On the whole, marital intimacy is much more practical than emotional. Like marriage itself, it nearly always involves

5. Lacking such respect, intimacy may degenerate into sado-masochistic interaction, as shown by the principal characters in Albee's *Who's Afraid of Virginia Woolf?*

deliberate intention, and may even be arranged in terms of businesslike contracts between the partners. It often involves property and ownership, and (unlike sexual and love relationships) may become a social and public matter, involving registration, the sanctions of various official or socially approved institutions, and signing documents which become part of public records.

Society may make few formal stipulations for those who intend to marry, but it certainly determines by law and statute the conditions under which the partnership is to be maintained, and the conditions of its dissolution should this be desired by the marriage partners. These conditions, and of course the form of marriage itself, vary from society to society. In our culture there is a strong assumption that marriages should be monogamous and indissoluble, although as we all know many exceptions are allowed. Much of the social uproar that attends any new legislation about marriage and divorce arises because marital intimacy, involving largely practical bargains and arrangements, is not at all clearly distinguished from sexual and love intimacy, which involves perhaps the most profound, powerful, and important feelings of which human beings are capable.

The young adult who is unmarried cannot of course be regarded as psychologically abnormal. In this he is similar to the young adult who is virgin, or who has not fallen in love. The probability of being single decreases statistically with age as follows (these figures for Britain represent chances in 100 of being single):[6]

Age	Male	Female
20	90	65
25	40	20
30	20	12
40	12	9
50	9	1

6. Davies, 1966.

In addition, the mean age of men at marriage in England and Wales in the 1960s was $25\frac{1}{2}$ years; for women it was 23 years. About 80 per cent of husbands are older than their wives, the mean age difference being about $2\frac{1}{2}$ years when the husband marries between 25 and 35 years, and about 1 year when he marries younger than 25 years.[7] Thus, being single is statistically a normal state for young adults, but becomes more unusual as they grow older. Even the young adult who *remains* single is not necessarily abnormal, any more than the one who *remains* virgin, or who *never* falls in love; but he may be more prone to develop certain kinds of psycho-social difficulties in later life. Marital intimacy, although perhaps less crucial for individual psychological health than the intimacy of sex and love, nevertheless facilitates healthy development in our society in important ways.

We have distinguished marital intimacy from intimacy in sexual and love relationships. In most research studies these different forms of intimacy are inextricably intertwined. Nevertheless, some of the findings of such studies do illuminate to some extent the psychological features we have been discussing – those which seem to determine the mutual attraction of human beings to one another, and the changes in their developing intimacy.

Early studies of the marital relationship attempted measure the suitability of individuals for marriage, and the likelihood of their achieving a happy marriage. Two researchers have investigated the premarital experiences and the subsequent marital happiness of hundreds of American couples. They found that the characteristics which best predicted happiness for the people surveyed had their origin in early childhood – the happiness of their parents' marriage, their fondness for their parents and their siblings, and the attractiveness of the opposite-sexed parent. In particular, higher scores for marital

7. Glick and Landau, 1950.

happiness were made by those who remembered their own childhood as happy. These studies emphasized that no other item of information was more significant: 'it far outweighs such items as adequacy of sex instruction, religious education, adolescent "petting" or even premarital intercourse'. Home discipline was also a good predictor for both men and women. Firm, but not harsh, discipline was most favourable for later marital happiness; irregular, unpredictable discipline the least.

More recent, and perhaps more sophisticated, studies have highlighted the fact that mutual attraction and marital relationships are exceedingly complex. Individuals may be attracted to each other either because their psychological needs are similar or because they are complementary. One study found that subjects tended to choose mates and friends because their needs were similar, not because they were complementary. An interesting sex difference appeared in this study: men selecting mates and female friends tended to look for the same things in both, while women preferred a mate and male friends who were different. It seems clear that the factors involved in choosing a mate, and in 'getting on' with that mate once chosen may be different. The matter is complicated also by the fact that a couple may have different opinions in their marriage relationship without being aware of them; assumed agreement tends to exceed actual agreement between partners, and marital satisfaction is often positively associated with assumed agreement. It has been suggested also that the marriage relationship has unique characteristics, which involve the needs of the partners in ways which are quite idiosyncratic; the individual partners may have quite different needs in their other social relationships.

Several studies have suggested that there is a strong tendency for husbands and wives to be similar, or homogamous, in age, origin, religion, social class, education, and intelligence.

They tend also to have lived close together. New marriages tend to be 'matrilocal' – the new family more often lives with or near the wife's parents, than with or near the husband's; and more visits tend to be made to the wife's parents. Attachment to the mother often persists after marriage in the wife but not in the husband, and the wife's mother tends to become more involved as 'granny' to the new family. There is therefore some evidence to support the old adage, 'A son is a son till he takes a wife, but a daughter's a daughter all her life'.

New families normally form part of a network of kin and friends. Friendships formed by each partner before marriage may not survive the marriage as new friendships are formed by the young couple. These new friendships are often with other couples in similar circumstances, and who may also be supported more or less extensively by their kin. When the ties of kinship are weak the young couple are more likely to develop new patterns of living.

In discussing these studies, and their rather oblique relationship to marital intimacy, we have begun to overlap with *social* intimacy – relationships with friends, neighbours, workmates, and others not involved in specific sexual, love, marital or kin relationships. Social intimacy, and the conditions under which it occurs, has been extensively studied by social psychologists. Findings here have been disappointingly inconclusive and vague. We still do not know why people come together socially. The similarity or complementarity of people's needs have been found to determine mutual attraction only under certain conditions, and not consistently even then. The basic difficulties are that similarity and complementarity are not easy to specify or measure; that people may act on similarity in some situations and complementarity in others; and that the individual's perception of similarity and complementarity may be different from the objective state of affairs. There are probably far too many variables and individual differences for clear-cut answers to be expected in this area. We are left therefore with only general descriptions of social intimacy, and perhaps a few tentative suggestions about its nature and the conditions in which it occurs.

The establishment of social relationships generally does seem to be significantly affected by such factors as social class, and by sex and age. Social intimacy, however, depends not only on obvious demographic variables but also on personality. The 'warmth' or 'coldness' of an individual, usually assessed from his manner and behaviour, may be crucial in determining friendships. One researcher manipulated warmth and coldness in an experimental situation and found, not surprisingly, that subjects were much more eager to interact with warm people and were much more formal with colder personalities.

There have been many sociometric studies of friendships in which individuals are asked to say which person in a given group they would like to be with in a given situation. Generally speaking *A* likes *B*, not because *B* is intrinsically 'nice' (*C* and *D* may *not* like *B*) but because of something in the relationship between the two people concerned – compatibility. Liking can be determined by the extent to which any person satisfies the needs of the other and does not himself make demands. Reciprocity also appears as *A*'s tendency to like *B*, if he knows that *B* likes him. It has been suggested, too, that friendships and partnerships develop because some enterprises cannot be carried out alone and a partner is chosen to help out. Such partnerships are not formed initially because of personal or social needs, although these may develop, but as a means of attaining a given goal. Thus one basis for friendship is simply a common aim. People within a given group tend to be liked more if they conform to its principles, express its ideals, and contribute to its activities.

All social relationships, it has been suggested, are like economic bargains, or an exchange of gifts, so that neither partner will stay in a relationship that is insufficiently rewarding. We need not assume, however, that rewards must be equal or similar in kind for both partners.

Because it is always difficult to say which aspect of an individual's personality will be responsive to particular aspects of the personality of others, prediction in personal relationships is exceedingly complex and unreliable. Prediction may be improved slightly by knowing the personalities of all the people concerned. Some features which can give guidance are dominance–submission, intelligence, and introversion–extraversion. The prediction of detailed sequences of social behaviour is extremely difficult because there is always a continuous mutual modification and feedback, both positive and negative, in any continuing relationship.

Social intimacy does seem to develop with time and repeated social contact, so that the longer two people interact the more they will tell each other about themselves. A study of pairs of college room-mates found that self-disclosure increased during the first nine weeks, then levelled off in all pairs; and that intimate disclosure was increased when the two people were isolated and confidences were mutual. This study does not explain, however, why different pairs reached different levels of intimacy.

In theory, therefore, one would expect that two people who like each other would continue to interact until they became inseparable. This does happen, but not always. Progressive interaction probably ceases when social intimacy has increased to the point where the individuals are unable to synchronize the increasingly complex feelings and social techniques required to maintain their relationship. It seems that in social intimacy there is a point of diminishing returns.

We should dwell for a moment on this point, for we are often encouraged to believe that 'togetherness' is such a good thing that we can never have too much of it. Certainly we are gregarious animals, but our social intimacy varies with our sensitivity to others. Very few of us can feel as warmly towards mankind as we do towards people we know well; in fact, the larger the society the cooler our regard. We tend to be loving with our sex-mates and spouses, affectionate with our relatives, amicable with our friends, polite to our neighbours, formal towards our acquaintances, indifferent towards strangers, and wary of foreigners.

Even if we confine ourselves to intimacy with those to whom we feel close, it is a matter of common observation that we can sometimes feel too close. Lovers have quarrels, good friends fall out, relatives sometimes feel they are seeing too much of one another, and so on. Intimacy in any human relationship can increase to a point where it begins to encroach on and become blocked by the other needs and the alternative intimacies of the people concerned. Schopenhauer once likened men to hedgehogs, forced to huddle together for warmth, yet repelled by each other's prickles when sufficiently warmed. Psychologists studying social intimacy might do well to consider Schopenhauer's model when setting up their experiments.

The final form of intimacy, the kind involved in work relationships, has already been touched on in the above discussion. Intimacy between workmates and colleagues becomes predominant only in matters pertaining to earning a living, or establishing a career. In our society we are perhaps encouraged too actively to compete with one another; but the young adult who achieves intimacy in his work relationships will be able to refrain from competing all the time – he will cooperate as well as compete, share both work and credit, and accept the need to be a learner, a follower, or an apprentice, before becoming a professor, a leader, or a master.

The young adult is therefore confronted with a formidable psychological task. He must achieve intimacy with sex, love, and marriage partners, with family, friends, and neighbours, and with workmates and playmates. He must also integrate these relationships in a way which allows him to move smoothly into the next phase of his development. As Erikson has described it, intimacy should involve 'mutuality of orgasm, with a loved person, of the opposite sex, with whom one is able and willing to share mutual trust and respect, and with whom one is able and willing to regulate the cycles of work, procreation, and recreation, so as to secure to offspring too a satisfactory development'.

It might seem unrealistic to expect young adults to be successful in all these relationships. We should remember however that to achieve self-abandon is to enrich one's personality; the greater the intimacy the greater the enrichment, and the greater the capacity for further intimacy. On the other hand, only exceptional young adults achieve a high degree of intimacy in all the areas distinguished above. More ordinary individuals will find that some intimacies can be developed only at the expense of others.

ILLNESS IN YOUNG ADULTHOOD

Our general point of view in this section is that young adults who fail to achieve intimacy may do so in the following ways: they may not achieve intimacy at all; they may achieve only a partial intimacy; or they may become over-preoccupied with one form of intimacy at the expense of other forms. All failures here entail an exaggerated sense of self, and a lack of capacity for self-abandonment. We shall attempt to apply these principles to each of the intimacy-relationships (sex, love, marriage, etc.) outlined in the preceding section.[8]

8. In doing so we are handicapped to some extent by two factors. First, when illnesses in young adults are considered as failures to resolve current crises (and not as regressions to earlier stages) we cannot use agreed or well-defined technical terms to describe them;

Sexual intimacy, when successful, entails a sexual act that is unitary. Failure in sexual intimacy may occur when the sexual act is not unitary but becomes arrested (or is exaggerated) in one of its aspects. If we arbitrarily and somewhat artificially subdivide the unitary sexual act into the phases 'fore-pleasure', 'orgasm', and 'after-glow', we may classify the various failures of sexual intimacy in terms of the young adult's over-concern with one phase at the expense of the others, i.e. his inability to abandon himself to the full sexual act.

An over-concern with fore-play leads not to sexuality but merely to sensuality. That is, the young adult may come to enjoy sensory titillation more than sex, and thus may never experience more than the sensual preliminaries of the sexual act. Fore-play will then have become an end in itself. Even when it produces sexual arousal it will tend to result merely in masturbation. Lowen has pointed out that the preoccupation with fore-pleasure and sensuality is in fact often associated with the basic inability to experience strong sexual feelings. A young adult may therefore engage in sex not because he is aroused but in order to become aroused. Limited by the lack of feeling or aliveness in his body, he cannot achieve even a minimum satisfaction of climax unless he resorts to bizarre techniques – lurid fantasies, 'kinky' behaviour, etc. Such techniques tend to become progressively less effective, so that he resorts to increasingly bizarre behaviour to achieve variety and to re-awaken his senses. He may even become addicted to sexual orgies, in which he attempts to produce new sexual excitements by means of technical gadgetry, anonymous promiscuity, exotic surroundings, or drink. These crude exercises in sensuality

---

there are no such terms. Secondly, our classification of illness in young adults will inevitably be influenced by social as well as psychological factors. Thus, the psychological disorders described here may not be regarded universally as psychological disorders.

soon lose their effect, however, and cannot stave off eventual boredom, dissatisfaction and depression.

Such young adults often attempt to conceal their emotional limitations, and their need for bizarre stimulation, by professing an exceptional lack of sexual inhibition. They often advocate sex without love. They are knowledgeable about sexual techniques and behavioural variations, and talk a great deal about the need to be 'objective' and 'scientific'. What they suffer from, however, is 'sex in the head'. They are not sexual aficionados, devoted to physical interaction with the opposite sex; they are merely sexual sophisticates, devoted to erotica and their own sensations. For them, sex is never a way of expressing feeling for the partner, but merely a 'performance' in which they are always more concerned with their own skill and artistry. In fact, both their sexual virtuosity and their compulsive need to impress the partner both derive essentially from their own well-founded fear of sexual failure. (Extreme cases may show impotence and frigidity.) All these preoccupations make the young adult self-conscious, inhibit his spontaneity, reduce his capacity for self-abandon, curtail the full sexual act, and inevitably prevent the occurrence of sexual intimacy.

Some sexologists have proclaimed an art of sex, in which the ideal is that each partner consciously and deliberately brings the other to climax. Some have even described the relationships as one of mutual 'serving'. We have agreed that part of sexuality consists of knowledgeable physical manipulation and being a good lover; but we have suggested also that sexuality cannot be regarded as nothing but such manipulation. A good lover is not the same as an adult sexual partner. Our point has been that an over-preoccupation with esoteric techniques may lead the young adult to regard fore-pleasure not as a means of sexual intimacy, but as an end in itself.[9]

9. Lowen went further: he suggested that over-preoccupation with satisfying the partner led inevitably to a decrease in overall sexual

It is quite possible that men and women differ in their attitude to technical sexual prowess. Men seem to regard their sexual capacity as central to their self-respect, perhaps because the man's failure in the sexual act usually means the failure of both partners. In contrast, the woman's pride in herself seems to derive not only from her sexual ability, but also from other functions, for instance, her role as a wife and mother. Thus, a wife's sexual infidelity seems to be intolerable to her husband because it threatens his virility; while the husband's infidelity may be tolerable to his wife so long as she retains his affection and support in her marriage and family. Certainly society tends to regard the cuckolded husband as an object of ridicule, but the wife left for another woman as an object of pity and sympathy.

To suggest sexual prowess may have a different psychological significance for men and for women is not to imply a double standard of sexual morality. As we have already suggested, the sexual relationship is essentially one of complementariness and, in that sense at least, of equality. In any case, double standards of sexual morality are now being changed rapidly, partly by laws and statutes, but also by the availability and use of modern contraceptive techniques. The effects of these changes, however, although profound and far-reaching, are probably still too recent for their full impact on current social attitudes to be felt.

Physiologically, the young adult who is over-concerned with fore-play will not achieve orgasm, but only climax as dis-

---

satisfaction. He considered that over-identification with the partner's feelings was not even genuinely heterosexual; it denied the oppositeness and hence complementariness of two individuals who should be mature and competent enough to take care of their own needs. If one sexual partner had to become the servant of the other, spontaneity and mutuality were lost. In extreme cases the whole sexual relationship could become a dishonest sensual game in which one served the other, who in turn tried to give satisfaction by pretending to have orgasms.

tinguished earlier. Although, as Lowen suggested, he may attempt to stimulate orgasm, his behaviour in sexual encounters really expresses his fear of full sexual abandon, and indeed may be understood as a kind of defence against it. 'Sighs, cries, moans, and groans tell little except that something is happening and may betray suffering rather than indicate pleasure' (Lowen, 1966).

In fact, on Lowen's criteria, Kinsey's (1948) list of six so-called orgastic responses may be regarded as behavioural concomitants not of success but of failure in sexual intimacy.[10] Kinsey listed:

1. Reaction limited to genitals with little or no bodily reaction. No significant feeling in climax. One-fifth of all Kinsey's male subjects regularly experienced this reaction.

2. Tensing or twitching in particular parts of the body, which is otherwise rigid. A few spasms with no emotional after-effects. This reaction occurred in 45 per cent of the males studied.

3. 'Legs often become rigid with muscles knotted and toes pointed, muscles of abdomen contracted and hard – shoulders and neck stiff and often bent forward, breath held or gasping, eyes staring or tightly closed, hands grasping, mouth distorted ... whole body or parts of it spasmodically twitching'. There were also groans, sobbing, or violent crying. No marked emotional after-effects. One-sixth of males. As Lowen suggested, this behavioural evidence suggests torture, rather than ecstasy.

4. Laughter, talking, sadistic or masochistic feelings, frenzied movement. Lowen commented that these reactions, which occurred in 5 per cent of subjects, were probably hysterical.

10. Kinsey was of course studying sexuality in terms of mechanical, physiological response. He stated explicitly that 'all cases of ejaculation have been taken as evidence of orgasm'.

5. As for (4) but 'culminating in extreme trembling, collapse, loss of colour and sometimes fainting of subject'. This to Lowen seemed hardly distinguishable from a panic reaction.

6. Pain and fear, sometimes with recoil from partner as climax approaches.

We turn now from failures to achieve sexual intimacy because of over-concern with fore-pleasure, to those due to over-concern with orgasm, and after-glow.

Those young adults who over-emphasize orgasm correspond roughly to Freud's *libidinal types*[11] (see Appendix, Table I). The libidinal type does achieve orgasm and not merely climax, but his sexual intimacy is nevertheless limited. His own orgasm is his sole aim. If he behaves tenderly towards his sexual partner he does so only as a means of enhancing the partner's response and thus increasing his own erotic pleasure. He himself remains self-centred, absorbed only in the gratification of his own instincts. The partners of such an individual are usually captivated at first by his libidinality, and do respond with genuine feeling to his apparent wish for intimacy. Eventually, however, they realize that they have been used by a partner who is preoccupied essentially with his own sensations, and is incapable of sustained intimacy. This is the heart-breaker, the virile and compulsively lusty Casanova or Don Juan type of young adult.

The third type of failure in sexual intimacy is represented by the young adult who becomes too preoccupied with those feelings which are usually the consequence of satisfactory intercourse, namely, the 'after-glow' experience. This type of adult, however, does not achieve these feelings by means of sex; on the contrary, he specifically avoids both the sensuality of fore-play and libidinality of orgasm. He usually denies the physical

11. Although Freud differentiated libidinal types into 'compulsive', 'erotic' and 'narcissistic' sub-groups, we shall consider them together and talk of 'the libidinal type'.

senses, and may show a marked distaste for the body and bodily contact. Thus the only sexual satisfaction open to him is imaginal, as in romantic daydreams and fantasies. In a sense, this type of young adult is the converse of the sexual sophisticate. Whereas the sexual sophisticate wants sex without love, this individual wants love without sex. He becomes a so-called 'platonic lover'.

Such a young adult will forever attempt to increase sexual tension by increasing the distance between himself and his partner; but he never discharges the tension in sexual union. He dreams of 'love' of an ineffable, imaginal, and spiritual sort; he transmutes himself and his partner into soul-mates, or some other mental abstraction which corresponds to no physical reality. Although he insists on creating a physical distance between himself and his partner, he does not do so in order to maximize sexual promise, but to minimize any possibility of its eventual fulfilment. This creation of distance may take positive or negative forms. The positive form consists of an artificial idealization of the partner ('You're far too good for me'). The negative form is an artificial self-denigration ('I'll never be good enough for you'). The platonic relationship becomes neurotic therefore when the separation is artificial, and the restriction on full sexuality is unnecessary, i.e. when there is nothing to stop the partners from expressing themselves in any way they want. Descriptions of this kind of 'love' (which often has psychological undertones reminiscent of the Oedipal situation described in Chapter 3) abound in poetry and literature. Most of our classic love stories are tragedies in which love is thwarted, unrequited, or unconsummated, and the lovers themselves are kept apart for all eternity.

So far we have seen how young adults may fail to achieve sexual intimacy because they have become over-preoccupied with its sensual, libidinal, or imaginal aspects. Sexual intimacy may also be impaired because it conflicts with other forms of intimacy in young adulthood. It may conflict even with love.

Some young adults deliberately choose to refrain from expressing their sexual feelings towards someone they love, because to do so would cause some kind of interpersonal catastrophe. They may decide, consciously and with full intent, that to gratify their need for sexual intimacy with the loved person would simply not be worth the damage it would cause. It might, for example, wreak havoc on certain personal values, such as friendship, loyalty, mutual consideration, tenderness, and of course love for the person (or other persons) concerned.

Similarly, both sex and love intimacies may be achieved at too high a cost, i.e. at the expense of other intimacies. Antony and Cleopatra, for example, may be regarded as, literally, 'love-sick'. That is, they insisted on having too much of one good thing, at the expense of every other good thing available to them. Their absorption in each other was so exclusive of every other form of intimacy that they ignored the entire world, counted it well lost, and ended disastrously in consequence. More normal forms of the same tendency are often seen in intense young couples who, because they are preoccupied with their own mutual intimacy, behave even in social groups as though they were alone.

Up to this point we have attempted to discuss disorders of sex and love solely in terms of the intimacy/self-absorption crisis of young adults. There are of course many other specific sexual disorders which are not explicable entirely in terms of intimacy, but require reference also to earlier stages of development – they involve regressive as well as genital sexuality.

Some young adults engage in different sexual relationships with different partners. For instance, a young man may 'play games' with his wife, be the 'great lover' with his mistress and dream perpetually of the incredibly perfect girl he nearly married. Multiple sexual relationships as such are probably not abnormal in the exploratory phases of early adulthood, but if they become too numerous, or if they continue too long, the individual may eventually find himself 'fragmented' and unable to achieve intimacy in any of his sexual relationships. He may come to believe that 'you should never sleep with the girl you love, or love the girl you sleep with'; he may become impotent with his wife, and capable only with prostitutes; and so on. Many 'infidelities' are probably due to this kind of disintegrated failure to achieve sexual intimacy.

Sexual relationships are not always formed with an actual person of the opposite sex. Sometimes sexuality is displaced on to some representation of, or substitute for, the opposite sex, which is then used as a stimulus for fantasies. This kind of young adult, almost always male, is sexually aroused only by pictures, statues or verbal descriptions of females and sexual behaviour. The enormous sales of pornographic books, blue films, girlie magazines and so on suggest that such individuals are very common in our society. In terms of intimacy, these sexual displacements may be considered abnormal when they are preferred to actual sexual encounters. Such young adults never get over their preference for pin-ups to people, and fantasies to real personal relationships. They continue to play with paper dolls, and thus avoid actual heterosexual interaction, and progressively reduce their chance of ever achieving intimacy. For these young adults the preferred sexual outlet is usually masturbation.

Sometimes the sexual instinct becomes focused on some part of the opposite sex, such as hair or clothing, which is then responded to as if it were the female. These sexual fetishes occur in infinite variety and often occur with other sexual deviations such as homosexuality or transvestism. Illness here usually involves earlier conflicts as well as those of young adulthood. Sexuality may be expressed in ways that are even less directly related to genitality. The voyeur or Peeping Tom, for example, prefers to look rather than to do; his counterpart, the exhibitionist, prefers to be looked at.

Another broad category of disorder includes people whose preferred partner is not of the opposite sex but of the same sex (see also Chapter 3). Homosexuality is regarded by most clinicians as a sexual abnormality. This attitude has not been altered significantly by recent changes in the laws pertaining to homosexuality. In terms of sexual intimacy there is an essential sterility in homosexual relationships. Sexual mutuality is necessarily precluded. Biological consequences are also impossible. Heterosexual couples may not produce offspring; but homosexual couples cannot. Most of us accept the basic premise that man is essentially a reproductive animal, so that anyone whose sexual behaviour is directed away from the opposite sex tends to be considered abnormal.

People who have sexual relationships with inappropriate age groups (children, old people), with dead bodies, or with inappropriate species (animals), nearly always have severe illnesses, usually of a psychotic sort. Indeed, their behaviour is seldom genuinely sexual. Sex is often used to express something other than sex. Rape, for example, is much more aggressive than sexual. Readers who require more detailed discussions of these deviations should consult the many textbooks on the subject.

When the young adult has such problems with sex (and love) he is likely to have problems also with most other forms of intimacy. For example, marital intimacy is likely to be unsatisfactory. Marriage, like any other agreement to live together, may provide the conditions for self-abandonment; but in itself it can never *guarantee* that marital intimacy will develop satisfactorily. In fact, when two people lack the more personal forms of intimacy, the closeness involved in marital arrangements may actually worsen their problems. The end result is of course divorce. Divorce in itself cannot be taken as evidence of a couple's inability to achieve marital intimacy, but only of their inability to achieve it with each other; repeated divorces, however, do suggest a more general problem.

In our society, failures in marital intimacy are now statistically predictable. According to the Registrar General (1964), divorce rates reach a peak after about 3 years of marriage and remain high until 11 years after. Thus rates are high between 25 and 35 years, decline in the late 30s and decline further in the 40s and 50s. They are relatively high for all durations of marriage when the wife's age was under 20 at marriage, when the marriage was childless, or when only one child was born. Divorce rates do not differ greatly between occupations of social classes. In general, about 25 per cent of all marriages may be expected to end in divorce; about half of all divorcees have been married less than 10 years; and more than two-thirds of all divorcees remarry.

Similarly, social intimacy may fail to develop in a wide variety of relationships (with relatives, friends, workmates, playmates, etc.). Again, any one form of such intimacy may conflict with any other form; and any one form of intimacy may in itself become under-emphasized or over-emphasized. A person might, for example, go to great lengths to avoid any contact with his relatives, because of earlier traumatic or disenchanting episodes in his family life. Alternatively he might give first priority to the needs of relatives because he is convinced that in all circumstances 'blood is thicker than water'.[12] Similarly, he might avoid friendship and develop into a 'loner', becoming

12. In view of the genetic, environmental, and unconscious factors involved in growing up within a family the strength of blood ties is hardly surprising. The blood ties of young adults however, should sometimes yield to other forms of intimacy. Conflict often arises when relatives assume, merely because they are relatives, that they have a right to behave towards young adults in ways that are grossly dis-

gradually more misanthropic as he repels more and more people by his aloofness. Alternatively, he might sacrifice all other forms of intimacy to those involved in friendship. Finally, intimacies in work and play relationships may conflict with each other, or become exaggerated in relation to other intimacies. A husband, for example, may sacrifice his wife and family for the sake of his work, or sacrifice both family and work for the sake of drinking companions at the golf club, and so on.

To list all the ways in which a young adult may fail to develop intimacy would be a formidable task.[13] I hope that a sufficient number of examples have been given to enable the reader to compile such a list for himself if he wishes.

REGRESSIONS TO YOUNG ADULTHOOD

There is a certain awkwardness in talking of regressions to young adulthood. We tend to assume that once adulthood (even young adulthood) is reached, the individual is by definition mature. To speak of anyone regressing to maturity seems a contradiction in terms. This derives however, from a habit of mind. As we pointed out in the preface, maturity means behaving according to our age, whatever our age may be, and is not therefore a characteristic of any one age group. The contrary habit of mind is perhaps encouraged by the fact that clinical terminology for regressive illnesses all refers to pre-adult age levels. Nevertheless, the fact that we have no specific labels for an illness does not mean that the illness does not exist.

---

courteous, and in extreme cases may be outrageously antisocial. The classic mother-in-law who arrives unannounced for an extended stay at her married daughter's house, and then proceeds to take over, criticizing the daughter's household arrangements, her family, and of course her husband ('I always said he was no good, my dear'), is a joke only in cartoons, not in real life.

13. Among the many other forms of psychological failure not dis-

Many older people do continue to behave like young adults, and in that sense may be said to be regressing to young adulthood. Having made the point, however, we do recognize also that many regressions to young adulthood are well tolerated socially, and might not be considered pathological in the strict sense by all clinicians.

Normal regression to young adulthood may be estimated by our responsiveness to advertisements which focus on the main psychological preoccupations of young adults, or which associate these with various products. Although advertisements have used all the forms of intimacy already discussed, the one with most universal appeal is of course sex. This is more than the glamour appeal of advertisements discussed in Chapter 3; it involves not merely the wish to be considered attractive to the opposite sex, but the wish to achieve the adult end-result of that attractiveness, namely sexual intimacy.

Sometimes the appeal is direct, in the form of technical information or instruction regarding the achievement of maximum sensual sensation and sexual potency. Many women's magazines feature articles on how to 'hold' a man, once he has been attracted; that is, how to achieve and maintain intimacy in sex and love relationships. Advertisements offer many aids to relaxing and 'letting yourself go' in all kinds of social, work, and play situations, implying that self-abandon and mutuality are easily purchased, and had better be enjoyed instantly because 'it's later than you think'.

Advertisements whose appeal is indirect simply juxtapose the commercial product and the predominant interests of young

cussed in this section are the false roles adopted by some young adults. These all involve self-absorption in one form or another. Nevertheless, the tendency to adopt false roles is not always pathological in early adulthood; it becomes so when it persists into later adulthood. False roles are therefore discussed as regressions in the following section.

adults. Here again the great attention-getter is sex. Nubile young women in indecorous poses will always gain the public's attention, no matter what the product. One current television commercial features the slow, sexy advance of a sultry, dark-haired beauty whose suggestive undulations almost (but not quite) make the viewer forget that she is offering only a jar of coffee. So long as man continues to be a reproductive species, sex in advertising, especially in the form of a young siren dressed in clothes which are two sizes too small for her, will never go out of fashion.

Intimacy, in all its forms, represents a value which we maintain to the end of our lives. To this extent therefore it cannot be abnormal to continue to be preoccupied with it. Abnormality begins when the form of intimacy that is preferred in later life is one which is predominant and natural in young adults: that is, when the intimacy is inappropriate to the individual's age. It is perhaps natural for young adults to be preoccupied with playing the field sexually, and to want to enjoy multiple love affairs. (Whether they do so in fact will of course depend on their own standards and preferences.) A normal adult of forty-five or fifty, however, although he may be libidinally aroused just as easily will not be so preoccupied with his impulse, and indeed may be slightly amused by it in the context of *his* natural interests (see Chapter 7). Other things equal, he is not at all so liable to act on his impulse. But the older adult who does tends to degenerate into the rather pathetic ageing playboy, still priding himself on being a devil with the women, and a real hell-raising man-about-town.

In general, the tireless search for sensual and social pleasure, the incessant preoccupation with heterosexual relationships, the indefatigable pursuit of the means of getting on in a career (all of which are part and parcel of being a young adult) become regressive when they persist too long, in their crude form, or fail to be blended with other values, in older adults.

So far we have been discussing the regression of older adults to intimacy in its positive forms. Older adults may regress also to the negative forms of intimacy, to the self-absorption or isolation (see Appendix, Table II) shown by young adults who have been unable to resolve their psychological crisis satisfactorily. In these cases, as with regressions to negative aspects of any developmental phase, the pathology is more marked. If anxiety predominates the individual shows hesitancy and fear in any relationship which requires spontaneity, mutuality, and responsiveness. He becomes shy and defensive in any social group. If depression predominates he becomes dissatisfied with his personal life, suffers a general feeling of disenchantment, feels that he is missing something important, and that he is somehow incomplete. In a phrase, he asks, 'Is that really all there is?' The general form of identity pathology is the individual's sense that he has not lived his life but merely accepted (or adopted) a role.

Such roles may become false when they express only limited, partial, or more juvenile forms of intimacy in sexual and marital relationships. For example (as Lowen pointed out) a woman may adopt a daughter role in which she demands love without sex; she may then talk of 'permitting' her husband to use her body sexually. Or she may adopt a pre-adolescent sister role, so that the marital relation becomes one of mutual support, with neither individual ever expressing intense or deep feeling. This is basically an asexual attitude which tries to ignore the essential differences between male and female. A third role is that of sweetheart, involving a romantic idealism in which sex is used almost as a defence against intimacy. Such women (sometimes described popularly as 'psychic virgins') are basically unresponsive, but nevertheless take pains to make themselves attractive to the opposite sex. A fourth role is that of the 'perfect wife' who does all the right things but without the appropriate feeling, and eventually comes to regard her domestic image as more important than intimacy. Lastly, there is the mother role adopted by the woman who indulges her husband as if he were her naughty boy, excusing even his infidelity. Such women usually become mother-martyrs, quietly but insistently proclaiming their own self-denial and sacrifice.

Similar limitations of marital intimacy may show in regressive male roles. The son role is adopted by husbands who continue to be spendthrifts and prodigals, passing all power and responsibility to their wives. Men who adopt the brother role usually blame their wives for the asexual relationship, ignoring the fact that she is merely responding to his big brother attitude. This is 'the boy next door', beloved of mothers of marriageable daughters. Here, however, the young man's sustained virtuousness is often a defence against his own impulses, and his idealization of women usually conceals a lack of healthy self-respect. Again, the knight-hero role is adopted by romantic Casanovas whose aim is the seduction of virgin princesses outside their own marriage. Since they are afraid to become genuinely committed, their technique is merely 'hit and run'. There is also a 'perfect husband' role adopted by men who identify entirely with domesticity and make being a husband a way of life. The last male role is that of father, where the individual becomes dynastic, patriarchal, and power-hungry, with strong anal needs for authority and control. The only marital relationship that such men can tolerate is one of master and slave. Their attitude towards their wives is usually one of 'there, there, little woman'. By suppressing the woman, they prevent her from ever achieving an adulthood that might challenge their manhood.

Regression to false intimacy may of course show in the adoption of merely social roles as well as the sex, love and marital roles exemplified above. Psychology, in its current pre-occupation with social roles and role-playing generally, sometimes seems to be assuming that adopting a role, or several roles, is the same thing as living a life. Our point here is that adopting a role may be repressive and restrictive. In role-playing there is always a certain self-consciousness, a loss of spontaneity, and a failure in self-abandon; thus role-playing may diminish the possibility of intimacy.

Most societies consistently attempt to manufacture social intimacy and 'togetherness' among their members by defining certain social roles publicly, sponsoring their attractiveness, and encouraging their adoption. Politicians, businessmen, and indeed all public figures, now offer the public not themselves or their work, but their 'image'. They are not concerned with what they really are, but only with what others think they are. Their decisions tend to be influenced not by the intrinsic value of a given alternative, but by how it will look to the voters or the general public. In extreme cases they may even be tempted to choose the worse of two alternatives, simply because their public relations advisers have terrified them into believing that their image would otherwise become spoiled. Neither images nor roles, however, are the same as 'the real thing', although the differences are often difficult to specify precisely. The failure to recognize such differences may itself be regarded as evidence of regression to a false intimacy.

Many adults actually come to prefer a social intimacy that is manufactured. Some British holiday camps, for instance, offer a formalized and regimented intimacy where togetherness is obligatory. It is created entirely by the social skills of the organizers. The paid professional master of ceremonies becomes adept at being 'pally' and works up false enthusiasm about communal activities. Hoggart, in *The Uses of Literacy*, described one such attempt to produce intimacy, where the holiday camp organizers went so far as to label the W.C.s 'Lads' and 'Lasses'. An equally false note is struck by the television broadcaster who tries to inject intimacy into his programme by implying that the viewer has invited him as a guest ('Thank you for letting me come into your home').

Since intimacy is a matter of spontaneity and self-abandon in personal relationships, we should perhaps recognize a special group of adults who, because of the nature of their work, may be more prone than others to regress to false intimacy. These of course are the 'experts' on personal relationships, such as psychologists, psychiatrists, psychiatric nurses, social workers, ministers, public relations officers, and so on. Experts do become intimately involved with their clients, but in such professional relationships there is always a certain detachment, a need for perpetual self-awareness, and an element of conscious manipulation which in fact precludes genuine intimacy. The occupational hazard for the expert is that he may come to believe that his professional intimacy is genuine intimacy, and thus adopt a false and regressive role. When this happens the falsity is particularly difficult to detect. In fact it may be said that here it 'takes one to know one'. Any criticism, say on the part of the client, is liable to be countered with a barrage of erudite analysis from the professional who, because he *is* the professional, usually has the last word. In psychotherapy a patient who quite properly rejects an erroneous interpretation from the therapist is sometimes confronted with the portentous question, 'Why are you resisting this interpretation?' Such brainwashing reflects the fears and needs of the therapist, not the patient, but it may represent also the only kind of personal relationship that the therapist can tolerate. Some therapists do choose their work because they cannot achieve intimacy outside it, and tend to hide their regressive needs for false intimacy behind learned jargon – 'resistance', 'transference', 'counter-transference', 'contracts', and the 'the doctor–patient relationship'. The ordinary individual finds it almost impossible to reach the person who is concealed behind professional jargon, particularly when the jargon looks and sounds as though it expressed genuine intimacy.

The falsity of such roles may show also in the expert's need to impose his professional intimacy on all his personal relationships, whether inside or outside his consulting room. That is, he *never* drops his professional role. There are physicians who treat everybody as if they were patients, psychiatrists who interpret everything psychoanalytically, psychologists who 'psychologize' the everyday lives and experiences of all their friends, social workers who treat people as 'case studies', nurses who use the royal 'we' in ordinary conversation, ministers who never take off their dog-collars and view their family and friends only as sinners whose souls must be saved; and so on. This kind of person, whatever his profession, never sees others as people, but only as external objects whose purpose is to confirm and support him in his own professional role. He tends to interact socially only with colleagues who 'speak the same language', or with potential clients who can be trained to do so. In general, such individuals demonstrate that the professional or expert in intimacy is no more immune to regression than anybody else; indeed, the nature of his work makes him more liable than most to regress to the false intimacy of young adulthood, and to exaggerate his professionalism into a way of life.

SUMMARY

We introduced this chapter by emphasizing that any psychological evaluation of young adults would be influenced to a considerable extent by social value-systems.

The goal of young adults was described as intimacy, achieved largely in terms of self-abandon (the voluntary yielding of identity) in sex, love, marriage, work, play, and personal relationships generally. We discussed intimacy in each of these relationships in turn, and suggested that psychological success for the young adult entailed the successful development and integration of all forms of intimacy.

Illness in early adulthood was regarded as 'self-absorption' and 'isolation', the failure to achieve intimacy, the under-emphasis or over-emphasis of one aspect of intimacy, or the failure to integrate its various forms. We discussed sexual inti-macy in some detail, relating sexual disorders to distortions of three different phases of the sexual act – fore-pleasure, ('sexual sophisticate'), orgasm ('libidinal type'), after-glow ('platonic lover'). Some regressive forms of sexuality were noted in pass-ing. Failures to achieve intimacy in love were exemplified, and a reciprocal relationship was suggested between sex and love, in which each type of intimacy tended to govern the satisfactory aspects of the other. This principle was extended and applied to intimacy in other personal relationships, in marriage, work, etc.

Regressions to early adulthood presented a certain semantic difficulty, but as in previous chapters normal regressions were described in terms of our response to advertisements whose appeal was based on intimacy, and on the young adult's natural tendency to enjoy multiplicity in personal relationships. Border-line regressions of older adults were discussed as the per-sistence of young-adult preoccupations in older adults. More severe pathology showed in those older adults who regress not to positive aspects of young adulthood (intimacy) but to nega-tive aspects (self-absorption and isolation). We described these briefly in terms of Levin's primitives (Appendix, Table II).

We listed certain forms of sexual role-playing as regressions to false intimacy and noted the danger of adopting false social roles, which might constitute an occupational hazard for pro-fessionals and experts in personal relationships.

CHAPTER SEVEN

Adulthood (30–65 years)

A man of ... forward-looking mind
WORDSWORTH, *The Excursion*

IN this chapter we are regarding adulthood as the period which begins in the early thirties and ends roughly with retirement. Apart from Erikson, and with the possible exception of Jung, none of the major developmental theorists have considered adulthood as a specific growth stage in the human life cycle. There is also a corresponding dearth of empirical and experimental investigation into the main psychological preoccupations of adulthood as such.

It is not easy to see why psychologists have largely ignored the adult stage. Researchers may have been discouraged by the methodological problems involved in studying as a group adults who are highly individualistic; by the traditional emphasis of psychoanalysis on earlier and more obviously formative growth phases; or even by the fact that they themselves tend to be in this age group. Whatever the reasons, the scarcity of psychological information about adulthood will ensure that this chapter is not only more discursive than the others, but shorter.

Adults are the people on whom young children depend, against whom teenagers rebel, and from whom young adults may learn. To put it the other way around, in very general terms, adults are regarded by children as protectors who are omnipotent and omniscient; by teenagers as authority figures who are hide-bound and 'settled'; and by young adults as persons of influence to be emulated, and eventually supplanted.

Insofar as adulthood is a period of responsibility, authority, and influence, adults are usually expected to be in charge of things. They are no longer trainees but graduates, and are expected to train those younger and less experienced than themselves. They are executives and policy-makers, and whether they uphold the *status quo* or try to change it they represent, more than any other age group, the way things are in society.

The period of adulthood, as defined here, covers more than three decades. Within this period there are far too many significant changes (biological, psychological, and social) for us to deal with it adequately as one unit of time. We may, however, consider the starting point of each decade as a point of change at which the adult may reappraise his function as an individual. The initial point of change, at about the age of thirty, may be the least significant of these milestones, because around this point and for some years afterwards the adult is extremely busy establishing himself in several areas simultaneously – in marital, social, vocational, financial, and other areas of his life. He is energetically preoccupied with nurturing his young family, stabilizing his domestic situation, negotiating commitments, planning his financial security, launching himself on a career or manoeuvering within it so as to maximize his potential in the near future, and so on.

The age of forty is probably a more significant point of change for the adult. At this time he is not so much establishing himself as consolidating. He is beginning to taste the fruits of his earlier efforts, in terms of increasing security, comfort, and influence. In his work he has confidence in his own capacities, knows how to apply his skills to the best advantage, and can distinguish between what is feasible and what is not. He knows the ropes, takes his experience and practical know-how for granted, and may become eager to try out ideas and policies which have germinated from earlier years.

The adult who has reached forty is of course able to look

forward and envisage the end of his working life. Until this time he probably considered retirement as a remote and unreal possibility. He may even begin to think about the end of his natural life, for it is when he is in his forties that many of his elderly relatives will begin to die off. He may find, too, that he is being treated differently by others. Unsought responsibilities may be thrust upon him. He may suddenly realize that most of the people he knows are younger than he is, and indeed seem to be treating him with the deference and consideration given (he thinks) only to much older people. He may be made to feel old when youngsters yield seats to him in public conveyances, offer to help him with the heavier chores, and call him 'sir'. His teenage children may begin to refer to his youth as 'the olden days', and regard him as being on the way down, while they are on the way up. The new sense of personal mortality created by others may be confirmed and enhanced by his own awareness of a decrease in his athletic capacities. Generally, he may become aware that his time is no longer unlimited.

The adult in his forties may look backwards as well as forwards, using his age as a vantage point from which to view his developmental achievements. He may re-evaluate his life, assessing what, and how well, he has learned from experience. He may review his own developmental crises, asking himself whether he has learned who to trust (Stage I); when to hold on and when to let go (Stage II); how much initiative is appropriate within realistic limits and his own known limitations (Stage III); how well he can apply the practical and social skills he has acquired (Stage IV); and the extent to which his identity (Stage V) has been confirmed, clarified, and developed by a growing stability in his marriage, work, and circle of friends (Stage VI). To the extent that he can integrate these achievements and see their culmination in his current life situation, he will be able to recognize and encourage their development in those younger than himself.

At the age of fifty the adult is not so much consolidating as consolidated. He knows what he stands for. His family will probably have grown up and left home; they may also have made him a grandparent. He may begin to delegate some of his responsibilities to younger men, supervising them from a benevolent distance. His physical capacity may have decreased noticeably, requiring an easing off in athletic activities; active sports may give way to more sedentary and contemplative pursuits.

Reaching the age of sixty makes most men aware of retirement and the need to bring their career to completion. They begin to plan actively for their post-retirement life. Women (apart from a few who continue their careers into their sixties) do not retire in the same sense as men, and many find that many of their ordinary activities become complicated because of their husband's retirement.[1] In this decade most parents, some of whom may have become grandparents, are usually in a position to help their grown-up children; they may arrange jobs, help financially, or at least baby-sit for adults still in the earlier phases of this period.

In this chapter we shall discuss the various forms of health and illness within the general framework of these decades of adulthood.

PSYCHOLOGICAL CRISES IN ADULTHOOD

Erikson considered health and illness in adulthood in terms of 'generativity' and 'stagnation' respectively. He defined generativity as 'primarily the interest in establishing and guiding the next generation'. By generativity Erikson meant more than

1. In considering domestic management (i.e. being a housewife) as a career we should perhaps distinguish between housewifery and homemaking. Many women are housewives but only exceptional women are homemakers as well.

parenthood; he included 'people who, from misfortune or because of special and genuine gifts in other directions do not apply this drive to their offspring, but to other forms of altruistic concern . . . which may absorb their kind of parental responsibility'. Generativity includes therefore any activity that is parental or care-taking, productive or creative, or that involves responsibility for others, or leadership in its widest sense.[2]

The most direct form of generativity, namely parenthood, is self-evident. In becoming a parent the individual is quite literally 'establishing and guiding the next generation'. Similarly the generativity of adoptive or foster parents, who look after other people's children, is obvious. It is probably true that, other things being equal, the real parents are the best caretakers for their own children; that is, the biological aspects of mating, together with the vitally important psychological effects of producing children from one's own body, and living thereafter in the closely intimate social setting of the family,

2. Society sometimes appears to be discriminating against those forms of generativity that do not involve actual parenthood. Income tax regulations, for instance, tend to penalize the single individual, even when he is exceptionally generative in other ways. Within this prejudice there is probably another, discriminating in favour of unmarried men and against unmarried women. The author has often demonstrated the prejudice in lectures, by asking the class for associations to the words 'bachelor' and 'spinster'. The first associations to 'bachelor' are usually 'gay', 'bold', 'free', etc., then become more derogatory, 'irresponsible', 'selfish', while the first associations to 'spinster' are usually 'dried-up', 'old maid', and later, 'lonely', 'sad', etc. The fact that bachelors are first envied and then disparaged, while spinsters are first disparaged and then pitied, may reflect the lingering pervasiveness of double-standard attitudes in society (see Chapter 6). Certainly the single man tends to be sought after socially, while the single woman tends to be excluded and left alone. This may be why spinsters recently began to refer to themselves as 'bachelor girls'. One way or another, our society seems to assume that most people get married and that anyone who does not must contribute, or be generative, in other areas to make up for it.

greatly increase the child's chances of obtaining adequate care-taking in terms of his physical, psychological, social, and even spiritual needs. On the other hand, there is no magic in the mere production of children which will necessarily guarantee that the child will in fact be adequately 'taken care of'. Parent-substitutes may sometimes do a better job of caretaking than the actual parents.

There are of course other ways of taking care of children apart from being, or acting as, a parent. Teachers may be generative in Erikson's sense, even if they are not themselves married and have no children of their own. There is no doubt that teachers, who often spend more time with children than parents do, have primary importance in 'guiding the next generation'; and indeed the care-taking responsibilities of teacher and parent often overlap. The effect of this overlap may be observed in the acrimonious interchanges between teacher and parent at some parent–teacher association meetings; or in the spirited debates (both at home and in the school staff-room) about who has the care-taking responsibility when the child is neither at school nor at home, e.g. when he is in the school bus.

Care-taking benefits are administered to adults as well as to children. That is, adults are sometimes taken care of by other adults. The family G.P., the psychotherapist, and the nurse, all have adults in their care, and to that extent have a generative function. They are care-takers in an extended sense. Employers and union leaders may, in varying degree, take care of the livelihood and welfare of employees; pastors take care of the spiritual needs of their congregation; statesmen and politicians sometimes take care of the social rights and standard of living of the electorate. In general, anyone who is actively solicitous for the welfare of others may be regarded as generative, especially when the care-taking is long-term. From this point of view, the function of the G.P., who may take care of three generations in a family, is probably more generative than that of the surgeon, whose care-taking (however vital) is of relatively short duration.

Another form of generativity is shown by those who, although they may not take care of people directly, nevertheless influence their lives and welfare by producing things. These are creative people, who invent new things, formulate new ideas, and suggest new ideals to benefit society. A connection between the generativity of creative people and that of actual parents is suggested even by ordinary language. We often talk of being fertile or prolific; we conceive or give birth to an idea; we even speak of having a brain-child; and so on.

We may, for our own convenience, group the generative functions of adults into three main categories: parental functions (whether natural or adoptive); care-taking functions (taking charge of, training, or helping others); and creative functions (producing, constructing, inventing, and so on). All these functions, in so far as they influence the next generation as well as the current one, will necessarily impose a certain *social* responsibility on the generative individual. That is, generativity in any of its various forms means more than merely producing or taking care of someone or something; it also involves accepting responsibility for the product's continued existence and its effect on others. Thus the parent of a child, the teacher who 'moulds' her class, the scientist who discovers nuclear fission, the artist who exhibits his picture, the television director of programmes, the lecturer, the author of a book: are all generative, in the strict sense, only if they recognize and accept responsibility for the effect on others of their creation. Unless social (and not merely personal) responsibility is understood to be an integral part of generativity, the criminally brutal parent, the sadistic teacher, the cynical mind-manipulator, and the maniac busily creating bombs for the destruction of society, would all have to be regarded as psychologically healthy in exactly the same sense as the benign reformer who invents a new labour-saving device.

Each of the main generative functions distinguished above tends to change in some degree as the adult moves through his adulthood. The production of children is, for obvious biological reasons, more appropriate in the earlier decade of adulthood. (The adoption of children usually occurs slightly later, when the adults begin to realize that they will not produce children of their own.) The *rearing* of children continues throughout adulthood and beyond; and parents, ideally, will change their form of care-taking as their children grow up. While the parent is changing as an adult to meet the various psychological requirements of each decade in his own adulthood, he will simultaneously be changing as a care-taker to meet the new requirements of his children at each new level of their development. Parents bring up their children, but children bring up their parents also. Many parents feel that in this respect they never quite catch up with their children. Just when the parent has learned to meet the needs of the child at one stage of its development, the child has moved on to the next stage. Presumably, when this lag becomes too great, and the parent fails to change with the child, psychological problems (of the kind we have outlined in previous chapters) are much more likely to occur.

Care-taking vocations and careers also continue throughout adulthood. Here too, the adult's generative function will change in scope and in quality as he acquires experience, and achieves promotion which involves greater care-taking responsibilities. Leadership aspects of generativity have been studied exhaustively by psychologists, but the findings of these investigations (for example, concerning the effect of leaders on group effectiveness) have often been contradictory. Researchers have been unable to describe a 'leader's personality' as such, largely because specific leadership characteristics are found to be effective in some, but not other, social situations. More recently, attempts have been made to consider leadership as essentially an interactive process, and to analyse its effectiveness in terms of both productivity and satisfaction of group members.

Creative forms of generativity have been investigated, indirectly as it were, in psychological studies of creativity as such. Some of these studies help to clarify the nature of creative generativity, while others give some indication of the changes in creativity which may be expected in different decades of adulthood.

Creativity is not merely an intellectual process. For example, McKellar found that creative thinking was largely an unconscious process. He distinguished reality thinking (R-thinking) from autistic thinking (A-thinking); that is, thinking which was directed towards the real world of facts, logic and problem-solving, as distinct from thinking which was associative, and was inner-directed towards the world of feelings, impulses, aspirations, dreams and fantasies. His point was that creativity involved A-thinking as well as R-thinking. This in fact confirmed the view of Wallas, who suggested that all creative thinkers reached their solutions in four main steps: preparation, incubation, illumination, verification. In the 'preparation' period the individual saturated his mind with a particular problem, and with all the relevant facts and theories; in the 'incubation' period, although the individual might pay little overt attention to the problem, his creative 'work' continued unconsciously, in the form of sifting, comparing, experimenting, and exploring various possibilities; the 'illumination' period, usually brief, consisted of a sudden 'aha!' experience; and was followed finally by a lengthy period of conscious, deliberate, and systematic 'verification' of the original idea.

Unconscious features in the creative process are suggested also by creative individuals themselves. Many creative people have insisted that they were merely expressive instruments, and were used or driven by a creative urge over which they had little or no control, and which they sometimes personified. In R. L. Stevenson's *Across the Plains*, for example, an author (often thought to be Stevenson himself) is described as experiencing dreams, in which 'little people' made up his stories for him, so that all the author had to do was write them down. Thus the creative process may not only involve unconscious factors, but may require a certain willingness on the part of the individual to relax and allow these factors free play. Creation, and indeed all forms of generativity may not reflect a deliberate effort to solve a specific problem so much as a spontaneous and almost self-indulgent activity which is enjoyed for the fun of it.

Attempts to analyse general personality characteristics of creative people have been made by several investigators. The following traits were found to be common in a wide variety of outstandingly creative individuals, regardless of their occupation. First, they showed a marked independence of thought and action. Creative people are not attracted to group activity where conformity is required, nor are they easily influenced once they have come to their own conclusions. On the other hand, they are less dogmatic than non-creative people, and are more willing to recognize their own irrational impulses. They prefer complexity and novelty, value and enjoy humour, and place a strong emphasis on both theoretical and aesthetic values. In general they may be regarded as more flexible and open to new ideas than less creative individuals.

One clear negative finding was that creativity was not necessarily associated with intelligence. For example, MacKinnon, who directed a series of studies, concluded that

our findings concerning the relations of intelligence to creativity suggest that we may have overestimated in our educational system the role of intelligence in creative achievement ... our data suggests rather that if a person has a minimum of intelligence required for mastery of a field of knowledge, whether he performs creatively or banally in that field will be crucially determined by non-intellectual factors.

This finding is qualified slightly by the fact that in creativity quality and quantity tend to vary together. There are of course exceptions to this general tendency. One person may produce only one or two outstanding works in a lifetime, while another may proliferate endless streams of trivia; but historically, most creative individuals have been productive as well as original.

The classic work on creativity, in its developmental aspects, is that of Lehman, who methodically worked out the relationship between age and creativity in a wide variety of human endeavours. In nearly all kinds of intellectual achievement, such as art, music, science, medicine, philosophy, technology, etc., he found that the rate of achievement was very low at 15 to 19 years (about 3 per cent of maximum rate), rose rapidly to its peak between 30 and 34, and fell steadily thereafter to 47 per cent between 45 and 49, and to nearly zero after 70. The curve for very high quality achievement, however, started later – in the early twenties – increased more rapidly to an earlier maximum (25 to 29 years), then subsided faster to nearly zero at 60.

Lehman's findings are of great interest, but of course they show only that creativity is greatest *on average* in the third decade. To obtain average trends he had to smooth out many wide variations between subjects, many outstanding exceptions, and many causal factors other than age. Creative people are by definition original, and we can expect individual variations to be most extreme and most frequent among them. Creativity varies not only by age, but also by the nature of the creative work. More sedentary forms of creativity may vary with age in different ways from the more athletic forms. For example, Lehman found that among contemporary (1912–32)

American musicians productivity not only increased to the age of 35, but also stayed steady thereafter till the age of 70. Again, Thomas Edison obtained 180 patents after the age of 60, and had 46 accredited military inventions after the age of 70; Benjamin Franklin was productive as a diplomat, inventor and writer into his eighties; and George Bernard Shaw was still publishing plays as a nonagenarian. It may be that our ordinary techniques for assessing human abilities become inadequate when we try to apply them to exceptionally generative individuals. Some psychologists, particularly in America, have already begun to show interest in developing more open-ended and versatile psychological assessment techniques which might be more appropriate for measuring creativity.

Psychological success in adulthood is more complex than success in any of the preceding developmental stages. The capacity for generativity depends to a considerable extent on the degree of psychological success achieved by the individual in earlier stages. Given this qualification, the successful adult will then achieve generativity in all its main forms: that is, parenthood (actual or vicarious), care-taking and leadership, and creativity in its widest sense. In addition, these forms of generativity will be well integrated with one another, and will be modified appropriately as the adult grows through the different decades of his adulthood.

ILLNESS IN ADULTHOOD

Illnesses in adults, in so far as they represent failure to resolve the current crises of adulthood rather than earlier conflicts, cannot be described in technical or clinical terms. There are no more diagnostic categories for adults than there were for younger adults discussed in Chapter 6. Also, the influence of social values continues to be an important factor in evaluating the psychological problems of adults. In this section therefore we are forced to use the ordinary descriptive terms of everyday language, and constantly to keep in mind that psychological illness in adulthood is always to be evaluated within a given social context.

Taking adulthood as a whole, there is a sense in which psychological illness is to be expected statistically, and hence may be regarded as normal. During adulthood, the individual reaches the half-way point in his life cycle, and has inevitably experienced many of life's vicissitudes. Since vicissitudes by definition imply both ups *and* downs, the adult will to some extent have had to expend energy, negatively as it were, on coping with adversity rather than seeking self-fulfilment. To this extent his degree of generativity in adulthood will necessarily be restricted. The degree of *possible* success in adulthood will always be determined to some extent by the individual's degree of success in earlier stages of his development. If earlier successes were partial, then success in adulthood will be correspondingly limited.

Even if an individual has been successful in resolving earlier developmental crises, his success as an adult depends also on opportunities for expressing and developing his generativity. For example, he may not be able to be a parent, not because of earlier neurotic conflicts about the opposite sex, but because there is nobody 'suitable' for him to marry when he is ready to do so. Inadequate or interrupted vocational training (because of war service, for instance) in earlier years may disqualify an individual from care-taking careers later. Some creative individuals may find themselves ahead of their time in that society rejects their creation and may indeed punish and persecute them for being generative in that particular way at that particular time, e.g. Freud, Socrates, Christ, the French Impressionists, etc. People who suffer these reversals of fortune sometimes react with a kind of over-compensatory generativity, which shows as a compulsion to take care of everybody. They may insist on being leaders even when leadership is not required, and even in situations where 'followership' would clearly be more appropriate.

The possibility of being generative is qualified also by biological factors, such as deterioration in physical health, which may occur as a direct result of ageing or because of earlier strains or excesses in the individual's life. Some limitations in generativity are imposed also by the biology of others, as it were. Children grow up and leave their adult parents, thus depriving them of this avenue for expressing their generativity. Parental responsibility and influence tend to fade away like the well-known Cheshire cat, and somewhere in adulthood it may disappear altogether – except perhaps for the smile. Adult parents themselves have parents, who are liable to leave them by dying, and thus force them to cope with bereavement reactions. These factors, and their inter-relationships, were neatly summarized by Davis (1966):

Consider fifty-year-old women living in England and Wales in the middle of the twentieth century. Fifty years is the commonest age for the menopause (although the average is a year or two younger). The average age of their mothers, supposing all had survived, would be 70 years old, and this is the commonest age of death in once-married women. The average age of their daughters is twenty-three years, which is also the average age of marriage for women. Many women thus meet within a few years of their fiftieth birthday crises in the relationships of greatest importance to them, those with husband, mother, and daughter.

What are the less 'normal' and more specific illnesses of adulthood? In the period of establishing oneself, between thirty and forty, certain illnesses tend to occur when a child is born. Generally, most of the patients who seek treatment in their thirties are women. One investigator found that in more than half his cases, mental illnesses associated with childbirth started in the first month after the birth and nearly half of those occurred in the first two weeks. The cluster of typical symptoms here usually involves conflicts in the mother's feelings towards her child (infanticidal impulses, delusions of the child's being dead, etc.); because of its time of onset, this illness is called *puerperal psychosis*. It has also been found that the symptoms are particularly common in older mothers who have already suffered mental illness; after pregnancies that were disturbed and complicated; and in cases where the infants were of low birth weight, or were premature. The marital relationships of such patients have usually been unsatisfactory, involving frigidity, mother-dependence, dominance in the wife, passivity in the husband, and so on. No association has been found between puerperal psychosis and social class, occupational class, legitimacy, illegitimacy, or social mobility.

Men as well as women may be adversely affected by the birth of a child. A husband may show a rather childish form of sibling rivalry (see Chapter 3) because he resents having his wife's attention diverted to the child. In extreme cases he may show the *couvade syndrome*. This reaction is usually described in terms of an analogy with certain primitive tribes, in which the male is given all the cosseting and care usually received by the expectant mother. In such tribes the man may show or simulate all the pregnancy symptoms (early morning sickness, pain in the lower back, etc.), act out the birth itself, and recuperate during an extended period of convalescence; while the woman simply has the baby. The specific reasons for the couvade syndrome are still not clear, but the men who become ill in this way tend to have had poor identification with their fathers, dependent relationships with their mothers, and to have been subsequently demanding and dependent towards their wives. Psychosis may also occur in men at or about the time of the child's birth.

In considering sex differences in adult illnesses we should

keep in mind that the person presenting himself (or herself) for treatment is not necessarily the only person in the family who requires it. One psychologist found that women coming to clinics often presented problems regarding their children; that two to three times more sons than daughters were brought also; and that, while the mothers showed a marked tendency to blame their sons for their illness, they tended to blame themselves for psychological problems in a daughter. These same women also presented marriage problems about as frequently as they did problems about their children. The husband may in such cases be a 'concealed' patient in the family situation. This is of course the age at which the adult male may become somewhat overwhelmed by the multiplicity of demands made on him, whether these have been imposed by others or by himself. He may struggle for a long time with duties that gradually become millstones in terms of the psychological stresses they entail. In their thirties both partners may also have their marital and family relationships sabotaged by the so-called seven-year-itch – by a growing tendency towards sexual infidelity, perhaps because of disenchantment, boredom, or merely too little fun in their own marriage.

In the forty to fifty phase, where the adult is consolidating, he is perhaps most prone to suffer the adverse effects of family bereavement. The death of a relative may revivify earlier conflicts even in normal individuals. According to several authors, some adults seem to be predisposed, because of earlier stresses, to break down when bereaved. For example, among such people the loss of parents in childhood, and especially of the mother in early childhood, is unduly common. One researcher found that a significant percentage of psychiatric patients fall ill within a few months of a family bereavement. The number who had lost a spouse was several times greater than would be expected by chance, and the group of bereaved patients contained a majority of women over forty.

Although the death of a parent has not been clearly established as a cause of psychological illness, patients themselves often report that it is. In addition, they often regard their mother's death as more significant than the death of their father. The effect of bereavement varies of course with the person's involvement with their lost relative, both before and at the time of death; it depends on his vulnerability; and varies according to whether the death itself was sudden and traumatic, or was merely an expected termination of a prolonged illness.

Natural physiological changes, such as the menopause or climacteric, often occur in this phase of adulthood. These changes may enhance the effects of psychological stresses, or themselves initiate new problems for the adult. Many adults regard the climacteric as a disturbing signal of advancing age, an indication that their productive years are over, and thus as a proof of diminished generativity. Diffuse disturbances of personality, usually associated with glandular changes, are sometimes produced by the climacteric. Forty is often regarded popularly as the 'dangerous age' for men, in that they may become glandularly over-stimulated at the very time when their wives are having menopausal problems. Adults in the pre-menopausal period may react physiologically by producing 'late' children; they may become unusually active, or they may show sudden and unpredictable mood swings, paranoid preoccupations, and so forth. Most of these features reflect a transient disturbance which settles down again after the climacteric, but sometimes the disturbance is severe enough to require treatment.

In the fifty to sixty phase, when the adult is consolidated, he is commonly thought to be prone to a particular kind of depression. This includes features of agitation, anxiety, and hypochondriasis, and starts between forty and fifty-five years in women and fifty to sixty-five years in men, and has been called *involutional melancholia*. This illness is probably not a direct consequence of menopausal changes alone, as was once thought, because (a) younger depressed patients show a similar syndrome, and (b) a comparison of involutional and earlier forms of depression revealed nothing unique about the former which could not be explained in terms of age changes and the general life circumstances already discussed above. This suggests that if involutional melancholia is a unique form of depression its uniqueness is not psychological.[3]

Suicide rates (see also Chapter 1) reach a peak in women during the decade from 55 to 64 years, and although in men the rates increase until after 85 years, there is a steep rise in the fifties and sixties. Suicide is committed by more single than married individuals, by more childless adults than parents, and by more widowed than single persons. Suicide rates are high among divorcees, and are very high among elderly men living alone after retirement, especially if they are widowed, single, or divorced.

The last few years of adulthood, when the individual is past the age of sixty and his career is reaching its point of culmination, may produce two main types of psychological illness: those due to problems associated with imminent retirement, and those due to increasing physical disabilities. We shall consider these in more detail in the next chapter.

We may conclude this section by referring to Erikson's criterion for the failure to achieve generativity, namely 'a prevailing sense of stagnation and interpersonal impoverishment'. This of course varies in content, depending on the particular phase of adulthood in which the adult experiences it, but it may occur in any phase. Similarly, Levin's description of typical feelings (see Appendix, Table II) may refer to any, or

3. This finding supports our general approach to depression as a non-specific but basic symptom. Both depression and anxiety have been regarded as 'psychiatric primitives' (Levin), with many different forms, as listed in Appendix, Table II.

all, phases of adulthood in given cases. There are, as we noted earlier, no technical terms to describe failures in generativity. Nevertheless, those adults who fear the responsibilities and perils of leadership, feel that they have been unconstructive or that they have been poor parents, and generally that they have wasted their life, do show fairly typical patterns of observable behaviour. They tend to talk of lost opportunities in their lives, of having 'missed the boat' in comparison with their contemporaries. They tend to become self-centred, dedicating themselves almost entirely to their own comforts and their own narrowing interests. As Erikson put it, 'they begin to indulge themselves as if they were their own one and only (spoiled) child'. Such adults come to believe that nothing is too good for them, and that the best is only just good enough. When their life of self-indulgence is threatened they become petulant. They try to conceal their determination to get their own way behind a mask of concern for others – 'I just *know* that the children really *want* to do all this for me, so I'll let them.'

REGRESSIONS TO ADULTHOOD

By definition the only individuals who can regress to this stage arc those who are chronologically beyond it; that is, old people. We are confronted here with an artifact of our developmental framework itself. The later the developmental stage, the fewer regressions to it (and the more regressions from it) are possible. (This effect was balanced in the first chapters. That is, the earlier the developmental stage being discussed, the more regressions to it – and the fewer regressions from it – were possible.)

Older people who 'regress' to adulthood are mostly those who are attempting, despite ample evidence of its inappropriateness, to perpetuate adult generativity into old age.

This is more conveniently regarded as 'illness' in old age, and is therefore considered as such in the following chapter.

SUMMARY

In describing the adult crisis we recognized the continuing problems of terminology. We used Erikson's concept of generativity, indicating the general psychological goal of adulthood, and attempting to group various specific forms of generativity in two main ways. First by decade, where adults of 30+ years were described as establishing themselves; those of 40+ years were consolidating; those of 50+ years were consolidated; and those of 60+ years were engaged in the culmination of their adulthood. Secondly, different forms of generativity were grouped into parental, care-taking, and creative functions.

In describing adult illnesses we first made allowance for the effect on the adult of having achieved only partial success in resolving preceding developmental crises; the effects of a lack of opportunity in the person's life situation for expressing generativity; and the effects of inevitable exposure to certain stresses such as bereavement, physical changes, etc. We then considered illnesses within the time-and-function grouping of generativity used in the preceding section. That is, parental problems, bereavement and climacteric problems, depressive and suicidal problems, retirement, and physical problems were regarded as predominating in rough sequence through the decades of adulthood. We summarized this section in terms of Erikson's criterion of 'stagnation' and the various forms of pathological effect as quoted from Levin in the Appendix, Table II.

CHAPTER EIGHT

Old Age (65 years and over)

Men must endure
Their going hence, even as their coming hither.
Ripeness is all.

SHAKESPEARE, *King Lear*

THE age group containing those we call 'old people' has never been clearly defined, and indeed it may not be definable. The word 'old' is in fact used subjectively. When we are, say, five years of age we regard teenagers as old, adults of thirty as decrepit, adults of forty as ancient, and adults of fifty and over as having one foot in the grave. As we ourselves move through these different ages the number of people we consider to be old diminishes; and although the number of people who regard *us* as old increases correspondingly, we never really get to the point where we regard *ourselves* as old. There is always someone around who is older (or at least who is showing his age more) than ourselves, and in relation to whom we still regard ourselves as young. Our reluctance to use the word old at all shows in the many euphemisms we employ. Instead of talking about 'old people' we call them 'older', 'elderly', or 'senior citizens'. It is in fact surprisingly difficult to find anyone to whom the word 'old' legitimately applies. Septuagenarians express genuine surprise at the death of friends in their late sixties ('. . . and he was still a young man'), or refuse indignantly to accept welfare benefits to which their old age entitles them, on the ground that such benefits should go to the 'old folks'.

There is only one small group of people who are regarded as old by everyone, including themselves. These are the eighty-

and ninety-year-olds who are bedridden or physically depend-ent. Notice that even here it is not enough to be an octogenarian or a nonagenarian; to qualify for old age in this strict sense we must also be incapacitated or immobilized. Such a definition of old age is, however, far too restrictive for the purposes of our present outline, and we have, quite arbitrarily, chosen to regard old age as starting around sixty-five, the usual age of re-tirement.

This age group has, until fairly recently, been neglected by psychologists. Part of the recent upsurge of interest in older people has been promoted by the simple fact that there are more of them in our society now than there have ever been in the past. In Great Britain, for example, the number of people over sixty-five has doubled between 1910 ($2\frac{1}{2}$ million) and 1950 (5 million), and is expected to have increased again by more than fifty per cent in 1975 (8 million). The proportion of old people, and especially old women, in our society is now increasing because of birth control on the one hand, and earlier retirement on the other.

PSYCHOLOGICAL CRISES IN OLD AGE

If we are to discuss old people objectively we must first make explicit some of the adultomorphic prejudices that most of us seem to have against them. These prejudices are almost univer-sally taken for granted in our society, tacitly assumed by most psychological investigators of old age, and are now helplessly shared by many old people themselves. To list a few, we tend to assume that old people are so degenerated physically that they have no personality worth talking about, that this deterioration is inescapable and irreversible, that they cannot change and always need help, that retirement is a kind of social death which creates citizens that are not merely 'senior' but 'second-class' as well, and so on. Most of these prejudices stem from the mistaken conviction that we should evaluate old people according to criteria appropriate for younger age groups. The assumption is of course quite false, but it has contaminated so many psychological studies of old age that we shall in this chapter take time to expose it whenever we come across it.

In old age there is a natural tendency for physical organs to wear out and for physical processes to run down. Energy diminishes, resistance to illness decreases, and in general the body becomes slower and less flexible. But even the biologists, who until very recently have tended to equate ageing and cell death, are beginning to realize that the view of ageing as nothing but a molecular deterioration is far too simple to do justice to the facts. In realizing this the biologists are ahead of most psychologists, who continue to be preoccupied almost entirely with deterioration in old age. Psychology tends to be so over-impressed with the negative implications of biology that the positive features of old age have tended to be ignored or denied. Clearly, physical health in old people has to be considered in terms of its occurrence within that age group, not in relation to some other age group. We should not dream of disparaging a teenager's physique because he can no longer put his foot in his mouth as he did when he was an infant. Similarly we should not disparage the physique of an older person merely because he cannot gyrate to music with the same agility as he did when he was a teenager.

Granted that older people are slower and more cautious, they can often compensate more effectively than younger people. They may sacrifice speed, but only for the sake of accuracy. They may have less energy, but they can often apply it more economically. They may be less adaptable, but they are more experienced. Their short-term memory may be impaired, but their long-term memory is relatively enhanced. And so on. In many psychological studies of old people, however, the experimental tasks set simply do not allow these positive skills to come into play. Thus biased findings may arise simply from the fact that the evaluative standards used in these studies are those applicable to younger people; indeed, they are often the standards appropriate for people around the age of the investigators themselves. Such studies have loaded the dice against older people to such an extent that their pessimistic conclusions regarding the ageing process and the enfeebled capacities of older people have really been no more than self-fulfilling prophecies.

There are many myths about the physique of older people to which we have become habituated, and of which we are probably no more aware than we are of the taste of saliva in our mouths. One notorious myth relates to sexuality. The assumption that older people are 'past it' has led to a general disparagement of any continuing sexual interest on their part as lecherous, perverse, or even obscene; and to a fervent wish to redirect sexuality in old age to 'nice' sublimated forms of sexuality such as nature-study and the like. Such prejudice is no more worthy of serious consideration than the adolescent's reaction when he first realizes that his parents go to bed with each other. More important, this prejudice is based on false facts. Although the intimacy of couples in later years may be more marital than sexual (see Chapter 6), involving more mutual comfort and companionship than intercourse, it is now well established that heterosexual interests do not necessarily diminish in older people.

Masters and Johnson have listed some of the factors which do tend to diminish sexuality in old age. Many of these factors are not physical, but psycho-social. They are:

1. Monotony in sexual relationships. This is perhaps more important in cultures which insist on monogamy.
2. Preoccupation with a career or other pursuits.
3. Fatigue. In the over-50s any exhausting physical effort will tend to abolish or diminish sexual urges.

4. Over-indulgence in food and drink, just as it lowers the capacity to feel or achieve in other areas, also depresses sexual tensions. Alcohol, especially, is liable to produce a progressive anaesthesia, so that the chronic alcoholic experiences very little or no sexual tension.

5. Infirmity, mental or physical. Acute illness leads to only a temporary reduction or loss of sexual response; long-standing chronic metabolic disease, such as diabetes, often produces impotence. (In our culture, infirmity in women causes less deprivation to men than vice versa, because ageing men have more alternative sexual outlets than ageing women.)

6. Fear of sexual failure. Masters and Johnson state that the importance of this factor cannot be over-emphasized. In ageing men the fear of failure, which usually leads to their withdrawal from sexual activity, may be disguised as anger or pretended apathy, or may show as a search for stimulation from young women. (We might add that although younger people tend to find older people sexually unattractive we cannot infer from this that older people find one another equally so.)

It is quite clear therefore that continuing sexual interest is, to a considerable extent, determined by non-physical factors. In addition, these factors vary considerably from person to person. Many older people who have lost a spouse tend not to marry again because they feel that remarriage would be an insult to the memory of the dead partner. Men however, more often wish to remarry, and are more discontented with living alone, than women.

In general, there is now good evidence that the continuance of sexual activity depends not simply on growing older, but on the kind of life that the person has had in the past, and in particular on the sexual habits he has acquired in earlier years. Masters and Johnson state categorically that 'if elevated levels of sexual activity are maintained from earlier years, and neither acute nor chronic physical incapacity intervenes, ageing males usually are able to continue some form of active sexual expression into the seventy- and even eighty-year-old age groups'. Similarly, Kinsey *et al.* noted that in women sexual activity after the menopause is directly related to sexual activity in the pre-menopausal years, and concluded that 'there seems to be no good physiological reason why the frequency of sexual expression found satisfactory for the younger woman should not be carried over into the post menopausal years'.

All this evidence suggests strongly that the alleged decline of older people is a highly individual matter, and that the necessary decreptitude assumption is by no means justified. Even those who will believe only statistical formulae on old people as against direct observation of them are now confronted with the evidence provided by Reichard *et al.*, who found in older people a variety of psychological types, each of whom had chosen a different strategy for dealing with old age. These authors distinguished types very broadly, but in sufficient variety to suggest that the criteria for health in old age are as complex as those for any other age group:

1. *Constructive:* high self-esteem, self-aware, responsible, no major stresses in life, interests broad and developed from those of early life.
2. *Dependent:* passive, self-indulgent, comfort-loving, non-neurotic, satisfied with own standards.
3. *Defensive:* over-controlled, conventional, compulsively active, rigidly self-sufficient, fearful of retirement, no insight.
4. *Hostile:* anger directed outwards, not depressed, near-paranoid, unstable history, envious of younger people, fearful of death.
5. *Self-hating:* critical and contemptuous of own life, unhappy marriage, restricted interests, pessimistic, death regarded as a merciful release.

Although some of our pessimistic biases against older people have arisen indirectly from our physiological myths, many others have arisen more directly from old-fashioned social and family stereotypes. Just as physical ageing has been regarded as nothing but cell death, so retirement has often been regarded as nothing but social death. It is true that the psychosocial effects of retirement are profound (especially in men), and, where they have not been anticipated and prepared for by the individual, may be exceedingly adverse; but they are not necessarily entirely adverse. To a considerable extent they are so merely because they have always been expected and assumed to be.

Psychologists are only now beginning to be concerned with the social and motivational aspects of old age, and it is not surprising that their first formulations showed lingering traces of negative social stereotypes. The view put forward by Cumming and Henry that ageing was a process of disengagement of the older person from his society assumed that the disengagement process was inevitable. In addition, disengagement *from* society was stressed much more than disengagement *to* any other positive area of living. The implication was that unless deliberate efforts were made by the individual the 'natural' process of disengagement left him in a kind of social vacuum. In such a vacuum, of course, psychological deterioration would be quite inevitable. Cumming later restated the theory in terms of the *mutual* withdrawal of the ageing person and his society from each other, but of course this emphasized rather than modified the basic assumption, namely, that such withdrawal is inescapable for the older person. The misleading assumption implicit in the disengagement theory is that retirement into old age is *only* a disengagement. Ideally, to become disengaged from the concerns more natural to younger people, such as full-time regular employment, is, or should be, to become at the same time more engaged with other matters – in precisely the same way as this happens in the transition from any earlier age phase to the next.

One sub-section of society which exerts a powerful influence on the psychological stereotypes of older people is the older person's own family. It has been pointed out that disengagement allows the older person increased freedom from the control of the norms governing everyday behaviour. The grown-up children of such older people are not always prepared to allow deviations from norms to which they still conform. If there is a sense in which parents never stop regarding their children as children, even when fully grown, there is a corresponding sense in which children, even when fully grown, tend to persist in regarding their parents as parents. They may not *let* their parents change, even when change would be greatly to the parent's psychological advantage. Disengaged older people who are independent of their children need not answer to anyone but themselves, and their continued maturation within this unique state of freedom may be stifled by the restrictive disapproval of their own children. At worst, this disapproval takes the form of an insistence that the older person should accept a 'second childhood' in which he is forced to become a child to his own children, unable to make any decision without prior consultation with them. The fact that many older people do accept such care-taking in reverse from their children does not in any way imply that the arrangement is psychologically beneficial to either party. Indeed, there is evidence to the contrary. The resentment of grown-up children saddled with the care of aged parents is often matched precisely by the resentment of the parents who feel trapped and diminished by such care. They do not complain of not being loved, but of not being understood, by their children. There is sometimes a certain arrogance in the attitude of care-taking children towards their parents, an insistent presumption that 'of course we know what's best for you, better than you do yourself'.

Welfare organizations, or institutions such as old people's homes, often adopt the same patronizing attitude. Because the older person is dependent in some ways, they act on the assumption that he must be incapable in every way, despite ample evidence to the contrary. Welfare programmes are often promoted by youthful enthusiasts who suppose that old people must at all costs be kept physically active (although old age is presumably an age of contemplation as well). Eager young social workers continue to bewilder them with futile tasks, such as making raffia baskets, whose pointlessness is immediately apparent to the old people – who may for many years have coped with many more responsibilities than the would-be helpers.

Perhaps enough has been said to indicate the pervasiveness of adultomorphic attitudes in both biological and social theories of old age, and to show that psychology has not yet disentangled itself completely from such assumptions. Certainly ageing *may* cause the individual to degenerate socially and physically until he becomes a lonely isolate, 'sans teeth, sans eyes, sans taste, sans everything'; but we should remember that it is also a growth stage in its own right, with its own standards of health, involving an increased freedom from restrictive social responsibilities, and which may ideally exemplify a high level of maturity in the sense implied by Shakespeare when he wrote 'Ripeness is all'.

What can be said positively about the criteria for psychological health in old age? Very little. Our chance of psychological success as we near the end of our lives depends in large measure on whether our earlier experiences were good, bad or indifferent. More important however, is the old person's evaluation of those experiences. Erikson suggested that one central aspect of health (or, as he called it, 'ego integrity') in old age was 'the acceptance of one's one and only life cycle as something that had to be and that, by necessity, permitted of no substitutions'.

Such acceptance is by no means fatalistic. Most of us, confronted by an unpleasant experience, wish that it had never happened. And many people, even when later they look back on their lives with the perspective of old age, continue to wish that these experiences had never occurred. Erikson's point, however, is that the *successful* old person, even though he may have detested the experience at the time, can nevertheless accept that he learned something of considerable value from it. From this long-term point of view, bad times may eventually be seen not quite as blessings in disguise, but at least as necessary learning experiences.

For example, from a childhood experience of, say, school phobia we may remember, in our old age, not that the first steps in learning were traumatic, but that apparently crushing incapacities were overcome; from a severe humiliation in earlier life we may have gained insight into our own psychological make-up, although at the time we may have felt nothing but an ecstasy of embarrassment; and in general, from adversity we may learn how to deal with the salt as well as the sugar in life. Indeed, we may come to see a certain inevitability in past distressing experiences; that is, given the circumstances and our own stage of development at the time, we may realize that the adverse outcome was not fortuitous but completely predictable; for us, in those circumstances, it could not have turned out otherwise. Such an attitude is much more than mere nostalgic resignation, or a sad folding of the hands in the face of an inscrutable fate. It involves an active reappraisal of events within a more comprehensive evaluatory framework. Past and present events are seen not only within their own context of time and place, but also in relation to one's whole life as it continues. This presumably can be done only in part by adults who have not yet reached old age, simply because they have not lived long enough. Nor is there any reason to suppose that this psychological goal of old age necessarily is achieved only by intellectual means. It is perhaps philosophical in its nature, but it does not require formal training as a philosopher to achieve it.

This positive attitude, once achieved by the successful old person, may be extended beyond his own life to life in general. According to Erikson, ego integrity involves 'a pervading sense of the order and meaning of things', or the conviction that, at least on the long view, life does make sense. In its ideal form, this presumably involves an almost global extension of the ego, beyond oneself, beyond one's family, beyond one's circle of friends and acquaintances, beyond one's social group, beyond one's nation, and even beyond one's own international age group. Life-experience comes to be considered not only in terms of individual men, but in terms of all men, mankind, humanity in general, or, as Erikson describes it, 'my kind'.

If this sounds too abstract and metaphysical we might consider one aspect of which we all have direct experience, namely, our attitudes to our own parents. We begin our relationship in childhood by being utterly dependent on them; in our teens we become violently critical of them; in young adulthood we may try to shoulder them aside, exulting in our new-found independence; in adulthood we may be indulgent towards them (or to their memory); and only in our own old age do we really understand them. Of course, if we have become successful old people, we may have begun to suspect much earlier that we ourselves contributed at least a tiny part to all the past family misunderstandings about which we felt so intensely at the time. This kind of insight requires a breadth of vision which is rarely achieved when we are too deeply involved in the on-going process of living and especially when we are younger.

These psychological achievements in old age derive in part from the fact that the older person is nearing the end of his life. Old people have by definition had a relatively long past. They also have a relatively short future. Their attitude to death, for instance, is quite likely to be considerably different from that of their younger contemporaries. Young children can hardly conceive of death as a reality; teenagers, whose lives are beginning to open out into a fascinating array of possible alternatives, consider themselves immortal – they may be able to conceive of death in the abstract, but not their own death; adults, who may have experienced death at second-hand (in their parents or other aged relatives) do perhaps begin to grasp the fact that they too will die sometime. For older people, however, death is not only a reality (they may have seen not only their seniors but most of their contemporaries die off) but an imminent reality. It is therefore natural that they will show more interest in death, and in the possibility of a life hereafter, than do younger people. Such interests are not morbid, as they might be in a twenty-year-old, but merely realistic. (Generally old people have a relatively neutral attitude to death; it is their juniors who tend to fear it.) Those old people who daily scour their newspaper for details of deaths and funerals are not pathologically depressed; they are merely checking to see how many of their own age group they have outlived; and if they read not only the 'deaths' notices, but the 'births' and 'marriages' notices as well, they are certainly showing positive health as well.

What then should we be able to see in the psychologically successful old person? Erikson's criteria of 'integrity' (and what he later referred to as 'wisdom') could perhaps be expected to show in older people as a kind of good-humoured serenity. However, this serenity should presumably be more than a passive observation of the passing show of life; it should include an eager, alert, and interested personal involvement in ordinary affairs. The successful older person will be able to plunge enthusiastically into the moment, and also be able to stand back and look at himself and other phenomena from a variety of perspectives. One writer gives a more down-to-earth set of criteria for health in old age: congruence between the older person's interests and his actual opportunities; continuity between his present and past patterns of living; acceptance of old age and death; a certain degree of happiness due to relief from responsibilities; and (considered to be most important) adequate financial security.

Any attempt to outline criteria for psychological health in old age should take into account all the qualifications which we have touched upon above; the influence of adultomorphic attitudes on old people themselves; the effect of physiological myths and social stereotypes; the recognition of individual differences within the old-age group; the treatability of genuine physical deterioration; and the need for evaluative standards unique to old people. The criteria for health in old age are still vague, and one of psychology's major tasks in the future is their systematic, detailed, and scientific clarification.

ILLNESS IN OLD AGE

As we might expect, illness in old people is usually considered more in physical than in psychological terms. In one sense, this is merely an extension of our tendency to consider old people only in terms of deterioration, and to assume that many psychological and social areas of living are closed to them. But even so, to consider illness in old people in terms of those assumptions confronts us with a new problem, that of distinguishing defects due to pathological deterioration from defects that may be expected simply because the patient is old.

All illnesses *are* illnesses only in relation to some standard of normality. As we have already seen, the norms for old age have never been clearly established, but have been considered largely in terms of the norms for younger age groups. The word 'senile', for example, does not really connote a norm for old age unless it excludes the idea of deterioration. Senility, in the non-deteriorative sense, is perfectly normal in advanced years. It becomes pathological only when it occurs prematurely, has exaggerated features, or has been brought about by unnatural causes.

Traditionally, 'senility' has never been clearly equated with illness. Some groups of physical illnesses in old age have been collectively described as 'senile dementias', but the implication has always been that the old person has suffered an abnormally extensive and rapid physical deterioration, and is more likely to die than his contemporaries. Nor are the symptoms in dementia clearly or exclusively physical. Arteriosclerotic dementia, for example, is specifically associated with restricted circulation of blood through the brain and other abnormal physical symptoms. Yet the syndromes of both senile and arteriosclerotic dementia also include symptoms that are not physical but psychological and social; for example, loss of interest, diminished responsiveness towards others, loss of subtlety of emotion, short-term memory defects, excessive tiredness, hallucinations or delusions, aimlessness, confusion, weakened emotional control, delirium, antisocial behaviour, and so on. Now many of these psychosocial defects are equally characteristic of say, infants, whom we should not dream of calling abnormal on that account; infants are merely 'young'. On exactly the same basis, when old persons show such 'symptoms' they should be regarded as merely old, and not sick. This would highlight the other symptoms, such as hallucinations and delusions, delirium, strokes and so on, which are clearly pathological by any clinical standards – and indeed would be so in any age group.

If we are to avoid adultomorphic classification of the psychological symptoms in old people we must first establish statistical expectancies for symptoms within that age group. We have already suggested that depression about approaching death, while morbid in younger people, may be no more than a realistic acceptance of an imminent fact in older people; similarly with depression about retirement. The sad feeling that one's working life is ended, that one's ability to produce is beginning to atrophy, or that one is not of much use to anybody any more, may be produced, artificially as it were, by current social attitudes and expectations, often unspoken but nevertheless powerful, in the face of which an old person who has retired becomes not depressed but systematically and irreversibly discouraged. To call this natural reaction to an unnecessary and modifiable social expectation 'depression' is not only unimaginative but clinically misleading.

Granted that psychological illness in old people must be considered within the context of old age itself, what forms may it take? Erikson suggested that old people who are failing psychologically may experience a pervading despair; they may feel that time has run out, and that there is now no chance 'to start another life and try out alternative roads to integrity'. Milder forms of such despair may show as resignation. The feeling of despair may be hidden by an apparent disgust with life, an almost somatic revulsion at years not used but merely spent, or containing too many disappointments and disillusionments, so that a satisfactory culmination in old age has become impossible. The disenchantment of such old people is almost cosmic in scope. Milder forms of disgust may be represented by misanthropy, or cynicism, in which disgust becomes intellectualized.

These reactions usually involve a severe loss of self-esteem which may be expressed by old people as a conviction that they are only a burden to others. Some try, often with no success, to look on death as a merciful release; but this is more a fear of death than a preoccupation with it. This last example shows the essentially cyclical nature of the outline in this book, and thus relates this last developmental stage back to the first. In a sense, old people who fear death lack basic trust in the unknown which follows death – just as some infants lack trust in the unknown which follows birth. A final quotation from Erikson is appropriate: 'Healthy children will not fear life if their parents have integrity enough not to fear death.'

APPENDIX: TABLE I

PREDOMINANT ASPECTS OF GENERAL DEVELOPMENT
(Freud, Erikson, and Piaget)

CHAPTER	AGE	PHYSICAL	PSYCHOLOGICAL CRISIS	SOCIAL
1	Infancy: (0–2 years)	Oral: (a) sucking (b) biting (c) weaning	Trust v. Mistrust: incorporation (acquiring) dependency aggression (tearing apart) *Cognitive Mode*: adualism; autism	Individual persons
2	Early Childhood: (2–4 years)	Anal: muscular control retention and expulsion	Autonomy v. Shame, Doubt: control: self esteem (sense of worth) retentive: obstinate, stingy, compulsive expulsive: cruel, disorderly, destructive (obliterating) *Cognitive Mode*: egocentrism; infantile/moral realism; animism	Parental persons
3	Play Age: (5–7 years)	Phallic: infantile–genital locomotor	Initiative v. Guilt: Oedipal identification with parents (fantasies) acceptability of age and sex roles conscience intrusive/inclusive *Cognitive Mode*: mechanical/deductive; animate/inanimate; logical/social	Basic family
4	School Age: (6–12 years)	Latency: no major physical changes	Industry v. Inferiority: external world competence social relationships	Neighbourhood/ school
5	Adolescence: (13–19 years)	Genital: puberty	Identity v. Identity Diffusion: recapitulation sexual/social roles emancipation from parents	Peer groups/models
6	Young Adulthood: (20–30 years)	Genital: no major physical changes	Intimacy v. Isolation: personal involvement competition and co-operation	Partnerships
7	Adulthood: (30–65 years)	Genital: maturity, gradual senescence	Generativity v. Self-absorption: care-taking productivity, creativity	Divided labour and shared household
8	Old Age: (65+)	Genital: senescence	Integrity v. Despair: retirement ('disengagement') recapitulation death	Mankind/'my kind'

TABLE II

CHAPTER	(a) PREDOMINANT (NEGATIVE) EMOTION IN DEVELOPMENTAL STAGES (Levin)			(b) PSYCHIATRIC ILLNESS (Foulds et al.)
	ANXIETY CONTENT	DEPRESSIVE MOOD	IDENTITY PATHOLOGY	DIAGNOSTIC CATEGORIES
1	Fear of starvation	Feeling of being abandoned, alone, withdrawn	(Chaos)	Psychosis: (a) disintegrated (b) integrated Addictions etc.
2	Fear of and doubts about impending disgrace	Feeling of shame, of shortcoming	Sense of worthlessness of the self	Obsessive-compulsive neurosis Passive-dependent Passive-aggressive
3	Fear of punishment for intrusiveness, seductiveness, or rivalry	Feeling of not being lovable	A sense of the belittlement of the self and the ego functions	Hysteria
4	Fear of not knowing how	Feeling of not being good for anything	A sense of the uselessness of the ego functions	Inferiority complex
5	Fear of the failure to master new and conflicting inner drives	Feeling that the world is not good enough	A confusing sense of the contradictory expectations of others, one's own contradictory ego functions and ideals, earlier identifications and social stereotypes	Identity diffusion Adolescent adjustment reaction
6	Fear of spontaneity and mutual responsiveness	Feeling of being self-contained, avoiding co-operation or competition	An unsatisfactory sense of merely having a role in life	Libidinal types
7	Fear of the responsibilities and the perils of leadership	Feeling of being a poor parent, of being unconstructive	A sense of being one's own spoiled child, a sense of a wasted life	
8	Fear of death	Feeling of resignation, disgust, cynicism and despair	A sense of being a burden to others, a rejection of one's second childhood	

260

References

ABRAHAM, K. (1924) 'Origins and Growth of Object – Love', in *A Short Study of the Development of the Libido*. (English translation in *Selected Papers*. London: Hogarth Press, 1942).

ADLER, A. (1927a) *Understanding Human Nature*. New York: Chilton.

ADLER, A. (1927b) *Practice and Theory of Individual Psychology*. New York: Harcourt Brace.

ADLER, A. (1930) 'Individual Psychology', in C. Murchison (ed.), *Psychologies of 1930*. Worcester: Clark University Press.

BRIDGES, K. M. B. (1932) 'Emotional Development in Early Infancy'. *Child Development* 3, 324–34.

CHESS, S. (1959) *An Introduction to Child Psychiatry*. New York and London: Grune & Stratton.

CUMMING, E., and HENRY, W. E. (1961) *Growing Old: The Process of Disengagement*. New York: Basic Books.

DAVIS, D. R. (1961) 'A Disorder Theory of Mental Retardation'. *J. Ment. Subnorm.* 7, 13–21.

DAVIS, D. R. (1966) *An Introduction to Psychopathology* (Second edn). London: Oxford University Press.

DOUGLAS, J. W. B., and ROSS, J. M. (1964) 'Age of Puberty Related to Educational Ability, Attainment, and School Learning Age'. *J. Child Psychol. and Psychiat.* 5 (3–4), 185–96.

ERIKSON, E. H. (1950) *Childhood and Society*. New York: Norton.

ERIKSON, E. H. (1959) 'Identity and the Life Cycle'. *Psychol. Issues* 1, No. 1.

FENICHEL, O. (1945) *Psychoanalytic Theory of the Neurosis*. New York: Norton.

FOULDS, G. A. (1965) *Personality and Personal Illness*. London: Tavistock Publications.

FREEMAN, T. (1958) 'The Contribution of Psychoanalysis to the Problem of Schizophrenia', in T. F. Rodger, R. M. Mowbray, J. R. Roy (eds), *Topics in Psychiatry*. London: Cassell.

FREUD, A. (1965) *Normality and Pathology in Childhood: Assessment of Development*. New York: International Universities Press.

HARLOW, H. F., and HARLOW, M. K. (1962a) 'Social Deprivation in Monkeys'. *Scientific American*, November.

HARLOW, H. F., and HARLOW, M. K. (1962b) 'The Effect of Rearing Conditions on Behaviour'. *Bull. Menninger Clinic*, 26 (5).

HOLT, R. R. (1960) 'Cognitive Controls and Primary Processes'. *J. Psychological Researches* 4, 1–8.

KINSEY, A. C., POMEROY, W. B., and MARTIN, C. E. (1948) *Sexual Behaviour in the Human Male and Female*. London: W. B. Saunders.

LEHMAN, H. C. (1953) *Age and Achievement*. London: Oxford University Press (published for the American Philosophical Society).

LEVIN, D. C. (1963) 'A Systematic Theory and Nosology for Psychiatry'. *Canad. Psychiat. Ass. J.* 8/6, 374–84.

LEVIN, S. (1963) 'Libido Equilibrium', in N. E. Zinberg and I. Kaufman (eds), *Normal Psychology of the Aging Process*. New York: International University Press.

LOWE, G. R. (1969) *Personal Relationships in Psychological Disorders*. Harmondsworth: Penguin Books.

LOWEN, A. (1958) *The Physical Dynamics of Character Structure*. New York: Grune & Stratton.

LOWEN, A. (1966) *Love and Orgasm*. London: Staples Press.

MACKINNON, D. W. (1965) 'Personality and the Realisation of Creative Potential'. *Amer. Psychol.* 20, 273–81.

MASTERS, W. H., and JOHNSON, V. E. (1966) *Human Sexual Response*. London: J. & A. Churchill.

MCKELLAR, P. (1957) *Imagination and Thinking*. Aberdeen: University Press.

MCNEIL, E. B. (ed.) (1965) *The Nature of Human Conflict*. Englewood Cliffs, New Jersey: Prentice-Hall.

MCNEIL, E. B. (1966) *The Concept of Human Development*. Belmont, Calif.: Waldsworth Publishing Co.

MEAD, M. (1930) 'Adolescence in Primitive and Modern Society', in V. F. Calverton and S. Schmalhausen (eds), *The New Generation*. New York: Macauley.

MILLEN, J. W. (1963) 'Timing of Human Congenital Malformations'. *Develop. Med. Child. Neurol.* 5, 343–50.

PIAGET, J. (1928) *Judgement and Reasoning in the Child*. London: Routledge.

PIAGET, J. (1932) *The Moral Judgement of the Child*. London: Kegan Paul.

REFERENCES

PIAGET, J. (1952) *The Origins of Intelligence in Children*. New York: International University Press.

REICHARD, S., LIVSON, F., and PETERSON, P. C. (1962) *Aging and Personality: A Study of 87 Older Men*. New York: Wiley.

WALLAS, G. (1921) *The Art of Thought*. New York: Harcourt Brace.

WHITE, R. W. (1959) 'Motivation Reconsidered: The Concept of Competence'. *Psychol. Rev.* 66, 297–33.

WINNICOTT, D. (1964) *The Family and Individual Development*. London: Tavistock Publications.

WOLFF, S. (1967) 'Behavioural Characteristics of Primary School Children Referred to a Psychiatric Department'. *Brit. J. Psychiat.* 113, 885–93.

Index

MORE ABOUT PENGUINS
AND PELICANS

Penguinews, which appears every month, contains details of all the new books issued by Penguins as they are published. From time to time it is supplemented by *Penguins in Print*, which is a complete list of all titles available. (There are some five thousand of these.)

A specimen copy of *Penguinews* will be sent to you free on request. For a year's issues (including the complete lists) please send 50p if you live in the British Isles, or 75p if you live elsewhere. Just write to Dept EP, Penguin Books Ltd, Harmondsworth, Middlesex, enclosing a cheque or postal order, and your name will be added to the mailing list.

In the U.S.A.: For a complete list of books available from Penguin in the United States write to Dept CS, Penguin Books Inc., 7110 Ambassador Road, Baltimore, Maryland 21207.

In Canada: For a complete list of books available from Penguin in Canada write to Penguin Books Canada Ltd, 41 Steelcase Road West, Markham, Ontario.

Henry Walton

SMALL GROUP PSYCHOTHERAPY

'Nobody can learn how to conduct a therapeutic group merely from reading a book. But equally, nobody can engage in group psychotherapy without a body of theoretical knowledge, an appropriate vocabulary, and an understanding of the techniques on which this treatment method is based.'

The contributors to this book, all experienced practitioners, draw from a wide range of specialist interests to make clear the central procedures of group methods. The characteristics of the group situation, the composition of the group, the role of the individual member and the supervisory functions of the conductor, are set out in concise form. The idea of the 'therapeutic community is discussed, the difficulties experienced by the trainee therapist examined, and several areas of current research considered. How should we evaluate the effectiveness of psychotherapy in bringing about changes in behaviour and personality? Which are the specific features of the group situation that facilitate change?

A Penguin Education Book

Also by Gordon R. Lowe

PERSONAL RELATIONSHIP IN PSYCHOLOGICAL DISORDERS

The ability to 'relate' to others, to have satisfactory personal relationships, has been extensively studied by psychologists. From a very wide range of such investigations the author has selected psychological studies which have used a rigorous empirical or experimental method, and which focus specifically on personal relationships impaired by psychological illness.

The selected studies, mainly motivational, interpersonal and social, examine impaired relationships both in controlled laboratory or hospital settings, and also in the everyday interpersonal situations of real life. Most age groups are represented. Thus, in chapter 1, dealing with neurosis, considerable space is devoted to aggression and dependency in children. Chapter 4 considers some of the family stresses of middle-aged individuals suffering from depression; and chapter 5 concentrates on recent studies of old age which distinguish normal 'disengagement' from symptomatic loneliness, despair and misanthropy.

A Penguin Education Book